Ethnicity and Inequality

SUNY Series in Ethnicity and Race in American Life

John Sibley Butler, Editor

Ethnicity and Inequality

Robert Masao Jiobu

State University of New York Press

Published by
State University of New York Press, Albany

For information, address State University of New York
Press, State University Plaza, Albany, N.Y., 12246

Library of Congress Cataloging-in-Publication Data

Jiobu, Robert M.
     Ethnicity and Inequality / Robert Masao Jiobu.
          p.   cm. — (SUNY series in ethnicity and race in American life)
     Includes bibliographical references (p.).
     ISBN 0-7914-0365-3. — ISBN 0-7914-0366-1 (pbk.)
     1. Ethnicity—United States.   2. United States—Ethnic relations.
3. Equality—United States.   I. Title.   II. Series.
E184.A1J49 1990
305.8'00973—dc20

Contents

Preface   vii

1. Introduction   1
2. Ethnicity and Socioeconomic Inequality   27
3. Ethnicity and Socioeconomic Gains   93
4. Demographic Potential and Socioeconomic Status   115
5. Explaining Ethnic Inequality   157

Notes   189

Index   205

Preface

This monograph is about ethnicity and socioeconomic status in the United States. It is both an empirical analysis of data from the 1980 Census of Population and a theoretical exploration of ethnicity, competition, and socioeconomic status, including the underclass.

Scientific analysis rests on data, but with regard to ethnicity and socioeconomic status, even basic facts are hard to find. Consequently, the first task of this monograph was to construct data tables that were comparable across ethnic groups. If nothing else, these tables can serve as a reference for other researchers.

Actually, providing data was a by-product of the second task, which was to empirically analyze the relationship between socioeconomic status, in terms of occupation, and ethnic groupings, in terms of ancestry and race. The bulk of the monograph is devoted to that job.

The third, and broadest task was an outgrowth of the analysis. Data rarely speak for themselves, and to generate hypotheses, various theoretical perspectives had to be examined. In the course of doing that, several ideas emerged which, when combined with the empirical outcomes of the study, culminated in a framework for conceptualizing ethnic relations.

These tasks are timely and vital. Ethnic issues are becoming increasingly prominent, both in the United States and around the world. I cannot prove that assertion, but impressionistically at least, events such as the Armenian conflicts in the Soviet Union, the Basque conflicts in Spain, and the Hutsu conflicts in Burundi— three far flung places with different cultures but having in common ethnic unrest—suggest that ethnicity has taken on more importance than sociologists have heretofore realized, and with that importance has come prejudice, discrimination, hostility, and sometimes, death. In the United States, racism, sexism, anti-Semitism, and ageism are on the rise. The Federal government, many say, has retreated from its commitment to civil rights, and the Reagan years, for all their accomplishments, were not good for minorities. If these events and trends presage the future, then the issues of ethnicity and equality will soon be pressing on us harder than before. It would be well if sociology could lay the foundation for studying them.

Plan of the Book

The book has five chapters. The first concerns preliminary matters, such as the definitions of terms and the operationalization of ethnicity. The second chapter is the longest, examining past research on socioeconomic status with particular reference to ethnicity, operationalizing socioeconomic status and the underclass, presenting several correlates of socioeconomic status, and lastly, analyzing a model of underclass membership. Chapter 3 concerns a basic, perhaps *the* most basic, issue: does anyone gain from ethnic inequality? Chapter 4 explores the demographic structure underlying ethnic inequality, and finally, Chapter 5 offers a framework of ethnic relations.

In performing the analysis, I was guided by the maxim that the highest sophistication results from applying the simplest statistic that will answer the question. Therefore, I sometimes used basic bar graphs, while at other times I used multivariate techniques, a few of which have not been applied to sociological data before. In either case, though, the goal was to answer the question in the most statistically parsimonious way possible.

To further clarify the data, I occasionally do not report digits to the right of the decimal point. A few colleagues have commented that they found this practice slightly disconcerting at first, but that they soon became accustomed to it. The practice is predicated on two assumptions. First, although the Census Bureau produces some of the finest data available, I doubt if they are always accurate beyond a single whole digit. Reporting many digits to the right of the decimal place implies a degree of accuracy that does not exist. And second, one- or two-tenths of a percentage point, or one- or two-hundredths of a correlation coefficient, would not alter the conclusions that were drawn. In fact, the less cluttered the data tables, the more closely the reader can focus on conclusions. Still, tradition being what it is, if a strong custom existed about showing digits to the right of the decimal point, or if there was the possibility of ambiguity, I did report them.

I thank William Form for critiquing Chapters 2 and 5. His comments were trenchant and always helpful. I also thank Richard Haller for his advice on matters related to computers, without which this study would have taken much longer to complete.

1

Introduction

To say that we are a nation of immigrants is a truism, for no society of comparable size was populated so quickly by so many different peoples, most coming voluntarily but some coming in fetters. So massive was this influx that half of all Americans, it is believed, have an ancestor who passed through one port of entry, Ellis Island. And no icon symbolizes this immigrant past so well as the Statue of Liberty and the words inscribed beneath it:

Give me your tired, your poor,
Your huddled masses yearning to breath
    free,
The wretched refuse of your teeming shore,
Send these, the homeless, tempest-tossed, to
    me:
I lift my lamp beside the golden door.

These lines speak to the American Dream, the vision of the United States as an egalitarian society in which anyone—regardless of origin—can fulfill his or her ambitions through pluck, hard work, and perseverance. This is surely a splendid dream, yet for all its splendor, it has played a strangely divisive role in American history. From the very founding of the nation, the American Dream has been juxtaposed against immigration and ethnicity. The basic issue has always been simple: can immigrants of different races and unique cultures melt into the mainstream to become part of the great American mass? Or will these groups remain separate, perhaps partaking of a portion of mainstream culture, but holding forth as separate ethnic and racial entities?

For some groups, the American dream became a reality, while for others it did not. And despite the ideology of equality, the *others* are often clearly identifiable by their ethnicity and race. The facts contradict the Dream, creating an issue that defies easy solution and simple scientific explanation. Consequently, ethnicity remains a major concern of American culture, politics, and scholarship.

In this monograph, I study a facet of the concern: ethnic inequality and assimilation. Paradoxically, while white ethnic groups have been in the United States as long as any other (except Native Americans, of course) more is known about nonwhite assimilation, especially that of African Americans. While not neglecting the black case, I hope to partially correct the uneven distribution of knowledge.

Approach of the Study

Various theories are invoked to account for different dependent variables, and from that view, this monograph is eclectic. Despite this diversity, however, the investigation is guided by the single broad principle of "infrastructural determinism." This principle implies that infrastructural forces, such as institutional arrangements and economic variables, are of primary importance, that superstructure derives from infrastructure, and that social behavior has a firm basis in the material, pragmatic constraints of life.[1]

The emphasis on infrastructural determinism is in keeping with the *Annale* approach to history, which maintains that historical explanations are composed of layers, with culture and ideas resting on a substratum of demographic and economic causes. In that sense, infrastructure is more basic than superstructure, but of course, that is a limited sense. In reality, both exist and both are important.[2]

Even while one might agree that society consists of both infrastructure and superstructure and that both are important, most empirical research must focus on one or the other. To simultaneously investigate both is not possible as a practical matter—at least not in the present instance. For that reason, and also for the pragmatic reason that the data are now available, I have chosen to emphasize infrastructural variables while drawing on culture and historical knowledge to help interpret the findings.

The goal of this study is now practicable because the necessary data are now in the public domain: the U. S. Census Bureau's Microdata Samples. In 1980, the Census asked about ancestry for the first time, and when those responses are linked with socioeconomic, demographic, and ecological data, some fundamental insights into ethnic stratification should appear. Almost as a byproduct, a statistical portrait of ethnicity in America is drawn and the store of fundamental knowledge about assimilation and stratification is increased.

Genetic Determinism and Race

An issue that has existed at least as long as sociology concerns the relative importance of "nature" versus "nurture." Put bluntly, are some races innately superior to other races? If "yes," then social causes have substantially less impact on life chances than genetic causes; if "no," then the reverse is true. Either answer obviously has enormous political implications, which is why the issue has not faded away despite more than a century of debate. Because of this, it would be well to discuss the issue now.

Given the disagreement over nature versus nurture, it is ironic that so much of the controversy stems from agreement. Everyone agrees that *some* human traits are genetically determined and that *some* are culturally determined—the issue is *which*. As yet, this issue has not been resolved to everyone's satisfaction, and so the debate continues.

The application of genetic determinism to biological matters does not generate much controversy among social scientists. For example, no one disputes the contention that blacks are genetically more prone to sickle cell anemia than whites. Applications to social matters, however, lead to a much different situation. Sociobiologist Edward O. Wilson, perhaps the most prominent advocate of such applications, has written:

The question of interest is no longer whether human social behavior is genetically determined; it is to what extent. The accumulated evidence for a large hereditary component is more detailed and compelling than most persons, including even geneticists, realize. I will go further: it is *already decisive.*[3]

Wilson does recognize that direct evidence linking specific genes to specific social behaviors has not been found. His evidence rests solely on correlational data, that is, data showing statistical relationships between social behaviors, often loosely defined and poorly measured, and characteristics known or strongly suspected to be genetically determined. These are also often loosely defined and poorly measured.

Wilson further recognizes that the same hypotheses about human behavior can logically stem from a theory of cultural rather than genetic determinism. He wrote:

> It is nevertheless a curious fact, which enlarges the difficulty of the analysis, that sociobiological theory can be obeyed by purely cultural behavior as well as by genetically constrained behavior. An almost purely cultural sociobiology is possible. If human beings were endowed with nothing but the most elementary drives to survive and to reproduce, together with a capacity for culture, they would still learn many forms of social behavior that increase their biological fitness. But as I will show, there is a limit to the amount of this cultural mimicry, and methods exist by which it can be distinguished from the more structured forms of biological adaptation.[4]

Contrary to Wilson's claims, not everyone is convinced that cultural mimicry can be distinguished from genetic determinism.[5] Attempts to draw the distinction are, at their crux, based on a fundamental and simple correlational paradigm. Scores on a trait of interest, such as intelligence or personality, are grouped by race and then statistically compared. Controls for variables such as education and motivation may be introduced, but the controls have not been totally satisfactory.[6]

Race

Despite the problems with sociobiological reasoning, many scientists and lay people alike think of race as a conglomeration of biologically inherited traits, such as skin color and hair type. Based on possessing a particular set of these traits, individuals are classified into *races*.

A major problem with the above approach is specifying *which* and *how many* genetic traits are required to define a separate race. Presumably, only the important traits should be counted, but how is that determined? Whereas visible characteristics may seem to be the most obvious criterion of importance, they are not decisive. Many of the most important differences between people, differences that have led to immeasurable suffering and inhumanity, are not highly visible. Without supplementary clues, such as distinctive dress, it might be impossible to know the race, religion, or creed of casual acquaintances.

To put the matter conversely, how many genetically determined similarities must be present to classify people into distinct racial groupings? Would skin color alone suffice? Or does it additionally require hair texture, facial shape, eye shape? Although a broad cultural consensus exists—whites, for example, are classified as a single race—consensus on the details is absent. The British are white, and so are the French and Germans. Is each group a separate race? Or are they all the same (white) race? This question may also be asked of a specific group. Are the British a political and cultural entity composed of separate races such as Welsh and Scot? Or are the British a single race? The data used in this study are not consistent in this matter, a situation that is hardly surprising given the ambiguity surrounding the concept.

Classifying persons of mixed genetic-racial backgrounds poses another conceptual problem. Obviously, if racial categories have not been defined, the notion of a mixed background has no meaning. Even if racial categories have been defined, the notion has but limited meaning, for everyone has a mixed genetic background.[7]

Another problem with the genetic definition of race concerns faulty generalization. A simple logical error, but one made with disconcerting frequency, is to believe that because behavior X has a genetic determinant, so does behavior Y. Blacks are susceptible to sickle cell anemia for genetic reasons, yet does it follow from that fact that the genes also determine the black crime rate? Clearly not—at least not without a well-established theory and strong evidence, both of which are currently missing.

The logical error in the foregoing example may be fairly evident, but much less evident is the error of generalizing from within a group to between groups. For instance, studies of intelligence have compared the tests scores of parents with children, siblings with siblings, and sometimes, one identical twin with another.[8] The conclusions have usually been that (1) the heritability coefficient is quite high with (2) the implication that racial differences in intelligence are genetically determined.

While these conclusions appear to be entirely reasonable, part (2) does not necessarily follow from part (1). For obvious ethical and practical reasons, this point can never be subjected to scientific experimentation with humans, but it can be clarified by performing the following "thought experiment":

Consider two groups, X and Y, and assume that their races are different, that all cultural influences are identical except that Group X is exposed to cultural Factor Z while Group Y is not, and that Z can be measured by Test W. Further, assume that on Test W, Group X has a mean score of 100 with a standard deviation of 10 and Group Y has a mean of 0, also with a standard deviation of 10. Finally, assume perfect methodology and measurement.

Under the given circumstances, the difference between the group means must be due to Factor Z, because no other possible source of that variation exists. At the same time, individuals within each group differ as to their ability on Test W (indicated by the non-zero standard deviations), and under these hypothetical circumstances, those differences must be due to genetic factors because no other source of *that* variation exists. In other words, even on the same measures, genetics factors can account for the within-group variation while social factors can account for the between-group variation. One does not preclude the other. As biologist Stephen Gould stated, "variation among individuals within a group and differences in mean values between groups [blacks and whites, for example] are entirely separate phenomena. One item provides no license for speculation about the other."[9]

Rather than following the nature versus nurture debate farther (which would be empirically pointless because the present data set does not bear on it), one may consider anthropologist Marshal Sahlins's observation that nature unfolds within culture, and that culture imparts meaning to nature.[10] In our culture, race is very important. Laws, policies, norms, morality, and ethics are constructed with regard to it. Power and affluence are divided by it. And a vast amount of research and scholarly debate, including this monograph, studies it.

Ethnicity

The present study concerns *ethnic* rather than *race* relations, but unfortunately, distinguishing between the two is not easy. An old but still useful distinction was implied by the first sociology textbook: "Amalgamation is a biological process, the fusion of races by interbreeding and intermarriage. Assimilation, on the other hand, is limited to the fusion of cultures."[11] Based on the implications of this statement, race becomes a biological category and ethnicity a cultural one.

While that distinction advances this analysis, many specific issues remain, the most pressing of which concerns the cultural traits that define ethnicity. Although no consensus prevails, several suggestions have been offered. *The Harvard Encyclopedia of American Ethnic Groups* proposed the following: geographic origin, migratory status, race, language or dialect, religious faith, ties that transcend kinship, neighborhood and community, traditions, values and symbols, literature, folklore and music, food preferences, settlement and employment patterns, special interests in regard to politics in the homeland and the United States, and finally, institutions that specifically serve and maintain the group's internal sense of distinctiveness.[12] Other analysts have proposed similar but shorter lists.[13]

A difficulty with this approach is obtaining agreement on the items to be listed, and then obtaining agreement on how many of those items must be present before a collection of people can be characterized as an ethnic group. Researchers admit that their lists do not include all possible cultural traits, nor do researchers require a group to possess every trait. However, given the state of current knowledge, this approach is probably the best available solution, however imperfect it may be.

Power and Majority-Minority

Political power influences the definition of racial and ethnic categories, a point illustrated by William Petersen's study of Hawaiian census data. He concluded that changes in the criteria used to define the various groups rendered intercensus comparisons highly suspect. While appearing to be random, these variations actually reflected the view of the dominant group. Offsprings of unions between Hawaiians and non-Hawaiians were originally designated as *hapa-haoles*, or half foreign. Later, when the United States assumed control of Hawaii, the designation became Caucasian-Hawaiian or Asiatic-Hawaiian, and still later the designation become part-Hawaiian.[14] Nothing in the biology of these people changed; what changed was the group with the power to apply labels.

This general principle bears on the current practices of the Census Bureau and thus on the data to be analyzed later. In the 1980 census, the *householder* provided information on all persons in the household. The householder (person listed in column 1 of the questionnaire) either owned or rented the domicile. If no such person existed, then anyone aged at least 15 was substituted.

To indicate race, the householder selected predesignated racial categories. The categories were the common ones and did not reflect a consistent underlying logic. Hispanics were not considered a separate race and were included among whites. Asians might be considered a single race but were given specific categories, such as Chinese or Japanese. By this logic, white groups (Germans and

Swedes for instance) should be considered separate races too, but just the single *white* category was provided for them.

The reason for using this particular set of categories is difficult to fathom, but it undoubtedly has to do with the political importance of the groups. Even though minuscule in number, Chinese and Japanese immigration has constituted a political issue since the mid-19th century. Asian exclusion, and the token quotas allocated to other nonwhites under the 1924 immigration law, resulted from political fights.[15] On the other hand, not until the 1960s and the war in Southeast Asia did the Vietnamese become important enough to warrant a separate census category. Also resulting from political confrontation was the designation of Hispanics as whites. When the Census Bureau suggested making Mexicans a separate race, Mexican protest groups exerted enough pressure to thwart the proposal.

Political power is important in yet another context. It underlies the concepts of *majority* and *minority*. To be sure, if a society consists of two separate groups, then the numerical majority is the one that constitutes more than 50.0% of the total; if there are three groups, than the numerical majority constitutes more than 33.3% of the total, and so on. (In the latter situation, the term *plurality* might be substituted for *majority*).

By this simple numerical logic, one can speak of, say blacks, as being a minority in the United States and, in fact, most of the groups that have traditionally been studied under the rubric of *race or ethnic relations* are numerical minorities. Had attention remained exclusively focused on those groups, then the numerical definitions might have been adequate. Inadequacies appear, however, when the numerical criterion is applied to women in the United States or blacks in South Africa. Women are a majority yet they obviously do not command the majority of power. Blacks constitute an overwhelming numerical majority in South Africa but are surely a minority with regard to power. For sociological purposes, therefore, power may be a better criterion for *majority* than number.

Accepting the criterion of power, however, does not solve all difficulties. There are still the questions of how power should be defined and measured. Assuming those questions can be adequately answered, another vexing issue arises. By definition, a minority has less power than the majority, so to define the minority we must be able to identify the majority, but to do that, we must be able to distinguish between minority and majority—which is what we started to determine in the first place. Thus, a certain amount of circularity is inherent in this situation.

Furthermore, how can we determine whether a group has a *proportionate* share of power? While one is tempted to adopt the obvious—power proportionate to group size—that approach raises an additional problem. How is group size calculated? Should the total population of the local area be placed in the denominator of the fraction, or should it be the population of the state, the nation, or some other unit of analysis?

Although the problems involved in defining majority, minority, ethnicity, and race might appear to be insoluble, they can be worked through well enough—at least well enough to permit this research to proceed. As will be indicated later in this chapter and at points throughout the monograph, various procedures can be applied and certain assumptions about racial and ethnic groupings seem reasonable even without confirming evidence.

Assimilation

Stated most tersely, assimilation is the extent to which groups resemble each other. An important consideration when analyzing assimilation concerns the direction or flow of the resemblance: which groups are becoming like which other groups? For simplicity, assume a majority group, A, and a minority group, B. As related to assimilation, four possibilities exist: Group A merges with Group B and both become partially like the other (called the melting pot); Group A remains distinct and coexists with Group B (called pluralism); Group B becomes like Group A (called Anglo conformity or Americanization); or Group A becomes like Group B (here called minoritization). Let us consider each of these possibilities.

1. *Melting Pot.* In the late 1700s, author-statesman St. John De Crevecoeur rhetorically asked, who is an American? His answer: a new, freedom-loving race sprung from European stock.[16] This basic idea is the essence of the *melting pot,* a term popularized by playwright Israel Zangwill in the early twentieth century. He believed that the United States was a crucible of ethnic groups and that cultural and biological amalgamation would eventually result in a single, unique racial-ethnic group, a *"Homogeneous-Americanus,"* so to speak.

Zangwill thought the melting would produce good, but his was not a popular opinion. Many people feared that amalgamation would weaken America's genetic stock and debase the American character. For these reasons, sociologists Edward Ross and Frederich Steiner endorsed restrictive immigration, while Robert Park believed that although assimilation was inevitable, it should still be resisted.[17]

The type of assimilation implicit in the notion of the melting pot has obviously never come to pass. Even the hastiest glance at the current ethnic scene reveals dozens upon dozens of ethnic groups. That these groups exist means, *prima facie*, that they have not amalgamated.

2. *Cultural Pluralism.* Opposite to the melting pot is a situation in which each group maintains its distinctive identity, subculture, and infrastructure. At the hypothetical extreme, each group would be so distinct as to form a society unto itself. Although that extreme is somewhat unusual, ethnic groups often remain highly distinct even while submerged within a broader encompassing society.

In offering *cultural pluralism* more than 60 years ago, psychologist Horace Kallen anticipated many modern notions about assimilation.[18] He argued that ethnic groups could remain distinct while peacefully interacting with each other and with the majority through the common culture of American life and under the authority of the duly accepted government. This vision, although different from Zangwill's, is no less idealistic.

Another more recent and darker variation of cultural pluralism is *internal colonialism*.[19] Ethnic groups remain separate, but the equality envisioned by Kallen is replaced by the domination of the minority for the benefit of the majority. More specifically, an internal colony exists when the following prevails: the ethnic group is subjugated by political power; the social organization and culture of the minority is weakened; the majority controls all important institutions; the majority profits from the internal colony; and finally, the majority imposes a racist doctrine justifying the internal colony. The black racial turmoil of the 1960s prompted this model, but it applies to other groups and to other times as well.[20] (More extreme but not germane to this study are the forced relocation of a minority and physical extermination).

3. *Anglo Conformity.* Another model holds that while the minority becomes like the majority, the majority adopts little of the minority's ethnicity. In the case of the United States, this is sometimes called *Americanization* or *Anglo Conformity*. If the process takes place for a sufficiently long time, then the minority will eventually become identical to the majority. The 1924 Immigration Act implemented this goal by establishing a quota system based, for all practical purposes, on race and ethnicity. It was assumed that Western

Europeans would easily Americanize, that Eastern Europeans and Levanters would probably not Americanize very much, and that nonwhites would not Americanize at all. Hence, quotas were established approximately in proportion to the group's prospects for achieving Anglo Conformity—or more accurately, what was *believed* to be the group's prospects. This latter point warrants emphasis. In the cases of the Chinese and Japanese, a major argument for exclusion centered on their alleged unassimilability. Yet today, these same groups closely resemble the white majority in terms of socioeconomic status.[21] Beliefs about prospective assimilation can be incorrect.

4. *Minoritization.* Conceivably, the minority might not change while the majority becomes like it. This type of assimilation has no name, so let us call it *minoritization.* The most dramatic illustration of minoritization is historical: white settlers who chose to live among the Indians. Today, whites who marry nonwhites and adopt a nonwhite life style are another illustration. Some minoritization may also occur in local areas where a majority adopts many minority customs. Examples are Southwestern areas of the United States where Spanish and Mexican influences are strong, and pockets in the Midwest where various Scandinavian groups have had much influence. On the other hand, perhaps these examples should not be carried too far. Great gulfs between groups may still exist. State laws proclaiming English the official language can be interpreted as resistance to minoritization, as can exclusion, Anglo conformity, and discrimination. One would conclude, based on past research and common observation, that resistance to minoritization has been largely successful.

Assimilation Defined

As mentioned, assimilation can be defined simply as the extent to which groups resemble each other. For empirical purposes, however, an operational definition is required. Following past research, assimilation is here defined as the extent to which a group differs from another group along a given empirical distribution. Assimilation implies non-assimilation or, as it is called in this context, *differentiation.* For example, if Group A does not have the same education distribution as Group B, then the groups are not assimilated insofar as education is concerned. Stated otherwise, the groups are educationally differentiated.

This operational definition of assimilation assumes that it is a multivariate phenomenon.[22] A group can be assimilated along some dimensions and not assimilated along others. A group may be educationally assimilated but occupationally differentiated. As a group, for example, Italians might attain the same education as the Irish but not the same occupations. Blacks might attain the same income as whites while the intermarriage rate remains minuscule. Thus, both assimilation and differentiation can simultaneously describe a group.

It further follows from the definition that assimilation is a structural property at the group level of analysis. An individual can be a point in a statistical distribution, but the individual cannot comprise the distribution. To be sure, an individual could be described as more or less assimilated, but that would simply be a verbal convenience and is not consistent with the terminology adopted here.[23]

Operationalizing Ethnicity

The Census Bureau nominally defined ancestry as descent, lineage, nationality group, or the country of origin of the respondent's parents or ancestors. The specific question asked of the householder (the person who filled in the census questionnaire) was: "What is this person's ancestry? For example, Afro-Amer., English . . . Venezuelan, etc."[24] Approximately 400 specific ancestries were tabulated. As they stood, these groupings were not usable for present purposes, hence a series of refinements were applied, as follows.

1. Broader categories were required, but not so broad as to mask potentially important differences. For example, the Census Bureau lists *Welsh* and *Cornish* separately and, although they undoubtedly differ, American culture does not define them as distinct ethnic entities. Thus, they were combined with the broader category of *British*. Although this example may be self evident, it was an exception. The Census Bureau listed many unfamiliar ancestries, and to ameliorate this problem, the *Harvard Encyclopedia of Ethnic Groups* was chosen as the standard reference. When in doubt, the volume was consulted to determine into which ethnic group a specific ancestry should be placed.

The choice of the *Harvard Encyclopedia* was predicated on the assumption that it is the most up-to-date and inclusive compendium now available. It contains over 100 separate ethnic groups, each discussed by a person with special expertise on the group. The pieces roughly follow a standard outline, so substantial commonality exists among them. While not perfect, the *Harvard Encyclopedia* did serve as a useful and public criterion for resolving questions about where to place specific ancestral categories.

Using the *Harvard Encyclopedia* further helped to ensure that some consensus existed as to whether a group was an ethnic group *qua* group. Quite possibly, respondents might list a specific ancestry that did not have an established identity in the United States. It would have been perfectly legitimate for some respondents to list their ancestry as Umbrian, but do Umbrians constitute a distinctive American ethnic group?[25] Would it not be more sensible to place Umbrians within the broader category of Italians, as in fact, was done in the present case?

2. In a heterogeneous society such as the United States, many people claim a diverse ethnic background: Dutch-French, Irish-German, and so on. To accommodate this, the Census questionnaire allowed for single, dual, and, in some cases, triple ancestry (together, the latter two are called "multiple ancestry"). When multiple ancestry was listed, additional criteria were needed.

If the first and second ancestry were the same, then the respondent was placed in that category. To illustrate, if both the first and second ancestry were French, then the respondent was considered French. If the first and second categories were different, such as Swedish and Dutch, the person was considered to have multiple ancestry with the first (primary) ancestry being Swedish. If, to take another possibility, the first response was Welsh and the second response was English, then the respondent was considered British because both Welsh and English were part of the British category.

The Census Bureau anticipated that some triple ancestries would be "frequently reported," and coded 17 triplets, for example, German-Irish-Swedish. All triplets were coded as multiple ancestry, and the respondent's primary ancestry was assumed to be the first ancestry of the triplet. In this example, the respondent would be coded as having multiple ancestry with German as the primary ancestry. In practice, this procedure did not have a substantial impact on the data because only 2.8% of all respondents were initially coded as triple ancestry.

3. A numerical cutoff was imposed: at least 1,500 respondents were required in a category. Admittedly arbitrary, a minimum number was necessary to provide flexibility for statistical purposes.

A smaller number would severely limit the investigation. As it turned out, some categories had to be further regrouped to increase the number of respondents for analysis.

    4. Some respondents listed themselves as "Americans, North Americans, Caucasians/white." Those persons were placed in the generic category *Anglo American*.

    These criteria helped produce a manageable number of more rigorously defined groups. Table 1.1 shows the composition of the 20 groups that resulted from applying these procedures. Note that *British* includes, among others, Australians and non-French speaking Canadians. The underlying commonality for this particular grouping is British historical influence. For some purposes, distinguishing between those specific groups might be useful, but that was not true here. The Hispanic categories should also be explicitly mentioned. The Spanish consist of persons who list themselves as *Nuevo Mexicano, Californios, Tejanos,* or terms that distinguish them from other Hispanics. This group is historically distinct from Spaniards (people from Spain) and Mexicans. While the Spanish are often lumped with Mexicans for statistical purposes, many Spanish resent the practice.[26] As it turned out, these criteria produced distinct categories for Mexicans and Spanish, but not for other Hispanic groups. These other groups were placed in the generic category of *Other Hispanic*. Also forming a generic group were Asians. There were simply too few to classify them into separate categories, such as Japanese or Vietnamese. It should be noted that the category *Asian* includes people from India. The two *Other* categories, white and nonwhite, will sometimes be shown for sake of completeness but will not be interpreted because they are so heterogeneous.

Ethnicity and Race

    Ancestry and race often overlap; for instance, the typical Irish person is white; the typical Asian is nonwhite. While one expects the overlap to be high, how high is an empirical question. In Table 1.2, the racial categories provided by the Census Bureau have been cross-classified with the ethnic categories just defined. In several instances the overlap exceeds 99%. Even among the generic category of Anglo American, almost 93% say they are racially white. Conversely, 99% of Afro Americans list their race as black. The category of Native American includes various Indian groups, of whom 70% consider themselves white and 26% consider themselves Indian.

TABLE 1.1

Ethnic Groups Used in This Study

Ethnic Group	Specific Ancestry Included in Ethnic Group*
Afro American	Afro American, Black, Negro
Anglo American	American, North American, United States, White, Caucasian
Asian	Asian, Subcontinent, Near East
British	English, non-French Canadian, Australian
Czech	Czech
Dutch	Dutch, Hollander, Netherlander
French	French, French Canadian
German	German
Irish	Irish
Italian	Italian
Mexican	Mexican, Mexican American, Chicano
Native American	American Indian, Eskimo
Norwegian	Norwegian
Other Hispanic	Cuban, South American, Spanish speaking Caribbean
Other Nonwhite	All others listing their race as nonwhite
Other White	All others listing their race as white
Polish	Polish
Russian	Russian, Belorussian
Spanish	Californio, Tejano
Swedish	Swedish

*There are over 400 ancestry categories, so only selected ones are shown for illustration.

Among the Hispanic groups, the majority list their race as white, although a substantial number wrote in a Spanish category that was not listed on the Census Bureau questionnaire. That they did so implies they strongly identified with being Hispanic and rejected being classified as racially white. The broad category of Asian is composed of several groups that identify with specific races: for instance, 18% list their race as Chinese and 9% list it as Asian Indian.

Clearly, some ethnic groups are overwhelmingly white while others are overwhelmingly nonwhite. Regardless of *a priori* theoretical distinctions between ethnicity and race, in practice they are so highly related that in most instances, to speak of the ethnicity is to speak of race.

Ethnicity and Inequality

TABLE 1.2

Ancestry and Race*

Ancestry Group	Race												
	W	B	C	F	J	K	H	V	OA	AI	I	S	O
Swedish	100.0												
Norwegian	99.8												
German	99.7												
Italian	99.7												
Polish	99.7												
French	98.6	1.0[b]											
Russian	99.6												
Irish	99.5												
Czech	99.4												
Dutch	99.4												
British	98.5	1.2											
Anglo American	92.8	6.2											
Afro American	1.0	98.8											
Native American	70.4	2.6									26.0		2.3
Spanish	68.4	1.4[b]									27.5	3.0[b]	
Mexican	54.5										40.1	4.2	
Other Hispanic	57.8	3.2[b]									33.2	5.3	

	Race												
	W	B	C	F	J	K	H	V	OA	AI	I	S	O
Asian	8.2		17.9	20.3	15.7	9.1	4.5	6	6.3	9.2			1.8[b]
Other White	98.5												
Other Nonwhite	8.4[b]	84.2	1.6							2.1			1.6[b]
Missing	84.2	12.6										1.5	

*Percent of the ancestry category in that racial category. Values less than 1% are not shown. Row values do not equal 100% due to rounding.
[b]Fewer than 100 persons in this category.
Legend: W: White; B: black; C: Chinese; F: Filipino; J: Japanese; K: Korean; H: Hawaiian; V: Vietnamese; OA: Other Asian; AI: Asian Indian; I: American Indian, Aleut, Eskimo; S: Spanish write-in.

Interestingly, some overlapping categories are "non-logical," such as *Other Nonwhites* or *Asians* who list their race as white. Because of these cases, the ethnic groupings were refined. In Table 1.3 groups usually considered white (or nonwhite) consist solely of whites (or nonwhites). To illustrate, persons who listed their ancestry as Dutch and their race as black were placed in the category *Other nonwhite;* persons who listed their ancestry as Asian and their race as white were placed in the category *Other white.* While the procedure did not affect very many respondents, the result was a more rigorously defined set of ethnic groups than found in previous research.

Even after applying the above procedures, one might argue that the categories do not form a single dimension—ethnic groupings (such as Swedish) are mixed with racial groupings (such as Afro American). On the other hand, because the two dimensions are so highly related, one can argue that the categories reflect an empirical reality. To analyze an ethnic distribution is to analyze a racial distribution.[27]

Perhaps reflecting this high overlap, the distinction between race and ethnicity is often ignored in practice. For example, the term *race relations* is already reified in the titles of university courses, textbooks, monographs, articles, and popular culture. Many researchers substitute the term *ethnic* relations for *race* relations because, I suspect, they are uneasy with genetic determinism. Nevertheless, given the close relationship between the two variables, the substitution does not affect the content of the discussion. Because of that, I use *ethnic* throughout the remainder of this monograph.

Ethnic Group Composition of the United States

Using the ethnic categories as just defined, Figure 1.1 shows the ethnic composition of the United States. The British constitute the single largest ethnic group in the country—one out of five Americans falls in that category. Between the British and the second largest group, Germans, there is a gap of five percentage points, and between Germans and the third largest group, Afro Americans, a six percentage point gap exists. From there, the sizes of the groups steadily decrease by lesser increments until the smallest groups are reached at one percent of the total.

These data are not identical to some others, notably the special counts made in conjunction with the Current Population Survey of 1979. That research found the English comprised 22% of the popu-

TABLE 1.3

Ethnic Groups Used in this Study As Modified by Race

Ethnic Group	Race	Ancestry Categories Included in Ethnic Group*
Afro American	Nonwhite	Afro American, Black, Negro
Anglo American	White	American, North American, United States, White, Caucasian
Asian	Nonwhite	Asian, Subcontinent, Near East
British	White	English, non-French Canadian, Australian
Czech	White	Czech
Dutch	White	Dutch, Hollander, Netherlander
French	White	French, French Canadian
German	White	German
Irish	White	Irish
Italian	White	Italian
Mexican	Nonwhite	Mexican, Mexican American, Chicano
Native American	Nonwhite	American Indian, Eskimo
Norwegian	White	Norwegian
Other Hispanic	Nonwhite	Cuban, South American, Spanish-speaking Caribbean
Other Nonwhite	Nonwhite	All others listing their race as nonwhite
Other White	White	All others listing their race as white
Polish	White	Polish
Russian	White	Russian, Belorussian
Spanish	Nonwhite	Californio, Tejano
Swedish	White	Swedish

*There are over ancestry 400 categories, so only selected ones are shown for illustration.

lation, the Irish 24%, and the Germans 29%.[28] These figures differ substantially from those shown on Figure 1.1. However, the Current Population Survey counted the same respondents in more than one ethnic category and, moreover, the ethnic categories were not identical to those used here.[29]

Single and Multiple Ancestry: Ancestral Diffusion

Because the Census Bureau tabulated both single and multiple ancestry, assimilation may be studied in a unique way. Claims of single ancestry should decrease as an ethnic group assimilates—

FIGURE 1.1

Ethnic Group Composition of the United States, 1980

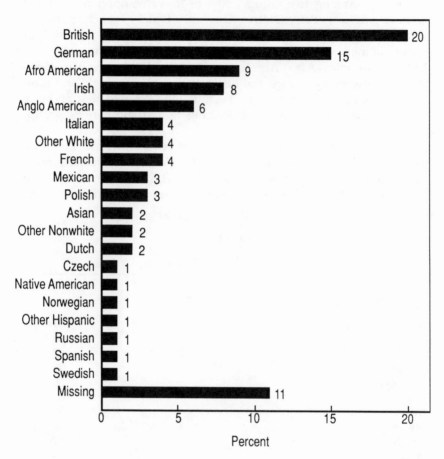

Percent

that is, assimilation across ethnic boundaries blurs the boundaries themselves. This process, implied by the concept of the melting pot, I call *ancestral diffusion*.

Overall, 60% of the sample claimed single ancestry, 29% claimed multiple ancestry, and the remaining 11% were missing. The 60% figure implies that the majority of Americans are ancestrally assimilated, but by the same token, 29% remain differentiated. Of course, whether this situation bespeaks "high assimilation" is a judgmental matter, not one of statistics. Statistically, however, considerable variation does exist among the groups (see Table 1.4). Among five groups, 50% or fewer respondents claimed to have single ancestry (Native American, Dutch, French, Swedish, and Norwegian). At the other extreme, among six groups 90% or more claimed single ancestry (Other Nonwhite, Asian, Mexican, Other Hispanic, Afro American, and Anglo American). However, for Anglo Americans the distinction between single and multiple ancestry might not apply. Persons who claimed that ancestry probably view themselves as belonging to a single generic group, *American*.

The findings are broadly consistent with American immigration history. Groups that met the most welcome should have most easily diffused into American society and, therefore, should be characterized by the lowest rates of single ancestry. That is so. The

TABLE 1.4

Ethnic Group by Single Ancestry

Ethnic Group	Percent Single Ancestry*
Native American	31
Dutch	36
French	42
Swedish	49
Norwegian	50
German	55
Irish	55
British	59
Czech	62
Polish	64
Russian	64
Other White	69
Italian	72
Spanish	79
Other Nonwhite	90
Asian	94
Mexican	95
Other Hispanic	96
Afro American	99
Anglo American	100

*Percent of the ethnic group that listed one ancestry.

lowest percentages of single ancestry are among Western European groups: Dutch, French, Swedish, Norwegian, German, Irish, and British. (The only category with a lower percentage, Native Americans, consists of indigenous groups that were not affected by immigration law).

Also consistent with the foregoing line of reasoning are the results regarding Eastern Europeans. They were less welcomed to these shores, a fact reflected in the small quotas assigned to them by the 1924 Immigration Act. Accordingly, they should be less ancestrally diffused than Western Europeans, an expectation substantiated by the data. The percentages of single ancestry among Czechs, Poles, and Russians are higher than among Western Europeans.

The Spanish and Italians do not neatly fit into the Western-Eastern European dichotomy, but for the Italians at least, their relatively low rates of ancestral diffusion might be explained by ethnic hostility. They have been the butt of much discrimination and have formed tightly knit ethnic communities.[30] The same might be true of the Spanish. With much less research to draw upon, however, that explanation must be regarded as highly speculative.

The table also shows the pronounced effect of color (white versus nonwhite) on ancestral diffusion. Groups usually considered to be nonwhite (Other Nonwhite, Asian, Mexican, Other Hispanic, and Afro American) have the highest percentages of single ancestry, in all cases exceeding 90%. If racial and ethnic hostility explain the lack of ancestral diffusion, the nonwhite cases fit the explanation.

Place of Birth and Ancestral Diffusion

Another expectation regarding single ancestry relates to the proportion of immigrants within a group. All else equal, groups with a large number of immigrants should be less assimilated because the foreign born have had less opportunity to be formally and informally socialized into American culture. Overall, six percent of the sample is foreign born, but that figure masks the wide variation between ethnic groups (see Table 1.5).

At one extreme, 62% of Asians were born abroad followed by 43% to 29% of the various Hispanic groups. At the other extreme, 0% (after rounding) of Anglo and Native Americans were foreign born. These data roughly correspond to what is known: specifically, that Asian and Hispanic immigration has increased markedly in the last two decades, and that Afro, Anglo, and Native Americans are basically indigenous groups.

TABLE 1.5

Foreign Born by Ethnic Group

Ethnic Group	Percent Foreign Born
Asian	62
Other Hispanic	43
Mexican	29
Spanish	23
Other White	17
Russian	13
Italian	9
Czech	8
Pole	7
French	4
Dutch	4
Norwegian	4
Swede	3
German	2
British	2
Irish	2
Afro American	1
Anglo American	0
Native American	0

To further explain ancestral diffusion, information on place of birth can be combined with information on single ancestry. For instance, Italian immigrants are more likely to have only Italian forbears than American-born Italians, if for no other reason than number; in Italy there are more Italians to marry. In contrast, American-born Italians are a statistical minority living in a heterogeneous society, and they will therefore encounter many non-Italians. Also, Italians born in the United States are socialized into Italian-American rather than Italian culture. For these reasons, one would expect a higher proportion of the foreign born to claim single ancestry than the native born. The data bear out this possibility (see Table 1.6).

Some cells on the table contain fewer than 100 respondents (marked with the pound sign—#), and extra caution should be exercised when considering those figures. Moreover, the data are anomalous for Anglo Americans because none were foreign born and all claimed single ancestry.

TABLE 1.6

Single Ancestry and Place of Birth*

	Foreign Born	Native Born	Difference**
Dutch	89	34	55
Swedish	93#	47	46
French	80	40	40
Norwegian	88#	49	39
German	91	54	37
Irish	83	54	29
British	83	58	25
Russian	96	59	37
Polish	93	62	31
Czech	58	92	-34
Italian	98	69	29
Spanish	89	76	13
Native American	100#	31	69
Mexican	99	94	5
Asian	98	68	30
Afro American	95	99	-4
Other Hispanic	96	96	0
Other White	96	63	33
Other Nonwhite	93	89	4
Anglo American	0#	100	-100
Mean	94	76	18

*Percent single ancestry.
**Foreign minus native.
#Fewer than 100 respondents.

The data show that, overall, 94% of the foreign born claimed single ancestry, as did 76% of the native born—a difference of 18 percentage points. When the contrast is drawn for specific groups, larger and smaller differences exist. For instance, 89% of the Dutch foreign born claimed single ancestry, but only 34% of the native born did so, a difference of 55 percentage points. Among Czechs, however, the pattern is reversed: the native born have a higher percentage of single ancestry than the foreign born. Except to say that Czechs are an old and some say, an unusually cohesive group, an explanation for this finding is not immediately forthcoming.[31]

With the minor exception of the Czechs, the overall conclusion is clear enough: as predicted, persons born in the United States usually have a more varied ancestral background than persons born abroad.

Assuming that single ancestry indexes a type of assimilation, then the overall rank order from most to least assimilated is

1. Western European
2. Eastern European
3. Spanish and Italian
4. Nonwhites

The ranking comes as no surprise. It conforms to what is known about the history of American ethnic relations: Western Europeans were preferred above all others, nonwhites were actively rejected, and Eastern Europeans and Levanters were between those two extremes. The ranking of Western Europeans also conforms to the widespread belief that they made the major contribution to American culture.

Although there is no doubt that Western Europeans are the majority in the United States, there remains the question of their precise number. Figure 1.2 speaks to that question, showing that Western Europeans make up 51% of the population, over twice the size of any other group. Even the conglomerate grouping of Others and Nonwhites combined comprises less than 40% of the total. Thus, numerically and perhaps culturally, Western Europeans can be considered the majority in the United States.

This finding reaffirms what is already widely believed. It is nevertheless important because it is derived from quantitative data rather than sheer assumption. On some occasions in the monograph, the broad categories shown in Figure 1.2 will be used, while on other occasions, the finer categories shown on Table 1.3 will be more appropriate.

Summary and Conclusions

On *a priori* grounds, race and ethnicity are distinct concepts, the former defined by some aspect of biological make-up and the latter by culture. As the data imply, however, the distinction may be more verbal than behaviorally real. In American society, the overwhelming number of people list their ancestry in a way that coincides with their race. Afro Americans list their race as black,

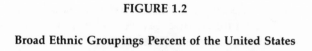

FIGURE 1.2

Broad Ethnic Groupings Percent of the United States

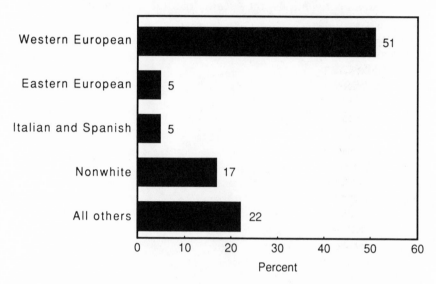

Europeans list it as white. Even among Hispanics, whose race is often debated, 30% to 40% deliberately wrote in a Hispanic designation on the Census questionnaire rather than checking the pre-assigned category of *white*. That they would make such an explicit effort suggests great depth of feelings behind their answers. This does not mean, though, that all ethnic distinctions should be ignored. Within broad groupings, ethnicity does define an important difference (e.g., between French and German within the white grouping), but between broad groupings, color is the overriding difference.

The overlap between ethnicity and race also means that both can empirically be used as part of a single dimension. Dimensions such as "British, Dutch . . . Mexican, Black" or "European . . . Nonwhite" are conceptually meaningful. Although they may seem strange at first glance, they are really no stranger than a more commonly seen dimension such as "White . . . Black, Filipino, Chinese." In that usage, Black, Filipino and Chinese are subcategories of nonwhite, while Filipino and Chinese are simultaneously subcategories of Asian. Yet the dimension does not jar our conceptual sensibilities, undoubtedly because we are so accustomed to seeing it

(for example, in Census Bureau codebooks). The distinctions between race and ethnicity, and between the subcategories within
them, are mainly matters of agreed usage. They are conventions
and, like all conventions, they seem "natural" and need not rest on
any logic or data.

2

Ethnicity and Socioeconomic Inequality

Socioeconomic status refers to the structured inequality found in all societies and is possibly the single most important facet of a society's organization. It both determines and simultaneously *is* the fate of individuals as well as entire categories of people, including ethnic groups. To designate a group as a minority is to recognize that the group has but little status and not much power, wealth, prestige, comfort, freedom, mobility, or opportunity. To an important extent, then, the study of ethnic relations is the study of inequality.

In an egalitarian society, such as the United States aspires to be, individuals can climb the socioeconomic ladder as high as their drive and ability will permit. It is said that "any boy can become president." Of course, this aphorism excludes more than half of all Americans, which suggests that some ascriptive characteristics must be at work, and that individual motivation is not the sole determinant of upward mobility. This recognition helps refocus the issue. Rather than casting it in terms of the social psychology of individuals, the issue can be cast in terms of groups and societal structures. Very basic questions can be asked. The following are examples, meant to illustrate some basic issues and their importance:

1. How many ethnic groups are there? Although seemingly obvious, this is not an idle question. As already shown (in Chapter 1), the number of groups is a function of the criteria used to define them, and in turn, the criteria are a function of complex social forces.

2. How are these groups ranked? To answer this question, the ranking criteria must be made explicit, a task to which this chapter is devoted.

3. Is the ranking system applicable to all groups, or is it specific to a given group? If the ranking criteria apply only to one group, then it might be impossible to derive a general explanation.

These questions, though seemingly simple, are fundamental. Without knowing the answers to them, attempts to develop sophisticated theories will founder. For example, a theory of ethnic relations that assumes—mistakenly—that a given ranking system prevails will generate erroneous hypotheses; and a theory that does not acknowledge the existence of certain groups will produce an incomplete explanation. Fortunately, census data now available are well suited to answering such questions. This is especially true of the 1980 Census of Population because it asked, for the first time, a question of ancestry.

Background

Two broad perspectives for interpreting inequality have assumed major standing: the Marxian and the Weberian. These will be briefly reviewed as backdrop for considering ethnic variations in socioeconomic status.

Marxian Approach

Any discussion of the Marxian approach risks becoming a discourse on the "correct" interpretations of Marx. In this regard, Erik Olin Wright stated, "As anyone familiar with the recent history of Marxist thought will know, there is hardly a consensus among Marxists over any aspect of the concept of class"[1] Wright, nevertheless, does offer another interpretation, which is that Marx distinguished between class structure and formation.[2] As a structure, class consists of empty slots. The organization of the slots remains constant but different individuals occupy slots at various times. Formation refers to the development of organized entities and collectivities within a class. These can emerge, change, and go out of existence without altering the basic structure of the class system. Thus, class structure is static while class formation is dynamic.

In a capitalistic society, private ownership of property leads to the formation of classes. People find themselves related to the means of production either as owners (bourgeoisie) or as workers (proletariat). Because the profit motive drives capitalism, owners continually and relentlessly exploit workers, a process that polarizes the two classes. As the gap between the classes widens, each becomes more internally homogeneous, increasing the potential for conflict between them.

According to a basic Marxian belief, the system favors the upper classes because they can convert their position into power along multiple institutional fronts (such as politics, law, and education), thereby using the system to their advantage. The often heard assertion that capitalist systems produce governments, economies, families, and other institutions with a capitalist orientation exemplifies this logic.

An alternative logic exists, of course. Weberian analysts both agree and disagree with the Marxian approach, and as a consequence, come to much different conclusions.

Weberian Approach

Weber rooted his analysis in power, describing stratification as "... phenomena of the distribution of power within a community."[3] His definition of power—the ability to realize one's will against the resistance of others—was broad, leading him to differentiate between types of power. He wrote, " 'Economically conditioned' power is not, of course, identical with 'power' as such. On the contrary, the emergence of economic power may be the consequence of power existing on other grounds."[4] After establishing the concept of power, Weber then argued that stratification flowed from it. He divided stratification into three types: class, status, and party. Only the first two will be discussed here because the third, party, leads into the realm of political power and authority, topics that are not relevant to the present concern.

With regard to class, Weber first identified the concept of *life chances*, or fundamental outcomes such as success, happiness, and wealth. Life chances were determined by economic forces, in particular by the power to exchange goods and skills for income in a labor or commodity market. A *class* was a grouping of people whose life chances were determined by the same economic factors.[5] Hence, class derived from the marketplace, or more accurately, marketplace power.

The second of Weber's dimensions is social *status:* "... every typical component of the life fate of men that is determined by a specific, positive or negative, social estimation of *honor*."[6] Weber felt that status led to the development of *status groups:* distinct social collectivities that were maintained by giving preferential economic treatment to group members, marital endogamy, and other elements of life style. Weber also argued that although property is not always a precursor to status honor, "... in the long run, it is, and with extraordinary regularity."[7] This means that as an empirical matter, class—an economically derived category—would be highly correlated with status, especially in the long run.

Carried farther, status groups evolve into castes, but usually only when the underlying differences between the status groups are ethnic or racial. Weber is not clear about the relationship between caste segregation and ethnic segregation. He says that in a caste situation, ethnic groups live alongside each other in relative harmony, but that at the same time, caste transforms the relationship between groups into vertically structured system of super- and subordinate relationships. He wrote:

> In their consequences they differ precisely in this way: ethnic coexistence conditions a mutual repulsion and disdain but allows each ethnic community to consider its own honor as the highest one; the caste structure brings about a social subordination and an acknowledgment of "more honor" in favor of the privileged caste and status groups.[8]

Weber's statement anticipated, in inchoate form, ideas that would later become prominent among American race relations scholars, especially the application of caste to black-white relations.

Although Weber's scheme possesses a logical neatness, some aspects are nevertheless confused. He said that honor determines status; that economics determine class; and that status and class frequently overlap. This seems inconsistent, for if status and class overlap, then which factor—honor or economics—determines status? Presumably, because honor is expressed in life style, and life style rests on an economic substratum, economics ultimately determine status. While the correctness of this interpretation can be debated, it is consistent with many modern researchers who use occupation to operationalize stratification.

Weber only briefly mentioned occupation, simply saying that an occupational group was also a status group. That is because occupation confers a life style that becomes the basis for social honor.[9] Life style is economic, and so occupation is also economic. As Wright has noted, "frequently, in fact, when sociologists equate blue-collar workers with the working class and white-collar workers with the middle class, they are thinking of occupations in terms of market capacities more than technical conditions per se."[10] This point has present relevance, for it opens the way to operationalizing status with data collected by the Census Bureau. To rely on the old analogy of geologic strata, each layer of the structure represents a quantum of income, education, occupation, and prestige (unfortunately, the last cannot be measured with census data).[11]

While I usually follow this Weberian logic, I do not use a strict Weberian terminology. I define *status* as a position within a structure. When education, income, and occupation are used to measure status, I call it *socioeconomic status*. This fits well with current terminology, and with operationalizations based on census data.

Ethnicity and Socioeconomic Status

The relation between ethnicity and socioeconomic status is not well understood. Although the relationship has been investigated before, those investigations have usually been tangential to other aims. The amount of accumulated knowledge is thus unexpectedly small and fragmented, but that does not mean the knowledge is valueless. Quite the opposite, it has implications for ethnicity in general, and for the specific dimension of socioeconomic status being studied here.

One of the most influential and now classic investigations in this area was conducted by John Dollard: *Caste and Class in a Southern Town*.[12] First published in 1937, his monograph set out, in great ethnographic detail, the social organization of American race relations as it then existed in one Southern locale. He compared black-white class structures, identifying three classes among whites. The lower class ("poor whites") were basically manual workers without "proper" ancestry, capital, or talent. They envied and resented middle- and upper-class whites, and middle-class blacks as well. The white middle class consisted of small business owners, professionals, and managers. They held both lower-class whites and blacks in great contempt. Rather than descending from the upper class, middle-class persons ascended from the lower class, according to Dollard. That was because upper-class standing could not be achieved; it was inherited. The forebears of the upper class were noted political, military, and business leaders, and although the current generation did not necessarily meet that past eminence, they nevertheless kept their class standing.

The strata found among whites could also be found among blacks. Like whites, the black lower class consisted largely of manual workers. However, unlike the white middle class, which included many business people and professionals, the black middle class consisted mostly of ministers and teachers. This group drew a sharp distinction between themselves and the black lower class, and stressed conventional behavior. They also stressed education, which meant that upward mobility might be achieved rather than being completely ascribed. Dollard candidly admitted to not knowing very much about the black upper class, but did say that the number was quite small.[13]

To Dollard, race had become caste and had replaced slavery as a means of maintaining white dominance. Within each racial group, class was the primary segregating variable, while between groups race-caste constituted an insurmountable barrier. Paradoxically, the existence of this barrier permitted whites and blacks to interact, especially along economic lines. White businesses sought middle class blacks as customers, landowners, and renters. In many instances, blacks provided services for whites, and the black middle class acted as a link between the two communities. As long as the barrier of race-caste existed, these economic and social relationships could be pursued without undermining the basic tenet of white superiority.[14]

In 1945, St. Clair Drake and Horace Cayton brought out a multi-volume study of Chicago's black community. They included a lengthy discussion of social class, and wrote, "Everybody in Bronzevill recognizes the existence of social classes, whether called that or not."[15]

Although Drake and Cayton used the term "class," they measured it with education, rent, and occupation, an operationalization consistent with the Weberian notion of socioeconomic status. They estimated that 5% of blacks were in the upper, 30% were in the middle, and 65% were in the lower classes. The corresponding values for whites were 10%, 40%, and 50% respectively.

Cross-cutting the horizontal stratification layers among blacks were vertical dimensions consisting of "church centered" activity and the respectability derived from it, and "shady activities," or illegitimate pursuits that were openly conducted throughout the black community with the complicity of the white power structure. The lower the strata, the less the church centered activity and the greater the shady activity. At the very bottom of the socioeconomic system was a layer that presumably was totally shady. Drake and Cayton called it the "underworld" but did not discuss it (indeed, they did not even list it in the index).[16]

Gunnar Myrdal also noted a shady element in the black socioeconomic system, and used the same term. He emphasized that the hierarchical distinctions within the shady strata rested on wealth and power, while within the broader black community, education was the primary criterion for determining socioeconomic standing (a point also made by Dollard).[17] The reason was the lack of black wealth. Myrdal wrote, "But there is so little of it [wealth] in the Negro community. And education is such a high value to this group, which has to struggle for it, that it is understandable why education is more important, relatively, for Negro status than for white status."[18] Because education was more readily attainable than wealth, the distance between the upper and lower strata was shorter, and the potential for upward mobility was, therefore, higher among blacks than whites.

Like Dollard, Myrdal recognized caste but argued that caste "caused" class in the sense that caste forced blacks to create a parallel stratification system. A lower, middle, and upper class existed among both groups, but the proportion of blacks and whites in each strata was different: "Any reasonable criterion used to describe the white lower class would, when applied to Negroes, put the majority of the latter in the lower class."[19] Unlike whites, employment by the government, the acquisition of some education, or home ownership was sufficient to place a black in the black upper class.

Myrdal's description of the black middle class was brief and confused. It apparently consisted of persons who held modest, relatively insecure jobs, and who possessed some education. The exceptions were black school teachers. Contrary to many analysts, Myrdal considered them to be middle rather than upper class.[20] Seemingly, that would even contradict his own assertions about the nature of the black class system.

E. Franklin Frazier's study of black life traced the origins of the black middle class to the few free blacks who existed prior to the Civil War, the ideology of free enterprise adopted by black business, the small group (about one-tenth) of educated blacks, and to the more open opportunities available when blacks migrated to the urban north.[21] The feature of his class analysis that has always been most salient concerns the over-conformity of the black middle class. It clearly dismayed him, and he wrote, "In the world of make-believe, middle class Negroes engage in all sorts of conspicuous consumption which set them apart from the Negro masses."[22] The same features has been noted by Drake and Clayton when they spoke of the "cult of clothes" that was an important part in black middle class life: "Prosperity has made possible an extreme elaboration of the 'cult of clothes' which serves to integrate the world of 'Society' and the world of Church in upper-class and middle-class circles."[23] In many ways, these comments remind one of Thorstein

Veblen's early notion of conspicuous consumption, wherein taste becomes defined in terms of costs, and status becomes synonymous with the acquisition and display of costly accoutrements.

The contention that blacks over-conform to a life style they envy can also be interpreted as an ethnic specification of a widely accepted notion, perhaps most thoroughly articulated as the "Dummont-Banks model" with reference to fertility in Victorian England. One logical kernel of the model widely applies: persons seeking upward mobility take on the trappings and values of the strata they aspire to.[24] Or in Weber's terminology, those wishing to join a higher status group adopt and overdo the higher group's dress, manners, and beliefs. When upward striving occurs at higher income levels, those persons are sometimes called the _nouveau riche_, implying that some aspects of status cannot be acquired through purchase.

While blacks have garnered much attention, the socioeconomic situation of white ethnic groups has not been ignored. As part of the investigation of Yankee City, Lloyd Warner and Leo Srole published a monograph devoted to ethnic relations.[25] In it, they examined the socioeconomic position of American Irish, Jews, Armenians, Greeks, French-Canadians, Italians, Poles, and Russians. The authors argued that the economic system of Yankee City could be divided into three broad strata, as shown on Table 2.1.[26]

This scheme explicitly links occupation with both social class and status, and resembles schemes to be discussed momentarily.

TABLE 2.1

Socioeconomic Categories Used by Warner and Srole[a]

Socioeconomic Level	Occupation	Predominant Class Identification	Status Score
Manual	unskilled labor	lower	1.0
	skilled labor	upper lower	2.0
	skilled craft	upper lower	2.5
White collar	management-aid and operations	lower middle and upper middle	3.0 4.0
Professional		upper middle	6.0

[a]Warner and Srole, 1945: 58–59.

Warner and Srole applied a status measure to individuals in each ethnic group to obtain a mean rating as follows:[27]

Irish, 2.5; French Canadian, 2.2; Jews, 3.3; Italians, 2.3; Armenians, 2.6; Greeks, 2.3; Poles, 2.0; Russians, 2.0, Natives ("Yankees"), 2.6.

While we might expect natives to outrank most groups, in fact they had approximately the same status as Armenians and the Irish (skilled craft). Jews had the highest mean status score (white collar) whiles Russians and Poles had the lowest (skilled labor). These scores may seem somewhat low, but we should not forget that the study was conducted during the 1930s when the first generation of immigrants still predominated. The scores could imply high mobility, especially since the authors stated that, "With the exception of the French Canadians, the societies in which the ethnics had their roots were all characterized by a class system similar to the feudal type."[28]

Warner and Srole argued that upward mobility resulted from successive replacement. As one group moved upward, another took its place. This was possible because expansion increased economic opportunities, making it possible for new ethnic groups to *replace* (rather than *displace*) older groups. Warner and Srole were, in effect, arguing for structural mobility, or mobility that occurs because the system itself expands, creating slots that ethnic groups can fill without coming into direct competition with the majority.

More recently, Herbert Gans analyzed ethnicity and class among Italian-Americans *circa* the 1960s in the Boston West End. He subsequently updated the study in 1982.[29] Gans used participant observation to gather his materials, and did not take a systematic census of occupations, income, education, or other socioeconomic measures. Still, based on some statistical data and observation, he did suggest that the overwhelming majority of West Enders were in the working class. If we assume that his information refers mainly to Italians, and if we agree that unskilled work defines the lower class, then approximately 20% of Italians were in the lower class and only 1% were in the upper class (professional and managerial occupations).[30] This is not so different from the black distributions described earlier. Unlike blacks, however, West Enders did not use education as a major criterion for distinguishing between the strata. They limited the contrast to the highly educated versus the noneducated while emphasizing conventional morality, sacrifice, and loyalty toward the group as characteristics distinguishing among classes.[31]

Gans asserted that two contrasting hypotheses may be developed to explain the differences between West End society and the majority middle class: (1) West End society resulted from Italian American ethnicity; or (2) West End society resulted from working class culture. If the second hypothesis is correct, then class is more important than ethnicity. Conversely, if the first hypothesis is correct, then ethnicity is more important than class. Gans argued for the class hypothesis: "As I have tried to show, the similarities in ways of life over the generations have resulted from the similar economic and social positions that the Southern Italian and the West Enders have occupied in the larger Italian and American societies respectively."[32] By simple generalization, this conclusion should apply to other ethnic groups as well.

The conclusion is partially built into Gan's definition of class as "strata-with-subculture that *grows* out of the structure of the national economy and society."[33] Socioeconomic and class structures are integral components of ethnic group organization, and if they derive from the broader society, the group will probably resemble the broader society in those respects. The same process would also help homogenize the subculture attached to the strata, rendering it not ethnically unique. In contrast, the studies of blacks just reviewed suggest that Gan's conclusion applies most readily to whites. Nonwhites encounter a race-caste barrier, which substantially affects their socioeconomic organization.

The foregoing studies have spanned several decades and considered disparate groups in various regions of the United States. They have had different goals and have used different methodologies. As we might expect, the result is a montage of findings and hypotheses, yet commonalities do emerge. These are stated below:

1.   The studies emphasized class-related behaviors and attitudes, a clearly important realm of inquiry but one which cannot be pursued with the data being analyzed here.

2.   Few studies drew a sharp distinction between class and socioeconomic status. However, they often used criteria such as occupation, income, and education to distinguish between the classes, implying the importance of socioeconomic stratification.

3.   With regard to blacks, the studies argued that race constituted caste. With regard to white ethnic groups, ethnicity was not

as important as class or socioeconomic status in determining life chances because race did not constitute a caste barrier.

4. The final commonality was the assumption (often unstated) that the structure of socioeconomic status found among the ethnic groups mirrored that found among whites. While the emphasis given to factors such as wealth or education varied between groups, no group had developed a radically different system.

Taken collectively these commonalities define a basis for linking ethnicity to socioeconomic status. The most detailed and most successful attempt to do so is Milton Gordon's work.

Ethclass

Milton Gordon has probably confronted the issue of ethnicity and socioeconomic status more directly than any other writer. He devised a typology and wrote, "I propose, then, that we refer to the subsociety created by the intersection of the vertical stratifications of ethnicity with the horizontal stratifications of social class as the ethclass."[34]

This concept follows from Gordon's observation that while the stratification system of the minority mirrors that of the majority, the minority could still remain ethnically distinct. That was possible because assimilation takes place along two dimensions: cultural, such as customs or language, and structural, such as kinship or friendship networks. Gordon felt that cultural assimilation occurs quickly and widely, but that structural assimilation does not. Thus, ethclass, a structural dimension, can exist even while ethnic groups culturally merge with the majority. He wrote the following:

> American society is criss-crossed by two sets of stratification structures, one based on social status, economic power, and political power differences, regardless of ethnic background, the other a set of status and power relationships based precisely on division of the population by racial, nationality background and religious categories.[35]

To illustrate Gordon's scheme: upper-class Poles have a life style similar to that of the majority of upper class but usually marry upper-class Poles; middle-class Poles have a middle-class life style but usually marry middle-class Poles, and so on. In this manner, the ethnic group maintains its distinctive structure, develops a stratification system similar to the majority's, and adopts cultural elements of the majority into its life style. Put another way, ethclass forms. It, in turn, is interlaced with national institutions and organizations, such as the federal government, to constitute an ethnic *subsociety*.[36] Finally, Gordon said that ethclass is transferable: a person in a given ethclass could move to another community and take up the same ethclass as before.[37]

Gordon's concept has an intuitive appeal. It combines ethnicity with stratification in a way that makes sense and that is supported by common observation. Equally important here, portions of the ethclass can be investigated with the available data.[38]

Harry H. L. Kitano applied the concept of ethclass to Japanese Americans but modified it to include generation, resulting in what he termed *ethnic-gen* class. It is especially relevant to Japanese Americans because of all the ethnic groups in the United States, they attribute the most importance to generational standing.[39] The current research considers Asians and not Japanese Americans specifically; however, generation has implications that go beyond a single group. As already demonstrated, the foreign born (first generation) are less ancestrally diffused than the native born (second or later generation).[40]

Underclass

In the *Declining Significance of Race*, William Julius Wilson sparked an ongoing debate by claiming that race no longer determined the life chances of *some* American blacks: "although racial oppression . . . was a salient and important feature during the preindustrial and the industrial periods of race relations in the United States, the problems of subordination for certain segments of the black population and the experiences of social advancement for others are more directly associated with economic class in the modern industrial period."[41] Possibly because this contention created so much controversy, his statements about the black underclass passed relatively unnoticed until the publication of his book, *The Truly Disadvantaged*.[42]

Wilson characterized the underclass as a strata suffering from long-term poverty, heavy dependence on welfare, and chronic unemployment. Many people in the underclass do not seek work, and many are criminals or otherwise deviant. Of the underclass families that do exist, most are black, urban, and headed by females.[43] The underclass occupies the lowest rung on the stratification hierarchy, upward mobility is rare, and if it occurs, the move is to the lower class. While that technically qualifies as upward, it does not represent entry into the socioeconomic mainstream.

Like his ideas about the underclass, Wilson's ideas about the structure of socioeconomic status were noncontroversial. He closely adhered to the Weberian tradition, defining class as a group with more or less similar goods, services, and skills to offer for income. Again following Weber, he argued that economic class determines life chances.[44] He assumed that the structure of black socioeconomic status parallels that of the white majority, a belief coinciding (whether intentional or not) with Gordon's analysis of the ethclass. Wilson implied that the following strata exist among blacks:[45]

Middle class: white collar, skilled crafts, and foremen
Working class: semiskilled operatives
Lower class: unskilled laborers and domestics
Underclass: the truly disadvantaged

We might note the absence of a black upper class. Either it does not exist, or if it does, it is so small that Wilson feels safe in ignoring it. As will be seen momentarily, the proportion of blacks (and certain other groups) in the upper layers of the stratification system is, indeed, small. We might also note that if long-term poverty is an essential defining characteristic of the underclass, then persons caught in temporary poverty should be found throughout the socioeconomic system. An engineer might fall into short-term poverty after losing a job, but will not end up permanently in the underclass.

Assumptions

The preceding discussions of socioeconomic status, ethclass, and the underclass indicate that the following assumptions can be made:

1.   The majority imposes its stratification system on the minority. Or, using the terminology presented in the first chapter, parallel majority and minority socioeconomic structures result from Anglo conformity rather than from minoritization.

2.   If the first assumption is correct, then the socioeconomic structure of the minority must resemble the majority's. This does not mean, though, that the distribution of persons across the structure will be the same. For example, 10% of the majority might be in the highest strata as compared to 2% of an ethnic group. In general,

we would assume that ethnics will be underrepresented in the upper echelons and overrepresented in the lower ones. In fact, such a distribution is part of the definition of being a minority.

3. Another assumption is that "more is higher"—the more education, income, and occupational prestige a group has, the higher its position. Closely related is the assumption that "higher is more powerful"—the higher the socioeconomic status of a group, the more power it has in the sense of influence and control over its own destiny and that of others.

Of the three assumptions, the latter two seem well supported and relatively noncontroversial. The first (that the majority imposes it structure on the minority) has little direct evidence for it, but given the indirect hints found in the literature and the widespread acceptance of Anglo conformity, the assumption seems reasonable.

Categories of Stratification

Over thirty years ago, Joseph Kahl and James Davis examined nineteen indicators of socioeconomic status. Relying on factor analysis to discover the overlap (commonality) among the measures, they concluded that occupation was the single best indicator of socioeconomic status.[46] Some twenty years ago, Peter Blau and Otis Dudley Duncan pointed out two common approaches to measuring socioeconomic status: the first summarizes and orders occupations into a ranking; the second has respondents score specific occupations as to prestige.[47] Though not perfectly correlated, the two approaches yield the same basic result: "The status scores offer a useful refinement of the coarser classification but not a radically different pattern of grading."[48] Remarkably, given the quick and frequent changes that most sociological findings are subject to, these conclusions still remain appropriate. Across both time and culture, socioeconomic status has proven to be among the most enduring and constant of social structures. This is true even when operationalizing socioeconomic status with occupation. While we might think that the rapid changes caused by advances in technology would make for instability, the over-arching organization of occupations has stayed much the same over the years.

When operationalizing socioeconomic status with occupation, sheer numbers present a difficulty. The federal government alone has identified over 20,000 occupations and even more than that must exist. Since no one can accurately rank that many occupations, a categorization scheme must be used, and the scheme developed by Alba Edwards of the Census Bureau over fifty years ago remains useful. An example (Table 2.2), taken from Dennis Gilbert and Joseph Kahl's book, shows the structure of occupations along with income, education, and estimates of prestige.[49] The latter scores denote the "social standing of the occupation" and are based on surveys conducted by the National Opinion Research Center (NORC).[50]

A basic consistency exists among the measures. The ranks of median prestige generally correspond to the ranks of occupation. The same is true of median education, although that measure does not vary substantially across the middle strata. Least consistent of the three measures is median income. Managers and administrators, for example, earn more than professional and technical workers, yet the former have less prestige and education than the latter. Other income inversions of approximately the same magnitude can also be noted: sales compared to technical, and craft compared to clerical. One possible reason for these discrepancies is the width of the occupational categories. Professionals include physicians, who have high incomes, along with teachers, who have more modest incomes. Although the rankings among the measures do not perfectly correspond with each other, a substantial amount of overlap exists. Gilbert and Kahl concluded the following:

TABLE 2.2

Occupation, Income, Education, and Prestige[a]

Occupational Group	Income	Education	Prestige
Executives, administrators, and managers	31,000	15	75
Professionals	29,000	17	82
Technical	20,000	14	82
Sales	22,000	13	67
Clerical	17,000	13	65
Craft	18,000	12	68
Operatives	16,000	12	58
Laborer (except farm)	10,000	12	46
Farm worker	8,000	13	55[b]

[a]Adapted from Gilbert and Kahl, 1982, p. 69.
Income: median income in dollars, 1983; *education:* median school years completed, 1983; *prestige:* median NORC prestige score, 1961.
[b]Estimated.

The Edwards scheme, then, is less than perfect as stratification measure. However, it is doubtful that Edwards or his successors at the Census Bureau could have done much better given the difficulty of reducing the multitude of occupations represented in the work force.[51]

Delbert Miller echoes this sentiment, advising researchers to "choose Edward's socioeconomic grouping if a relatively broad classification is satisfactory for your problem."[52] With some modification, his advice will be followed here.

Table 2.3 shows the occupational structure that has been adopted for this study along with examples of specific jobs. Note that the occupational hierarchy slightly differs from the one shown on the previous table. One difference is that the positions of the professional and managerial groups have been reversed. This was done because the data (Table 2.2) indicated that although professionals do not have the most income, they do have the most education and prestige. Another difference is the combining of technical, sales, and clerical jobs into one category, and operatives and laborers (including farm) into another. The distinctions between these jobs did not seem large enough to warrant separate consideration. Moreover, combining them reduces the number of categories, an outcome desirable on methodological grounds. Even with the large sample being used, the combinations of ethnic groups and strata could easily produce sparse tables—that is, the number of cases in a cell might be too small for reliable analysis. Also, note the separate category for service occupations. This coincides with current Census Bureau practices and reflects the assumption that service occupations have assumed major importance in the economy. Finally, the underclass was added to the bottom of the hierarchy.

Operationally Defining the Underclass

Wilson characterized the underclass with a series of overlapping attributes—for instance, lack of labor force participation, long-term unemployment, and welfare. People not in the labor force are by definition, unemployed. They are also likely to be impoverished and, if impoverished, to be on welfare. Wilson also mentioned female-headed families and being black, but not all blacks and not all female-headed families are in the underclass.

Other analysts have offered hints about measuring the underclass (although not necessarily using that term). Clement Cottingham identified chronic poverty as the key.[53] Whether extending over

TABLE 2.3

Socioeconomic Categories and Occupation

Broad Occupational Category and Examples

Professional
Engineer, computer scientist, teacher, medical doctor, dentist.

Managerial
Legislator, chief executive officer, accountant, purchasing agent.

Technical
Technical, sales, administrative support, technologist, technician, sales, secretary, clerk.

Craft
Craft, precision production, farm, mechanics, repairers, precision production, farm operator.

Service
Launder, servant, fire fighter, police, cleaning person.

Labor
Laborer, operator, fabricator, machine operator, assembler, motor vehicle operator.

Underclass
Long term poverty, not in labor force, illegal occupations.

generations or short-term, poverty is associated with unemployment, welfare dependence, and hopelessness. Poverty is so intrinsic that the idea of a non-impoverished underclass is an oxymoron. Consequently, I used the following poverty variables to operationalize the underclass:

1. Poverty in 1979, measured by the federal government's poverty index. This index is based on two government studies. In 1955, the Department of Agriculture found that a typical family of three or more persons spent approximately one-third of their income on food. In 1961, the department devised an "economy food plan" taking family size into account. The poverty cutoff level was subsequently set at three times the estimated cost of this food plan, with the precise dollar amounts being adjusted for inflation. The index is not adjusted for transfer payments, assets, other sources of sustenance, or geographic variations in the cost of living.

If the total income of a family falls below this cutoff, then the entire family is considered poor. Poverty is also defined for persons not in families, with adjustments made to take their smaller households into account.

In 1979, the poverty cutoff for a family of two adults with two children under 18 years of age was an income of $7,356 per year, before taxes. For an unrelated individual, it was $3,686 per year.[54] These are hardly princely sums. As defined by the poverty index, the poor are very poor indeed.

2.   While the index operationalizes current poverty, the concept of the underclass connotes long-term poverty. The 1980 census does not contain such an item, and so a proxy was substituted: long-term unemployment, specifically, not having worked since 1978. The period of approximately one-and-a-half to two years (recall that poverty refers to 1979 and the Census was taken in 1980) would seem to operationalize "long-term unemployment." In effect, persons who were below the poverty cutoff in 1979 and who, in 1980, had not worked since 1978, were defined as the underclass.

The year 1978 was chosen on a somewhat but not totally arbitrary basis. In Figure 2.1, poverty has been plotted against year last worked. While the general outcome is as expected—the earlier the year last worked, the greater the percentage of poor—the trend is not linear. The percentage of poor markedly increased between 1979 and 1978, creating a "skree point" (place where a large discontinuity exists). This suggests that 1978 is an appropriate cutoff for long-term unemployment.

In addition to poverty and long-term unemployment, criteria were imposed to restrict the definition to a delimited category of people:

•   Age of 16 years or older, because the Census Bureau does not include anyone under that age in the labor force regardless of their work activity.

•   Not in school full-time, on the assumption that full-time students, whatever their current socioeconomic position, are in transitional status.

•   Not inmates of institutions, because the Census Bureau does not measure poverty for those persons.

If the occupational structure shown previously in Table 2.2 constitutes a unidimensional ranking, then the underclass may be interpreted as having the lowest occupational rank.[55] That interpretation does, however, introduce some ambiguity. Poverty and long-

FIGURE 2.1

Percent Poor by Year Worked

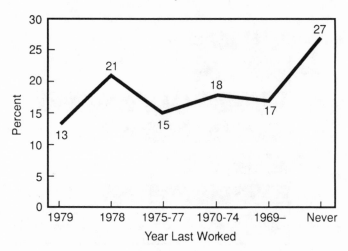

Year Last Worked

term unemployment jointly define the underclass, which means that underclass persons do not have official occupations. Because of this ambiguity, some researchers may find an alternative view more satisfactory: occupation as an index prestige, power, economic standing, or status (in the Weberian sense). From that view, the underclass has the least amounts.

None of the foregoing procedures directly measures behaviors, subculture, life chances, or what both Marx and Weber termed *class*. Poverty also consists of psychological dimensions, but they could not be operationalized with the present data either.[56] The current research can only organize measures, such as education, occupation, and income, into a ranking of socioeconomic slots. The organization remains constant while the relative numbers of each ethnic group in those slots varies. If we wish to make statements about *class*, we must assume that it varies systematically with stratification measured in this way. According to the literature reviewed earlier, this assumption is reasonable.

Structure of Socioeconomic Status

The socioeconomic structures of America in 1979–1980 is given in Figure 2.2. Because the occupational categories shown do not in-

FIGURE 2.2

Socioeconomic Composition of the United States

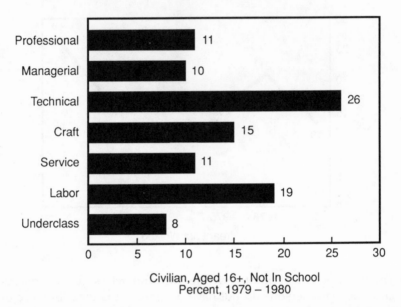

Civilian, Aged 16+, Not In School
Percent, 1979 – 1980

clude everyone in the population, the distribution does not correspond to those sometimes found regarding education (usually restricted to persons 25 or older) or group size (usually based on the total population).

The largest single occupational category is technical (26%). Labor is the next largest category (19%), followed by craft (15%). Service and professional are the same size (11%), while managerial is almost as large (10%). The smallest group by a slight margin is the underclass (8%). Although the technical category might seem unusually large at first glance, recall that it also includes occupations such as sales, secretary, and clerk. With that proviso, the figures on the graph are similar to those reported by other researchers.[57]

Table 2.4 presents data on income, education, and occupational prestige.

The professional group has the highest median education (sixteen years) of any occupational grouping. This finding agrees with previous research (see Table 2.2) and is not surprising because education is the major prerequisite to attaining professional status. The difference between the professional and the managerial group (two

TABLE 2.4

Socioeconomic Status, Education, and Income

Socioeconomic Category	Median Education[a]	Total Income[b]	NORC Score[c]
Professional	16	15,000	82
Managerial	14	18,300	75
Technical	12	10,000	82/65
Craft	12	13,400	68/58
Service	12	6,000	47
Laborer	12	10,600	58/46
Underclass	9	1,700	na

[a]Years of school completed; 1 = first grade . . . 16 = 4 years of college.
(*Note:* this not the same as the Census Bureau scoring.)
[b]Income from all sources, 1979.
[c]Index of occupational prestige, from Gilbert and Kahl, p. 69.

years) may not seem to be much, but it is substantial. It could represent completing fours of college versus two years or, if one interprets the data loosely, completing an associate of arts degree versus a baccalaureate degree. Interestingly, education does not distinguish among technical craft, service, or labor; all have the same median (twelve years). This finding may reflect American society, which emphasizes education regardless of occupational goals, provides public education, and mandates school attendance up to a minimum age. As a result, educational attainment across the middle range of occupations tends to be highly homogeneous. A barber is as likely to have completed high school as a computer technician.

In light of the relatively high levels of education characterizing the occupational system, the underclass median (nine years) is even more striking. This represents approximately the lower level of junior high school, an attainment far below that of the next highest category, labor. While the extent of the undereducation among the underclass should come as no surprise, it is still worth noting. Relative to other strata, or considered on an absolute scale, the underclass is severely undereducated.

The income rankings are not nearly as consistent as the education rankings. The second ranked occupational category, managerial, has the highest median income by over $3,000. There are also inversions between labor and service, and between craft and technical. In fact, the median for labor is higher than the median for technical, a group three ranks higher. Gilbert and Kahl reported similar patterns: inconsistency with regard to income, and consistency but little variation with regard to education (see Table 2.2).[58]

The NORC scores of occupational prestige were collated with the occupational categories, and are also shown in Table 2.4.[59] Not all jobs could be rated, so the matching between score and occupational group was crude, involving some "mental interpolation." Nevertheless, the scores do indicate the prestige of the occupational categories, if not the total precision, at least with enough precision to indicate relative ranking. As anticipated, the professional category ranks highest, followed by the managerial category. Depending on the particular occupation, the rating of the technical category varies from 82 to 65. Similarly, the ratings for craft and labor occupations vary, although not so widely. Although some inconsistencies exist, the NORC prestige scores generally vary with the occupational categories in the manner one would expect: higher occupations have higher prestige.

In sum, the following four indicators were considered:

1. The ranking scheme devised by Edwards and various modifications of it.

2. Education, which does not vary except at the extremes of the occupational categories.

3. Income, which is only crudely consistent across the rankings.

4. Prestige ratings, which are generally consistent with the occupational categorization.

When these data are considered along with the analyses previously reviewed, the overwhelming weight of evidence indicates that occupational rankings do measure socioeconomic status and, indirectly, social class as well.

Ethnicity and Socioeconomic Status

Although the preceding discussion suggests that occupational categories measure, or *are* socioeconomic status, that finding is in reference to the population as a whole. It does not refer to the relation between socioeconomic status and ethnicity, a topic about which social scientists know surprisingly little. To be sure, a fair amount is known about *some* aspects of *some* groups, but usually not very much is known about their socioeconomic status. For example,

example based on past research, it would be difficult to compare the socioeconomic status of blacks to that of Mexicans, or the socioeconomic status of the British to that of Swedes. The basic data are simply not there. If only on a descriptive level, knowing more about the socioeconomic status of these groups would constitute useful knowledge. That is the subject broached in the following analysis.

Educational Attainment

Observers routinely assume that education is a major cause of ethnic inequality. So widespread is this assumption that it has become part of the conventional wisdom of the social sciences. Yet, despite its widespread acceptance, it should not be taken for granted. The data just presented (Table 2.4) showed that education does not vary much between occupational categories, an outcome implying that education is not an overwhelming determinant of socioeconomic status. Those data did not, however, take ethnicity into account. If the data had been divided into ethnic groups, and within groups into occupation categories, then differences between and within groups could have been examined. That was not done because attention was then focused on evaluating socioeconomic schemes. Now, however, attention has shifted to ethnicity, and those comparisons will be undertaken.

Figure 2.3, which compares educational attainments for different ethnic groups, displays school years completed, from one, indicating nursery school, through 22, indicating eight or more years of college. Because the focus is on socioeconomic status, the medians are based on persons for whom a socioeconomic category could be assigned. This differs from the more common procedure of basing education on persons aged 25 or older.

Overall, the figure shows more uniformity than variation. Of the 21 groups, 18 have a median of 14 years of schooling completed (12th grade). The two highest medians are 15 and 16 years (first and second year of college); and the lowest is 12 years (tenth grade). Given past research, the high Asian median comes as no surprise. More surprising is the Russian median, the highest of any group. If we interpret the Russian category as a surrogate for Jewish ethnicity, then the outcome is consistent with what is known about American Jews. At the other extreme, Mexicans have the lowest median education, suggesting that they may now be the single largest group at the bottom of the socioeconomic pyramid.

FIGURE 2.3

Median Education (Years of School Completed)

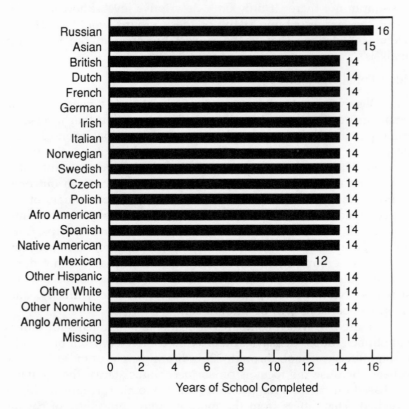

Years of School Completed

While these medians enable us to compare groups, they do not show the relationship between socioeconomic status and education, a comparison directly relevant to the task at hand. Those factors are shown in Table 2.5.

Without exception, the highest medians are associated with the highest socioeconomic category. The values for professionals vary along a narrow range of 18 to 20 school years completed, except for Native Americans, whose median is 16 years. Furthermore, the second highest medians are associated with the managerial category, the second highest socioeconomic group. Values range from 18 years (Russian and Asian) to 14 years (Mexican and Spanish). Across the mid-range of socioeconomic categories, a value of 14 years typifies Europeans. However, nonwhites exhibit more varia-

TABLE 2.5

Median Education[a]

	British	Dutch	French	German	Irish	Italian
Professional	18	18	18	18	19	18
Managerial	16	14	15	16	16	15
Technical	14	14	14	14	14	14
Craft	14	14	14	14	14	14
Service	14	14	14	14	14	14
Labor	14	14	14	14	14	14
Underclass	11	12	11	12	12	11

	Norwegian	Swede	Czech	Pole	Russian
Professional	18	18	18	19	20
Managerial	16	15	15	16	18
Technical	14	14	14	14	15
Craft	14	14	14	14	14
Service	14	14	14	14	14
Labor	14	14	14	14	14
Underclass	10	11	12	10	9

	Asian	Afro American	Mexican	Spanish	Native American
Professional	19	18	18	18	16
Managerial	18	16	14	14	16
Technical	16	14	14	14	14
Craft	14	14	10	13	14
Service	14	13	10	14	14
Labor	14	14	11	14	14
Underclass	7	11	9	9	12

	Other Hispanic	Other White	Other Nonwhite	Anglo American	Missing
Professional	18	19	18	18	18
Managerial	15	17	15	14	14
Technical	14	14	14	14	14
Craft	11	14	12	14	14
Service	13	14	13	14	14
Labor	12	14	13	13	14
Underclass	10	12	10	10	10

[a]Years of school completed, those for whom a socioeconomic category could be assigned.

tion, especially Mexicans and Spanish. Finally, the lowest medians are found within the underclass, where they range from 7 years to 12 years. Overall, education does vary by socioeconomic category, and in a way we would anticipate. The amount of variation is nonetheless rather small, with most of it occurring between the very highest and lowest categories.

Considering both the group medians and the medians within occupational categories, two summary points can be drawn with regard to education. First, within each group, the higher the socioeconomic category, the higher the education. However, across the midrange of socioeconomic status, education hardly varies at all. Second, few differences exist between groups. For instance, the modal education of nonwhite professionals is 18 years, which is identical to the corresponding white mode. Nonwhite laborers typically have a mode of 14 years, which is, again, nearly identical to the corresponding white value. Thus, even though differences exist, the groups appear to be more similar than different along this measure.

To explain this, at least two factors come to mind. The first is compulsory education. Whether mandated by law or by strong custom, most Americans spend a considerable portion of their childhood in school. This places a floor under educational attainment; some minimal amount will be obtained regardless of social and economic background. To be sure, this does not mean that everyone will receive the same quality of education, but it does reduce the variation between groups in the number of school years completed. The second reason is the nature of socioeconomic status. Certain levels of educational attainment are prerequisite to entering certain occupations. Physicians, to illustrate, must have a professional education. Consequently, anyone who becomes a physician will have completed a given number of school years regardless of ethnicity. The real issue, of course, is not whether minority physicians have completed the same number of school years as majority physicians (in general, they will have), but how education screens minorities out of the medical pipeline in the first place.

Income Attainment

Economist George Easterlin has statistically studied the question of whether money can buy happiness. He concluded that it can, which probably surprises no one.[60] Money has such obvious importance that to discuss it is to belabor it.

Figure 2.4 displays median income from all sources for people who could be assigned a socioeconomic category. Although sometimes only income earned from employment is used when comparing ethnic groups, in this instance, the total from all sources seemed to be more appropriate. That is because the total determines the life style associated with socioeconomic status. It should be noted, though, that employment income is tantamount to total income for most people, and so this choice of measure actually has little impact on the statistical outcomes. Possible exceptions to this are people in the underclass, many of whom receive transfer payments, and the few people who earn significant income from interest, dividends, and rents.

FIGURE 2.4

Median Income (Income from All Sources)

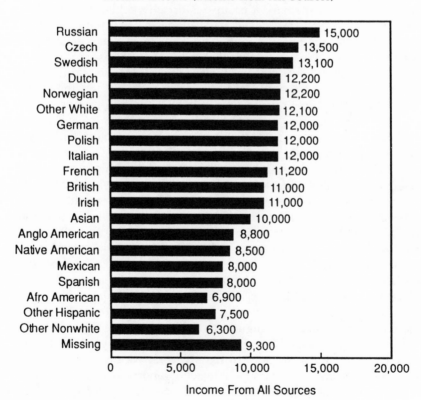

Income From All Sources

Unlike education, income substantially varies across groups. Russians have the highest median and, in some comparisons, by large amounts. For example, the Russian median is over twice the Afro American median, and almost that much larger than the Spanish and Mexican medians. The high median for Czechs may reflect their atypical immigration history. After World War II, Czechs came to this country in bursts, fleeing political persecution. Many of those fleeing were highly educated professionals, who evidently have been able to capitalize on their background. This explanation, however, does not apply to Swedes, and their relatively high income remains inexplicable at present. Also somewhat inexplicable is the relatively low Asian median. In the present case, the heterogeneity of the grouping might be an explanation. Included in it are the Vietnamese and other Southeast Asians, most of whom have very low incomes.[61] Also worth noting are the median incomes of the British, French, and Irish. They are all slightly to moderately below the Italian median, a group historically subjected to intense discrimination. Several analysts have suggested that the Italians are currently assimilating at a high rate, and these data suggest that insofar as income is concerned, that is indeed the case.

Although making sense of the specific comparisons can be difficult, at a broad level one comparison stands out: all the white groups have higher incomes than all the nonwhite groups. Color clearly affects income.

In addition to varying between groups, income should also vary by socioeconomic status. Table 2.6 displays the pertinent data.

Several inconsistencies appear in the relationship between socioeconomic status and income. Consider the professional category. Within it, the medians range from $21,700 (Russians) to $11,000 (Mexicans). These medians are lower than those for the managerial category, which range from $24,000 (Russians again) to $8,800 (Native Americans). The second highest socioeconomic category, in other words, often has the highest median income. Other inconsistencies abound: the fourth highest socioeconomic category, craft, usually has the third highest median income while labor, the sixth highest category, usually has the fourth highest income. The labor medians are considerably higher than the service medians, but service ranks above labor. Nevertheless, one outcome is consistent. The underclass medians are low (the Asian and Mexican medians of zero result from underclass people who report no income at all). Insofar as *reported* income is concerned, the underclass is severely disadvantaged vis-a-vis the rest of society.

TABLE 2.6

Median Income[a] (Dollars)

	British	Dutch	French	German	Irish	Italian
Professional	15,000	17,600	14,700	15,100	15,700	18,400
Managerial	20,500	21,000	18,700	18,000	16,900	16,100
Technical	10,000	11,400	10,000	9,900	10,000	10,000
Craft	14,200	12,600	14,600	15,000	14,100	15,500
Service	6,200	4,000	7,000	6,600	6,100	7,800
Labor	11,000	12,500	12,000	12,600	10,900	12,400
Underclass	1,800	2,300	2,400	1,800	1,800	2,000

	Norwegian	Swede	Czech	Pole	Russian
Professional	14,600	17,000	16,000	15,000	21,700
Managerial	15,800	23,100	18,000	24,900	24,000
Technical	10,300	10,600	10,500	11,100	11,000
Craft	16,200	14,800	15,500	16,300	14,800
Service	6,300	6,000	5,700	6,800	6,800
Labor	14,000	11,500	19,600	12,500	10,900
Underclass	3,200	200	1,500	2,400	2,800

	Asian	Afro American	Mexican	Spanish	Native American
Professional	19,000	12,000	11,000	17,500	19,900
Managerial	18,300	13,200	14,000	12,500	8,800
Technical	9,600	10,000	9,000	8,000	9,000
Craft	9,800	9,200	9,000	11,300	11,200
Service	7,700	5,400	6,000	6,400	6,200
Labor	9,000	9,000	9,000	8,800	8,000
Underclass	0	1,800	0	1,700	900

	Other Hispanic	Other White	Other Nonwhite	Anglo American	Missing
Professional	11,400	17,400	16,400	15,000	12,500
Managerial	12,300	20,200	20,000	16,400	16,000
Technical	10,000	11,500	8,000	8,500	9,500
Craft	8,500	16,200	9,000	12,300	12,600
Service	5,300	5,200	5,400	5,000	6,300
Labor	8,500	12,300	7,700	9,800	10,000
Underclass	1,900	1,500	600	2,000	1,900

[a]Income from all sources, those for whom a socioeconomic category could be assigned.

When considered as a whole, these data indicate that ethnic groups are more similar than dissimilar in terms of socioeconomic status. To be sure, there were substantial differences between groups as to median income, which was to be expected; but when income was specified within occupational category, a different picture formed. The relationship between median income and the occupational categories was essentially similar for all groups. Although it did not vary as much, the same may be said of the relationship between median education and the occupation.

These data suggests a point that is well known, but still worth reiterating. The components of socioeconomic status are related in a predictable fashion, and the relationships are the same for all ethnic groups—in the main. For example, among both blacks and whites, education is related to income. This does not mean, however, that equality prevails. Even though the same basic relationship exists, its strength can still vary between groups. Whites, for example benefit from their education more than blacks.[62] In addition and for whatever reason, each group does not have the same absolute amount of socioeconomic status. The current data indicate that the most glaring differences are in income, especially when contrasting whites to nonwhites.

The Socioeconomic Status of Ethnic Groups

Although composed of specific variables, socioeconomic status can be regarded as a global construct, a summary of social standing and placement in society. With regard to this broader construct, two questions about it and ethnicity can be raised: (1) What is the socioeconomic composition of each ethnic group? and (2) What is the ethnic composition of the American socioeconomic system? With regard to the latter question, we may, for instance, inquire about the proportion of professionals who are Irish as compared to the proportion who are Mexican. The results would reveal something about the ethnic structure of the American socioeconomic system, and Gordon presumably had that in mind when he spoke of the ethclass (the qualifier *presumably* deserves emphasis because he did not specifically mention this point). Concerning the first question, we may inquire about the proportion of Irish in the professional category as contrasted to the proportion of Mexicans in that category. Those results would reveal something about the distribution of each group across socioeconomic categories, indicating group standings *vis-a-vis* each other. Both lines of inquiry are important; they are just different.

Before considering results, some decision-rules require clarification. When discussing group differences, we need an operational criterion for determining if the groups differ. What does it mean, in other words, to say that a group is like another group? One criterion for answering this question is probability (tests of significance). However, as textbooks commonly warn, even small differences become statistically significant when based on large samples. That was the case here. Statistical tests did not prove very useful, although they are reported in some instances.

Semantic consensus may be more useful because it can be operationalized with reference to *only*. For example, if a difference between two groups is 5%, should that be described as *only* 5%? Or if the difference is 10%, should that be described as *only* 10%? And so on. When, in other words, can we appropriately use *only*, an adverb implying that a difference is small and lacks importance? I have previously found 10% to be a workable figure and so if a difference is 10% or smaller, it will be described as *only*, but if it is larger, it will not be so described.[63] By extension, this rule also applies to *small, slight, nearly, almost*, and other such words. Although the "rule of 10%" has no basis other than subjective feeling, it does have the virtues of being public and explicit.

Ethnic Composition of Occupational Categories

Table 2.7 shows the ethnic composition of the American stratification system. Every socioeconomic category is mostly composed of Western Europeans. The percentages vary from 60% or more of the professional and managerial categories to 38% of the underclass. Of specific Western European groups, the British are the most prevalent: 26% of professionals and managers are British; 22% of technical and craft; and 17% of service, labor, and the underclass. Germans are the next most prevalent, with values ranging from 18% of the craft category to 9% of the underclass. The Irish follow with a value of 7% in the underclass and a value of 10% in managerial and technical. After the Irish, the percentages decline substantially for Europeans (Western and Eastern): all the remaining percentages for specific European groups are 3% or less.

The nonwhite percentages are relatively small. For example, only 1% of professionals are Mexican, only 5% are black, and only 3% are Asian. In total, only 9% of professionals are nonwhite. However, nonwhites—especially blacks—make up a much larger proportion of the labor category (20%) and the underclass (27%). Both formal research and the mass media convey the impression

TABLE 2.7
Ethnic Composition of Socioeconomic Categories
(Percent of Occupational Category)

Ethnic Group	P	M	T	C	S	L	U
British	26	26	22	22	17	17	17
Dutch	2	2	2	2	2	2	1
French	4	4	4	4	3	4	3
German	17	17	16	18	14	14	9
Irish	9	10	10	8	8	8	7
Norwegian	1	1	1	1	1	1	1
Swedish	1	2	1	1	1	1	*
Total Western European	60	62	56	56	46	47	38
Czech	1	1	1	1	1	1	*
Polish	3	3	3	3	2	3	2
Russian	3	2	2	1	1	*	*
Total Eastern European	7	6	6	4	4	4	3
Italian	4	5	5	4	4	4	3
Spanish	*	1	1	*	1	1	1
Asian	3	1	2	1	2	2	1
Afro American	5	3	6	5	15	12	20
Mexican	1	1	2	5	4	4	5
Native American	*	1	1	2	1	2	1
Total Nonwhite	9	5	9	13	22	20	27
Anglo American	3	4	5	6	5	6	7
Other Hispanic	1	1	1	1	1	2	2
Other Nonwhite	1	1	2	1	3	2	4
Other White	6	6	3	4	3	3	3
Missing	8	8	10	10	11	11	13
Total other and Missing	19	20	21	22	23	24	29
Total Percent	100	100	100	100	100	100	100

*Less than one percent.
Legend: P: professional; M: managerial; T: technical; C: craft; S: service; L: labor; U: underclass.

that the underclass is overwhelmingly black. To be sure, the underclass contains more blacks than any other group, but whites and other non-blacks still constitute the overwhelming majority of that category. In a way, this is not surprising. There are more whites than any other racial category. So, based on sheer number, we would expect whites to dominate every socioeconomic category, and in general they do (this will be discussed further in a moment).

Socioeconomic Status of the Ethnic Groups

While the foregoing data indicate the possible structure of the ethclass, they indicate nothing concerning the well-being of each group. To that end, Table 2.8 shows the percentage of each group in the various socioeconomic categories.

A plurality of Western Europeans, Eastern Europeans, Italians, and Spanish are at least middle class. That is, approximately one fourth to one-third of each group is in the technical category. With two exceptions, moreover, approximately 10% of these groups are in the professional category. The two exceptions are the Spanish (6%) and the Russians (24%). That the Russian category undoubtedly includes many Jews, a group noted for upward mobility, helps explain their exceptionally high figure.[64] At the other end of the continuum, a fairly substantial proportion (7% to 20%) of Western and Eastern Europeans are in the labor category, but only 7% or less are in the underclass.

A different situation prevails among most nonwhites. Approximately one third of Afro Americans are in the combined categories of managerial, technical, and craft, but only 6% are in the professional category. Their distribution is obviously skewed towards the bottom of the hierarchy, with over 60% in the service category or below, and almost 20% in the underclass alone. The distribution of Mexican Americans resembles the black distribution, the major difference being that 25% of Mexicans are in crafts compared to 9% of blacks. The Mexican percentage in the underclass (13%) is the second largest on the table (excluding the miscellaneous groups). Asians do not fit the black and Mexican pattern. While 18% of Asians are in the professions, a sharp decline occurs between that category and the managerial category. Approximately 25% of all Asians are in technical occupations, and their proportions in labor and the underclass are approximately the same as the European groups. Contrary to the image presented by the media, Asians have not been particularly successful in avoiding the bottom rungs of the

Ethnicity and Inequality

TABLE 2.8

Socioeconomic Composition of Ethnic Categories
(Percent of Socioeconomic Category)

Ethnic Group	P	M	T	C	S	L	U	Total
British	13	12	28	16	8	15	7	100%
Dutch	11	12	29	17	10	18	4	100
French	11	10	29	15	9	20	6	100
German	12	11	28	18	9	18	5	100
Irish	11	11	30	14	10	16	7	100
Norwegian	15	12	32	13	10	15	4	100
Swedish	12	17	29	17	10	12	2	100
Total Western European	12	12	29	16	9	16	6	100
Czech	12	13	30	13	10	17	5	100
Polish	12	11	32	14	9	18	5	100
Russian	24	15	34	11	7	7	2	100
Total Eastern European	15	13	32	13	8	15	4	100
Italian	10	11	31	15	11	17	6	100
Spanish	6	8	27	9	15	24	11	100
Asian	18	7	27	9	14	18	6	100
Afro American	6	4	18	9	18	26	19	100
Mexican	5	4	14	25	14	25	13	100
Native American	4	6	24	23	10	25	8	100
Total Nonwhite	7	4	19	14	16	25	15	100
Anglo American	6	7	25	18	10	24	10	100
Other Hispanic	6	6	21	12	12	28	16	100
Other Nonwhite	7	4	19	16	15	24	15	100
Other White	16	13	27	13	8	16	6	100
Missing	8	7	27	16	11	21	10	100
Total other and missing	9	8	25	16	11	21	10	100

Legend: P: professional; M: managerial; T: technical; C: craft; S: service;
L: labor; U: underclass.

socioeconomic ladder. In large part, this undoubtedly results from the influx of Asian immigrants that has been going on since the late 1960s.

The upper echelons of the stratification system present less of a social issue than the lower echelons. The rich can look after their own interests, the poor require help. In this regard, the combined categories of labor and underclass contain 45% of all blacks, 38% of all Mexicans, and 35% of all Spanish. Put otherwise, the Mexican and Spanish proportions in labor and the underclass exceed the Western European proportions by a factor of at least 1.5, while for blacks, the factor is two. By any criteria, these figures represent a huge gap in equality.

Nevertheless, these findings should not deflect attention from the Western European presence in the lower strata. Slightly more than one out of five Western Europeans are in the labor or underclass, and one out of twenty is in the underclass alone. Eastern Europeans fare better but, if Russians are removed from that grouping, the percentages of Czechs and Poles are comparable to the Western European percentages in the labor category, and are almost as high in the underclass. While Europeans do well relative to most nonwhite groups, on an absolute basis, these figures are not trivial. People trapped in the underclass suffer from desperate unremitting poverty, and so even a small number constitutes a major social and moral issue for society.

Group Size

Since data showing the distribution of ethnicity and socioeconomic status (Tables 2.7 and 2.8) are simple percentages, they do not take into account the effect of sheer number. To illustrate, it is not surprising to find more Western Europeans in every occupational category because they are the largest ethnic grouping in the United States. Although this has no effect on the descriptive accuracy of the findings—the data are what they are—it does distort conclusions about equity and assimilation. The impact of number ought to be taken into account before arriving conclusions about over- or under-representation in socioeconomic categories.

A basic logic is available for this purpose. It runs as follows: if ethnicity made no difference to socioeconomic status, then we would expect the number of each group in each socioeconomic category to be proportionate to the group's size. This number, called the "expected" number, can be compared to the actual number of the group in the category.[65] If, for example, the actual number of blacks in the underclass is larger than the expected number, then blacks are "overrepresented" and conversely, if the actual number is smaller, then they are "underrepresented." For ease of comparison, the difference between the actual and expected numbers may be expressed as a percentage. A negative percentage indicates that the category contains fewer of the group than their size would suggest, a positive figure indicates the opposite, and zero indicates neither underrepresentation nor overrepresentation, or what I call *parity*. The data are shown on Table 2.9.

First, note the craft category. In it, there are disproportionately more British, Dutch, Germans, and Swedes than expected from their group sizes, but conversely, there are disproportionately fewer French, Irish, and Norwegians. In other words, four of the seven Western European groups are overrepresented, and three are underrepresented in crafts. This split occurs in no other socioeconomic category. Western Europeans are uniformly overrepresented in categories above it and uniformly underrepresented below it. In other words, craft appears to be a transition category.

Eastern Europeans evince much the same pattern as Western Europeans. Czechs and Poles are overrepresented above craft and underrepresented below it, especially the underclass. Russians exhibit an extreme accentuation of this pattern: they are 125% overrepresented in the professional category and −64% and −72% underrepresented in labor and the underclass.

Italians are at parity in the categories of professional, craft, service, and labor (that is, the figures are 10% or less). However, Italians are somewhat overrepresented in the manager and technical groupings and considerably underrepresented in the underclass. The Spanish display a different pattern. Disproportionately few Spanish are in the top portion of the socioeconomic hierarchy while the opposite holds for the bottom portion. Only in the technical category have the Spanish attained parity.

Native Americans are at parity in technical and service, but contrary to what we might think, they are not disproportionately clustered in the underclass. One possible explanation is the relationship the federal government has to Indian tribes. In effect, governmental assistance might constitute a floor that keeps native Americans out of the underclass but not out of labor and craft. Consistent with what we might think, however, native Americans are disproportionately underrepresented in the professional and managerial categories. Fewer Asians are in the managerial, craft, and underclass occupations than expected, but considerably more are in the professions. In fact, Asians are second only to Russians in terms

TABLE 2.9

Estimated Inequality: Percent Above or Below Parity[a]

Ethnic Group	P	M	T	C	S	L	U
British	24	27	5	6	−21	−19	−20
Dutch	0	20	7	9	−6	−3	−51
French	5	5	8	−4	−12	−6	−28
German	8	13	5	14	−11	−6	−43
Irish	4	16	14	−10	−4	−13	−16
Norwegian	37	20	18	−15	−8	−20	−46
Swede	17	74	10	13	−9	−37	−72
Total Western							
European	14	20	7	5	−13	−12	−29
Czech	14	31	12	−13	−10	−9	−37
Pole	13	16	20	−10	−20	−5	−44
Russian	125	57	26	−27	−33	−64	−72
Total Eastern							
European	43	29	20	−15	−22	−21	−51
Italian	−4	12	15	−4	−1	−9	−29
Spanish	−48	−17	4	−41	38	26	37
Asian	69	−24	2	−44	33	−3	−24
Afro							
American	−39	−62	−34	−41	74	37	134
Mexican	−54	−57	−46	64	31	31	59
Native							
American	−66	−43	−9	47	−3	35	3
Total							
Nonwhite	−33	−55	−31	−12	54	31	90
Anglo							
American	−49	−27	−6	16	−5	29	28
Other							
Hispanic	−47	−42	−23	−24	15	49	100
Other							
Nonwhite	−31	−58	−28	0	41	27	86
Other							
White	50	36	1	−14	−21	−13	−29
Missing	−23	−25	1	6	1	10	23
Total Other							
and Missing	−18	−19	−5	3	0	14	25

[a]*Parity:* the number expected based on group size. A negative number
indicates below parity, a positive number indicates above parity.
Legend: P: professional; M: managerial; T: technical; C: craft; S: service;
L: labor; U: underclass.

of overrepresentation in the professional category. It is reasonable to suppose that Asians have pursued higher education leading to professional-technical careers. Their underrepresentation in the managerial category could reflect this career line, as well as possible race discrimination. Why they should be so underrepresented in crafts, though, remains unknown, except that the immigrant streams from Asia historically have not included large numbers of artisans and craftsmen.

The patterns among blacks and Mexicans differ from those of Europeans, Asians, and Native Americans. In the higher occupational groupings, the number of blacks and Mexicans is considerably below what we would expect based on their number in the population. However, the reverse is true for lower occupational categories. Blacks are especially underrepresented in the professional, managerial, technical, and craft categories, but overrepresented in service, labor, and the underclass. In the underclass in particular, the figure is 134%, or more than twice that of any other group.

If these percentages divide along any criterion, it is white-nonwhite. Most white groups are underrepresented or at parity in the lower strata while most nonwhite groups are overrepresented. In the underclass alone, five of the six overrepresented groups are nonwhite while eleven of the thirteen underrepresented groups are white.[66] Except for Asians, the lowest socioeconomic categories contain the greatest disproportion of nonwhites.

The disproportion may actually be greater than these data suggest. The Census Bureau often undercounts people in certain categories, notably the poor, criminals, and transients—persons most likely to be in the lower strata. Any ethnic group that disproportionately falls into those categories will therefore be disproportionately undercounted, a situation describing blacks and probably Mexicans as well. Since the data already show that disproportionate numbers of blacks and Mexicans are in the labor category and underclass, adjustments for undercounting (if they were available) would change the percentages but not the basic conclusions.

Correlates of Socioeconomic Status

Even though the data file being analyzed is a national sample, it is not especially large for the task at hand. Once the file is divided into socioeconomic status categories, ethnic groups, and other groupings, the number of cases per cell rapidly declines, sometimes to fifty or fewer (including zero). This means that when showing the relationship between socioeconomic status and two or more variables, small cell frequencies will often be present. The most direct solution to this problem, a larger sample, obviously cannot be obtained now.

Consequently, some caution is required in judging the forthcoming data. The focus must remain fixed on patterns of numbers rather than individual numbers. Whereas individual numbers might reflect idiosyncratically small cell frequencies, patterns suggest stable relationships. Moreover, because sixteen groups will be analyzed (the miscellaneous groups are combined into one, "Other"), patterns relevant to a given hypothesis will be replicated sixteen times. If consistent patterns emerge, that would constitute a substantial body of evidence, certainly more than has been available before.

Intermarriage and Socioeconomic Status

Without exception, analysts believe that intermarriage is the ultimate form of assimilation, for intermarriage represents the blending of cultures, the fusion of social structures, and of course, biological melding. Although several explanations have been offered for intermarriage, none have stood up to rigorous empirical test and logical analysis, leading observers to agree that while intermarriage represents assimilation, explaining why it occurs has thus far defied social scientists.[67]

Here, however, interest centers not on explaining intermarriage per se, but on the simple correlation between assimilation, as indexed by intermarriage, and socioeconomic status. Research suggests that the two variables should be related. For example, in a seminal study of Mexican Americans living in Los Angeles, Leo Grebler and associates found that the higher the occupational status of grooms, the more often they married non-Mexicans.[68] Another study found that as education increased, so did the intermarriage among several ethnic groups in California, including Mexicans. This occurred regardless of generational standing and ethnicity.[69] Whatever theory we might invoke to explain these and similar findings, the fact remains that higher socioeconomic status is associated with higher outmarriage rates; and all else equal, that is the expectation here.

Procedures. Ancestry will be used as a surrogate measure for intermarriage. We have already examined ancestry as a means to classify ethnic groups, and we know that it involves race, religion, the respondents' knowledge of their progenitors, social identity, and self definition of ethnicity. Clearly, it is a complex variable, but one interpretation remains constant throughout the complexity: people claiming single ancestry are saying there has not been any intermarriage in their lineage, and people claiming multiple ancestry are saying the opposite. Whether or not we accept this statement at face value, the implicit claims regarding intermarriage remain, and so do the claims for assimilation. Research suggests that this interpretation of the ancestry variable makes sense. One study used it to test hypotheses concerning Hungarians, Italians, Poles, and Slovaks. The findings generally confirmed the expectation that structural opportunities influence single ancestry rates, and when coupled with the findings presented in Chapter 1, they increase our confidence in the intermarriage interpretation of the measure.[70]

Table 2.10 displays the relation between single ancestry and multiple ancestry. Initially, I thought that statistical tests of significance would be useful guides for decision making, but ironically, even though the tables are sparse, the sample is still large enough to render very small differences statistically significant. Hence, tests were of little use and a more "common sense" procedure had to be adopted. Those instances in which the multiple ancestry percentage exceeded the single ancestry percentage by three or more percentage points have been highlighted in bold type. If a trend exists—if multiple ancestry (assimilation) is associated with higher socioeconomic status—then the pattern of bold numbers should reveal it.

The criterion of three percentage points was chosen after the fact, but it was guided by the goal of discovering patterns. A smaller criterion resulted in too many differences being highlighted, a larger criterion in too few (or at least that was my subjective judgment). Of course, since the data are presented in Table 2.10, the reader can draw different conclusions.

Excluding the Other category, the data for the Spanish come closest to an archetypical pattern. The multiple ancestry percentages for professional, managerial, and technical exceed the corresponding percentages for single ancestry while the reverse holds for craft, service, and labor. Had the latter statement applied to the underclass, then the pattern would have been complete, but it did not. With that exception, the pattern indicates that multiple ancestry (assimilation if you will) is associated with higher socioeconomic standing.

TABLE 2.10

Socioeconomic Status by Ethnicity and Single and Multiple Ancestry[a]

Socioeconomic Category	British SA	British MA	Swede SA	Swede MA	Asian SA	Asian MA
Professional	12	14	**14**	11	**19**	0°
Manager	12	13	17	17	7	9°
Technical	26	**31**	27	**31**	27	27°
Craft	17	16	19	16	8	**18°**
Service	9	8	**12**	7°	**14**	9°
Labor	**17**	13	9	**15**	18	18°
Underclass	7	5	2°	3°	6	**18°**

Socioeconomic Category	Dutch SA	Dutch MA	Czech SA	Czech MA	Afro American SA	Afro American MA
Professional	**12**	9	5°	**29**	6	**13°**
Manager	**15**	9	**15**	7°	4	**13°**
Technical	26	**31**	29	**33**	18	0°
Craft	16	18	**18**	2°	9	**19°**
Service	**12**	9	7°	**16°**	19	6°
Labor	16	**20**	**19**	13°	26	19°
Underclass	3°	4°	**7°**	0°	19	**31°**

Socioeconomic Category	French SA	French MA	Pole SA	Pole MA	Mexican SA	Mexican MA
Professional	11	12	11	**15**	5	**11°**
Manager	10	10	10	**13**	**4**	0°
Technical	23	**34**	32	32	13	**44°**
Craft	**18**	12	13	**16**	25	17°
Service	9	10	9	8	**14**	6°
Labor	21	19	**19**	13	**25**	11°
Underclass	7	4	5	3°	13	11°

Socioeconomic Category	German SA	German MA	Russian SA	Russian MA	Native American SA	Native American MA
Professional	10	**13**	22	**28**	3°	4°
Manager	11	12	15	15	3°	7
Technical	27	**30**	34	34	24	24
Craft	**19**	16	**12**	9°	22	23
Service	10	8	7	7°	8°	**12**
Labor	18	18	6	7°	**29**	23
Underclass	5	4	**4°**	0°	**11**	7

TABLE 2.10

Continued

Socioeconomic	Irish		Italian		Spanish	
Category	SA	MA	SA	MA	SA	MA
Professional	11	12	10	11	4°	**11°**
Manager	10	**13**	**12**	7	8	**11°**
Technical	31	30	29	**36**	26	**37**
Craft	14	14	15	14	**11**	**3°**
Service	11	10	9	**15**	**16**	**11°**
Labor	17	16	**18**	14	**25**	**18°**
Underclass	8	5	7	**2°**	11	**11°**

Socioeconomic	Norwegian		Other	
Category	SA	MA	SA	MA
Professional	15	14	8	**18**
Manager	12	**11°**	8	**14**
Technical	27	**38**	23	**32**
Craft	**16**	**10°**	**16**	11
Service	**11**	**7°**	**11**	8
Labor	11	**20**	23	14
Underclass	**7°**	**0°**	**11**	3

[a]Percent single and multiple ancestry for those who could be assigned a socioeconomic category.
Bold: Difference of three or more percentage points between single and multiple ancestry.
°: Based on fewer than fifty respondents.
SA: Single ancestry; MA: multiple ancestry.

So clear a pattern does not hold, however, for any other group. Considering the three highest categories (technical, manager, and professional), no clear pattern can be discerned. In some cases, the rate of multiple ancestry is higher among these categories, and in other cases it is lower. A somewhat clearer pattern describes lower socioeconomic categories. Single ancestry is associated with both labor and the underclass among Czechs, Italians, Native Americans, Norwegians and Mexicans, and with labor *or* the underclass among the British, French, Irish, Poles, and Russians. If the definition of "lower" categories is expanded to include service, then the Dutch and Asians may be added to this list of groups. In sum, this tally accounts for thirteen of the fifteen groups. The overall conclusion suggested by these data is essentially negative: single or multiple ancestry is not consistently related to socioeconomic standing across the groups.

Place of Birth and Socioeconomic Status

The data in Chapter 1 have shown that place of birth (foreign or United States) bears a relation to multiple ancestry. Whether place of birth has an effect on socioeconomic status, however, is problematic. One might argue that the foreign born, being less socialized into American culture, will do less well than the native born. On the other hand, immigration laws favor high-level socioeconomic occupations, which implies that the foreign born will have high standing. Data relevant to these possibilities are shown in Table 2.11.

Only among Czechs does the archetypical crossover pattern emerge: for the professional and managerial categories, the percentages born in the United States are larger than percentages born abroad while the reverse holds for all lower categories except labor (however, note the small cell frequencies). Contrary to what was the case in the past, the foreign born are overrepresented in professional or managerial positions among several groups (Dutch, Asians, Afro Americans, Spanish, and Norwegians). At the same time, and complicating the matter, the foreign born are also overrepresented in lower socioeconomic categories. Their percentage in the underclass exceeds the native born percentage among French, Irish, Swedes, Czechs, Poles, Russians, Italians, Asians, Afro Americans, and Norwegians. Thus, for some groups, the foreign born are at a socioeconomic disadvantage compared to the native born, among other groups they are not, and among a few groups they are simultaneously at a advantage and disadvantage. Unfortunately, the data cannot indicate the reasons for these multiple outcomes, and perhaps not too much should be made of them anyway. The overall patterns are weak.

Gender and Socioeconomic Status

Gender is an important variable for several reasons. Most obviously, men and women have traditionally followed much different life trajectories. For example, in 1980 three-fourths of all men participated in the labor force whereas only half of all women did.[71] Not only do participation rates differ, but so do the types of jobs held by women and men. For instance, relatively few women are engineers or computer scientists while relatively few men are nurses or home economists. Manual labor is male dominated while the underclass is female dominated.[72] Facts such as these suggest that a relationship between socioeconomic status and gender should exist. Data relevant to this expectation are shown in Table 2.12.

TABLE 2.11

Socioeconomic Status by Ethnicity and Foreign and U.S. Birth[a]

Socioeconomic Category	British FB	British USB	Swede FB	Swede USB	Asian FB	Asian USB
Professional	15	13	20°	12	20	14
Manager	13	12	0°	17	6	11
Technical	26	28	40°	29	26	29
Craft	11	16	0°	18	8	11
Service	19	8	20°	9	14	14
Labor	9°	15	0°	12	19	17
Underclass	7°	6	20°	2°	8	3°

Socioeconomic Category	Dutch FB	Dutch USB	Czech FB	Czech USB	Afro American FB	Afro American USB
Professional	18°	10	0°	13	12°	6
Manager	29°	11	7°	13	6°	4
Technical	18°	29°	36°	29	18°	18
Craft	24°	17	7°	14	6°	9
Service	6°	10	14°	9	12°	18
Labor	6°	19	14°	17	18°	26
Underclass	0°	4°	21°	4°	29°	19

Socioeconomic Category	French FB	French USB	Pole FB	Pole USB	Mexican FB	Mexican USB
Professional	11°	11	7°	12	2°	7
Manager	14°	10	12°	11	2°	6
Technical	11°	30	29	32	7	19
Craft	17°	15	12°	14	31	21
Service	20°	9	5°	9	16	13
Labor	17°	20	19°	18	30	21
Underclass	9°	6	17°	4	12	13

Socioeconomic Category	German FB	German USB	Russian FB	Russian USB	Native American FB	Native American USB
Professional	7°	12	17°	25	0°	4
Manager	6°	11	4°	16	100°	5
Technical	31	28	21°	35	0°	24
Craft	15	18	25°	10	0°	23
Service	19	9	8°	7	0°	10
Labor	19	18	8°	7	0°	26
Underclass	1°	5	17°	1°	0°	8

TABLE 2.11

Continued

| Socioeconomic | Irish | | Italian | | Spanish | |
Category	FB	USB	FB	USB	FB	USB
Professional	0°	**11**	4°	**11**	9°	4°
Manager	10°	11	9°	11	8°	8
Technical	30°	30	13°	**32**	23	**30**
Craft	**20°**	14	**19**	14	9°	9
Service	**15°**	10	9°	11	15°	14
Labor	10°	**16**	37	15	30	21
Underclass	**15°**	7	**9°**	5	6°	**13**

| Socioeconomic | Norwegian | | Other | |
Category	FB	USB	FB	USB
Professional	**25°**	14	10	9
Manager	0°	**12**	7	9
Technical	**25°**	**32**	21	**25**
Craft	**13°**	13	12	**16**
Service	0°	**10**	15	10
Labor	0°	**16**	25	21
Underclass	**38°**	**3°**	10	10

aPercent of foreign and U.S. born for those who could be assigned a socioeconomic category.
Bold: Difference of three or more percentage points between foreign and U.S. born.
°: Based on fewer than fifty respondents.
FB: Foreign born; USB: U.S. born.

Unlike the two previous tables, the bold print forms a discernible pattern: a kind of zig-zag down the columns. The British provide an archetypical case. Males predominate in the categories of manager, craft, and labor while females predominate in professional, technical, service, and the underclass. In addition to the British, this pattern can be observed among the French and Germans, and almost the same pattern exists among the Irish, Swedes, Poles, Italians, and Spanish.

A few exceptions to the pattern exist. In the case of Native Americans, the relationship was reversed in the professional category: the male percentage exceeded the female percentage. For Russians, the pattern prevailed among the higher socioeconomic categories, but was ambiguous among the lower ones. The opposite applied to Mexicans and Norwegians. The slightly higher percentage of professional males among Italians, Asians, Mexicans, and

TABLE 2.12

Socioeconomic Status by Ethnicity and Gender [a]

Socioeconomic Category	British M	British F	Swede M	Swede F	Asian M	Asian F
Professional	12	15	12	12	19	17
Manager	15	8	21	11	10	5°
Technical	18	41	19	44	21	34
Craft	26	3	26	4°	12	5°
Service	6	12	5°	17	14	14
Labor	20	9	16	7°	21	16
Underclass	3	11	1°	4°	4°	9

Socioeconomic Category	Dutch M	Dutch F	Czech M	Czech F	Afro American M	Afro American F
Professional	9	12	9°	16	4	8
Manager	16	6°	13	12°	4	3°
Technical	22	38	23	37	12	23
Craft	4	6°	22	4°	16	3
Service	7	14	7°	12°	13	23
Labor	21	14	24	9°	39	14
Underclass	0°	10	1°	9°	11	27

Socioeconomic Category	French M	French F	Pole M	Pole F	Native American M	Native American F
Professional	10	13	11	13	5°	2°
Manager	14	6	15	6	5°	6°
Technical	19	41	23	45	15	36
Craft	25	3°	22	3°	36	5°
Service	7	13	6	12	5°	17
Labor	26	13	22	12	30	20
Underclass	1°	11	2°	8	4°	14

Socioeconomic Category	German M	German F	Russian M	Russian F	Mexican M	Mexican F
Professional	10	13	22	26	5	4
Manager	13	8	19	9	5	3°
Technical	18	43	25	47	9	23
Craft	28	3	18	1°	37	6
Service	6	15	6	8°	12	17
Labor	23	10	7	6°	28	20
Underclass	2	8	2°	3°	5	27

TABLE 2.12

Continued

| Socioeconomic | Irish | | Italian | | Spanish | |
Category	M	F	M	F	M	F
Professional	11	11	11	9	6°	5
Manager	**13**	9	**13**	7	**12**	5
Technical	20	**43**	19	**46**	16	**38**
Craft	**23**	2	**23**	4	**18**	1
Service	8	**13**	9	**13**	13	**16**
Labor	**22**	10	**22**	11	**29**	19
Underclass	3	**12**	3	**10**	5°	**16**

| Socioeconomic | Norwegian | | Other | |
Category	M	F	M	F
Professional	15	14	9	10
Manager	13	11	**10**	6
Technical	21	**44**	15	**36**
Craft	**24**	0°	25	3
Service	5°	**16**	8	**14**
Labor	**20**	9°	28	14
Underclass	3°	**6°**	6	**16**

[a]Percent of males and females for those who could be assigned a socioeconomic category.
Bold: Difference of three or more percentage points between males and females.
°: Based on fewer than fifty respondents.
M: male; F: female

Spanish might be attributed to male dominance in the those subcultures, although that is an after-the-fact interpretation.

These findings contain no major surprises. Males have traditionally dominated management, crafts, and labor while women have dominated technical (recall that this category also includes clerical and sales), service, and the underclass. Although the patterns are not quite so clear among nonwhites, the data do indicate that gender and socioeconomic status are related as one would expect. More importantly, these data also indicate that ethnicity does not make much of a difference. In general, the same basic patterns can be found among all ethnic groups.

Education and Socioeconomic Status

Education is one of the most powerful predictors of socioeconomic status, in large part because education and socioeconomic status are defined in terms of each other. Some analysts substitute education for occupation when measuring status, while other analysts combine the two variables in a summary measure (sometimes also including income).[73] As a result, if education is used to predict socioeconomic status, one sub-part of the concept is being used to predict the whole, which is partially tautological.

On empirical grounds, however, the tautology is not perfect. We already know that for the nation, median education does not perfectly vary with socioeconomic status (recall Table 2.4), although that finding might be due to the aggregated nature of the data. If the data had been partitioned into ethnic groups and a different measure of education used, a stronger relationship might have emerged. Consequently, in Table 2.13, education has been dichotomized into high school or less and some college or more.

The pattern in these data is exceptionally clear. In the three highest socioeconomic categories, the college percentage exceeds the high school percentage, and by substantial amounts (in some instances, in excess of twenty percentage points). This is true for the French, Irish, Asians, Afro Americans, Mexicans, Native Americans, and Norwegians. For most other groups, the college educated predominate in the two highest categories, and again by substantial amounts. These groups are the British, Swedes, Czechs, Poles, Russians, and Italians. Finally, for the Spanish, the college educated predominate among the four highest socioeconomic categories. For lower ranking socioeconomic categories, the reverse pattern exists. Beginning either with craft or service, the high school percentages exceed the college percentages, often by considerable amounts. We may therefore conclude that higher education is associated with higher socioeconomic status, and that lower education is associated with lower socioeconomic status.

Recapitulation

Of the four socioeconomic correlates studied in this section of the monograph, intermarriage and place of birth were not related to socioeconomic status in any consistent fashion. No overall patterns could be discerned in those data. In contrast, a clear relationship did exist between gender and socioeconomic status. Females predominated in the professions, technical, service, and underclass while males predominated in managerial, craft, and labor. An equally clear relationship existed for schooling: college education went with high socioeconomic status and high school educa-

TABLE 2.13

Socioeconomic Status by Ethnicity and Education[a]

Socioeconomic Category	British HS	CO	Swede HS	CO	Asian HS	CO
Professional	3	29	2°	24	3°	32
Manager	7	21	13	21	3°	12
Technical	28	29	30	29	18	36
Craft	20	10	21	13	15	3°
Service	10	5	12	7°	24	5°
Labor	22	5	18	5°	26	11
Underclass	10	1	4°	1°	12	1°

Socioeconomic Category	Dutch HS	CO	Czech HS	CO	Afro American HS	CO
Professional	3°	29	2°	27	1	25
Manager	8	21	9°	18	2	10
Technical	29	28	29	31	14	30
Craft	21	7°	14	13°	10	5
Service	11	8°	13	5°	20	11
Labor	23	8°	25	5°	29	15
Underclass	5	1°	7°	2°	23	5

Socioeconomic Category	French HS	CO	Pole HS	CO	Mexican HS	CO
Professional	3	27	1°	32	1°	26
Manager	7	17	8	18	3	12
Technical	28	31	34	28	12	25
Craft	16	12	16	9	28	10°
Service	12	5	10	5	15	8°
Labor	27	7	24	6	26	16
Underclass	8	2°	6	1°	15	2°

Socioeconomic Category	German HS	CO	Russian HS	CO	Native American HS	CO
Professional	2	28	4°	37	1°	12°
Manager	6	21	7°	21	3°	14°
Technical	28	29	38	31	20	39
Craft	21	11	18	7	24	18
Service	12	5	12	4°	12	5°
Labor	24	6	15	1°	30	9°
Underclass	7	1°	6°	0°	10	4°

TABLE 2.13

Continued

Socioeconomic	Irish		Italian		Spanish	
Category	HS	CO	HS	CO	HS	CO
Professional	2	27	2	29	1°	18
Manager	7	19	7	20	6°	15°
Technical	28	35	32	28	25	35
Craft	17	8	18	8	8	13°
Service	13	5	12	8	17	7°
Labor	23	5	22	5	29	11°
Underclass	10	2	7	2°	15	2°

Socioeconomic	Norwegian		Other	
Category	HS	CO	HS	CO
Professional	2°	31	2	26
Manager	7°	18	4	18
Technical	28	36	23	28
Craft	19	6°	18	9
Service	16	1°	12	6
Labor	21	7°	27	9
Underclass	7°	1°	13	3

[a]Percent for those who could be assigned a socioeconomic category.
Italics: Difference of three or more percentage points between high school and college.
°: Based on fewer than fifty respondents.
HS: High school or less; CO: one year of college or more.

tion (or less) went with low socioeconomic status. Although there is more to be said about these findings, it would be better to hold those comments until the underclass has been examined in greater detail.

Explaining the Underclass

The data have already shown that some percentage of every ethnic group is in the underclass. Although different procedures and data might produce somewhat different percentages, the essential point would remain: an American underclass exists and cuts across ethnic boundaries. Because of the issues this conclusion obviously raises, and because of the renewed interest sparked by William Wilson's work, a more detailed analysis of the underclass will be undertaken here.

Model and Variables

Several factors potentially determine underclass membership, and while many of those (such as psychological factors) cannot be dealt with here for lack of data, a basic model can still be constructed. Given the state of knowledge about the underclass, a basic model is still very much needed. In the present case, the goal is to identify several fundamental variables, and then to determine the net impact of each variable on the likelihood of underclass membership (by *net* I mean the effect of a variable after accounting for or controlling the effect of other variables in the model). The following variables could be identified and operationalized:

- Inner City
- Gender and single parenthood
- Ethnicity and subsamples

Inner City. Wilson views the underclass as an urban phenomenon, characterizing it by the terms *ghetto* and *inner city*. Although he does not explicitly say so, his view is a variation on the writings of Robert Park and Ernest Burgess. In a classic statement, they said that lower socioeconomic groups initially settled in the central portion of the city because they wanted to be near their work and because they could afford the housing in that area. As their economic situation improved, they then moved to better neighborhoods on the periphery of the city. Blacks were an exception to this process. They could not disperse because of race discrimination, and as a result, homogeneously black neighborhoods emerged and became centers of black communal life.[74]

The conception of the black ghetto as a relatively complete community persisted until the 1960s. At that time, changes in laws, economics, and politics led to a profound change in the nature of the ghetto. According to Wilson, waning discrimination has permitted middle-class blacks, who are the major reservoir of black leadership and socioeconomic resources, to follow the tracks of other ethnic groups and leave the ghetto. The result is that "today's ghetto neighborhoods are populated almost exclusively by the most disadvantaged segments of the black urban community . . ."[75]

The social isolation of the ghetto compounds this problem. Wilson believes that concentrating the poor in a homogeneously segregated area reduces their "access to jobs and job networks, availability of marriage partners, involvement in quality schools, and exposure to conventional role models."[76] None of this is new.[77]

The deleterious effects of ghettoized existence have been long known; however, Wilson's writings do add urgency to the argument.[78]

While the black ghetto has received the most media attention, the ghettoization of other groups should not be overlooked. Asians and Hispanics, in particular, live in urban cores, as do large portions of several European groups. The urban core may thus be more ethnically diversified than commonly realized. In addition, gentrification and other revitalization programs have attracted middle-class whites back to the core, thus adding both racial and socioeconomic diversity. Although Wilson emphasizes the black concentration, we should not therefore assume that the urban core is totally black.

Mostly poor and black, however, are specific subareas of the urban core. These areas best fit the notion of a black ghetto, but unfortunately, the data file being analyzed does not contain direct measures of ghettoization. Consequently, a "round-about" procedure had to be used. The Census Bureau defines a Standard Metropolitan Statistical Area (SMSA) as consisting of a large population concentration and the nearby communities that form an economic and social unit. Once a population concentration is considered part of an SMSA, the entire county is included. Each SMSA contains a central city, defined as the largest city within an SMSA (some SMSAs have more than one central city).[79] Basically, an SMSA is a large metropolitan area and the central city is its core. Note that the central city is not the same as a ghetto or inner city; those terms do not have official definitions.

Research showing the clear existence of ghettoized neighborhoods justified using the central city to operationalize the inner city that Wilson spoke of. When black census tracts are shaded with a pencil on SMSA maps, the ghetto immediately stands out as a defined, segregated, compacted area within the central city. And significantly, virtually all blacks in the central city live in the ghetto while virtually no nonblacks live there.[80] In other words, blacks who live in the central city live in the ghetto. This means that central city residence can serve as a proxy measure for ghetto residence. If used in this manner for the entire sample, central city would not be a very good proxy. As will be seen, however, ethnicity is also included in the analysis, and so we may safely assume that with regard to blacks, central city residence stands for ghetto residence, whereas with regard to other ethnic groups, it stands for central city residence, but outside the black ghetto.

Central city residence was scored as a binary (dummy) variable. Respondents living in the central city received a score of 1; otherwise they received a score of 0.

Gender and Single Parenthood. Gender has a major impact on poverty. The present data show that over three times as many women as men are in the underclass (13% versus 4%) and that the underclass consists overwhelmingly of women (74%). Other research has shown that gender affects earnings more than age, education, and work experience.[81] To describe facts such as these, Diana Pearce suggested the term "feminization of poverty."[82]

Poverty became feminized for several reasons. Sex discrimination is an obvious and much discussed phenomenon. After discrimination (which cannot be directly quantified with census data), the next most discussed reason is the female-headed household. Women traditionally bear the primary responsibility for raising children, a responsibility they retain even if unmarried. As a result, most single parents are women (84% in the present data), and they encounter great difficulty in finding work, gaining an education, being mobile, and benefiting from the numerous little things that contribute to upward mobility. Another reason poverty has been feminized is that women fall into the underclass faster than men climb out. Hence, the female proportion increases. Still another reason is age. Women live longer than men, and because the aged are often poor, larger proportions of women are poor.

Although the argument about single parenthood makes good sense, its appeal might mask another point, namely, that single parenthood affects men, too. Though proportionately far fewer, male single parents encounter much the same problems as female single parents: difficulty in scheduling work and finding child care, and other impediments to upward mobility.

The Census Bureau does not directly ask about single parenthood, so three questions were combined to produce a proxy measure. A respondent was considered a single parent if he or she was (1) the householder, (2) lived in a family household with a male householder, no wife present, or in a family household with a female householder, no husband present, and (3) the family had children, aged 17 or younger, present. Persons meeting these three criteria received a score of 1; persons not meeting any one of them received a score of 0.

This measure identifies single parents of either sex, but it mostly refers to female single parents because women constitute the overwhelming majority of single parents. To measure gender itself, women were scored 1 and men were scored 0.

The concept of the feminization of poverty assumes that poor women share a common destiny overriding other divisions, such as race and ethnicity. The assumption may be more ideological than factual. For example, in 1981, over twice as many black as white female headed households were impoverished, implying that white women must contend with gender discrimination but black women must contend with ethnic *and* gender discrimination.[83] The same effect might be generalized to women in other minority groups.

Ethnicity and Subsamples.   The present study uses a comparative approach. While each group could be compared to every other group, that would produce 136 comparisons—obviously an unmanageable number. So, to simplify matters, each ethnic group was compared to one "standard group," the British. They were chosen for two straightforward reasons. First, the British constitute the single largest group under study and so provide a large base for statistical analysis. Second, Western European influences dominate the cultural core of American society, and within that grouping, the British clearly represent the white Anglo-Saxon Protestant tradition and have played a dominant historical role in the development of the nation.[84]

To compare each group to the British, a binary variable was constructed for subsets of the sample. Consider Italians as an illustration. A subsample was drawn that consisted only of British and Italian respondents; Italians were scored 1 and non-Italians (British) were scored zero. The binary variable thus created captured the difference between being Italian and being British. The same procedures were followed for each ethnic group, but to streamline the results, the categories of Other and Missing were combined into one.

Hypotheses.   The foregoing discussion of the model may be summarized as a series of net hypotheses, or predictions about the effect of a variable taking into account all other variables:

• The following variables will increase the likelihood of underclass membership: being a central city resident, female, or a single parent.
• Being Western European, Eastern European, Italian, or Asian will decrease the likelihood of underclass membership, while being Native American, Spanish, Mexican, or black will increase the likelihood.

• The hypotheses, stated as *main* effects, also have potentially important *interaction* (*joint*) effects. For instance, gender may affect underclass membership and so may race, but when the two variables are combined, the effect may be especially large. A black female may have an especially high probability of being in the underclass. Given these possibilities and the present emphasis on ethnicity, the model includes the interaction terms between it and all other variables.

Categorical Model

It would seem at first that a relatively simple model could accomodate the foregoing hypotheses; but the situation is actually more complicated than the hypotheses suggest. Consider what happens if, for each subsample described above, we simultaneously crosstabulate underclass membership by all the independent variables. The result would be underclass by central city residence by gender by single parenthood by ethnicity. Table 2.14 displays an illustration. The table is far from simple. It has 32 cells, implying that several hundred cell-by-cell comparisons could be made. That is far too many to comprehend. Moreover, even with the large subsamples being used, the table might have many cells with small frequencies. Preliminary analysis did reveal, however, that the data met the standard criterion of having fewer than 20% of the cells with 5 or fewer respondents.[85]

Table 2.14

Illustration of a Categorical Model[a]

			In the Underclass				
	Dutch				*British*		
Male		*Female*		*Male*		*Female*	
SP	SP	SP	SP	SP	SP	SP	SP
CC	CC	CC	CC	CC	CC	CC	CC

			Not in the Underclass				
	Dutch				*British*		
Male		*Female*		*Male*		*Female*	
SP	SP	SP	SP	SP	SP	SP	SP
CC	CC	CC	CC	CC	CC	CC	CC

[a]SP: single parent; *SP*: not single parent; CC: central city residence; *CC*: not central city residence.

Given the size of the table, a more compact methodology would be helpful. Fortunately, one is available in the form of a linear categorical model. Without loss of information, the major relationships in the crosstabulation (Table 2.14) can be succinctly expressed as follows:

$$Y = X_1 + X_2 + X_3 + X_4 + X_1 + X_4 +$$
$$(X_1 \times X_4) + (X_2 \times X_4) + (X_3 \times X_4)$$

where Y is underclass membership, X_1 is central city residence, X_2 is gender, X_3 is single parenthood, X_4 is ethnicity, $(X_1 \times X_4)$ is the interaction between central city residence and ethnicity, $(X_2 \times X_4)$ is the interaction between gender and ethnicity, and $(X_3 \times X_4)$ is the interaction between single parenthood and ethnicity.

This view of the model suggests a potential complication: more interaction terms. The joint effect between every pair of variables might be included, as might the effect between every triplet and quadruplet. However, the model would then become lengthy, unwieldy, and most important, theoretically unintelligible. Few theories (if any) explicitly distinguish between main and interaction effects, and certainly not between all double, triple, and quadruple effects. For those reasons, the model contains only the interaction effects resulting from ethnicity, the primary focus of this investigation.

Results

Table 2.15 shows the descriptive statistics for each variable in the model. These statistics represent only persons for whom socioeconomic status could be ascertained; excluded, for instance, are children 16 or under and students. Consequently, the figures do not represent groups in their entirety, a fact that should be borne in mind when perusing them.

Concerning central city residence, relatively few Western Europeans reside there, although some variation does exist. The percentages range from 8% (Dutch) to 17% (Swede). In marked contrast, approximately one-fourth to one-third of Poles, Russians, Italians, Spanish, and Mexicans live in the central city, as do some 40% of blacks and Asians. Among nonwhites, only the value for Native Americans, a highly rural group, approximates that of Western Europeans. Regarding the percentage of females, the lowest value (37%) is for Mexicans while the highest values are for the Spanish

Table 2.15

Descriptive Statistics for Model Variables[a,b]

Ethnic Group	Central City	Percentage Female	Single Parent
British	13	44	3
Dutch	8	41	5
French	16	46	5
German	13	42	3
Irish	18	45	4
Norwegian	12	46	4
Swede	17	41	3
Italian	22	43	4
Czech	17	48	2
Pole	26	42	3
Russian	32	40	4
Asian	44	48	5
Afro American	45	52	14
Mexican	34	37	6
Spanish	35	53	9
Native American	12	44	7
Others	22	44	4

[a]Percent of those who could be assigned a socioeconomic category.
[b]Central city versus non-central city, female versus male, single parent versus non-single parent.

and blacks (52% and 53% respectively). The figures for single parenthood are typically 5% or less, but among blacks it is a comparatively high 14%.

These descriptive statistics provide an overall impression of the data, but they do not show the net effects required by the hypotheses. For that purpose, the categorical model shown in Table 2.16 should be consulted.

In Table 2.16, the minus sign indicates that a measure decreases the probability of being in the underclass. Those coefficients that are statistically significant are marked with a pound (#) sign.[86] Significance was assessed with the chi-square test. As is well known, chi-square increases as a function of sample size, which leads to paradoxical interpretations. With a large sample, we can be confident that nonsignificant chi-squares are, indeed, nonsignificant,

TABLE 2.16

Parameter Estimates of the Categorical Model

Variable	Dutch	French	German	Irish	Italian	Norwegian
Intercept	−3.00#	−3.02#	−2.78#	−2.64#	−2.51#	−3.48#
Central City residence	.31#	.01	.07#	−.04	.10#	−.52#
Gender	1.17#	.95#	.70#	.69#	.66#	.56#
Single Parent	.12	−.01	.15#	.16#	.32#	−.13
*Central City residence	.39#	.09	.15#	.04	.18#	−.44
*Gender	.49#	.26#	.01	.01	−.02	−.13
*Single Parent	.10	−.02	.14#	.14#	.31#	−.14
Ethnicity	−.18	−.20#	.04	.17#	.31#	−.66
Residual Chi square	12.45	18.04#	31.60#	56.01#	25.66#	8.20

	Swede	Czech	Pole	Russian	Spanish	Mexican
Intercept	−3.01#	−3.00#	−2.60#	−3.01#	−2.23#	−2.32#
Central City residence	.07	−.12	.10	.30#	.32#	−.12#
Gender	.71#	.82#	.69#	.42#	.52#	.82#
Single Parent	.13	−.07	.36#	.16	.34#	.14#
*Central City residence	.15	−.04	.18#	.38#	.40#	−.04
*Gender	.02	.14	.00	−.26#	−.16#	.13#
*Single Parent	.11	.05	.34#	.14	.32#	.13#
Ethnicity	−.26	−.18	.21#	−.25	.59#	.50#
Residual Chi square	9.63	6.41	15.21	7.82	16.34#	12.79

but by converse reasoning, significant chi-squares might be reflecting sample size rather than substantively important effects. Unfortunately, no statistical solution to this problem exists. We can only recognize it and take due care when interpreting results.

Central City. Considered across all ethnic groups, central city residence has mixed impact on underclass membership. The measure is not statistically significant among the French, Irish, Swedes, Czechs, Poles, and Afro Americans; but it is significant among all other groups. These findings cast considerable doubt on

TABLE 2.16

Continued

	Asian	Afro American	Native American	Other
Intercept	−2.60#	−2.15#	−2.32#	−2.34#
Central City residence	.24#	.04	.18#	.06#
Gender	.56#	.61#	.61#	.62#
Single Parent	.25#	.07	.21#	.16#
*Central City residence	.32#	.12#	.26#	.14#
*Gender	−.13#	−.08#	−.08	−.07#
*Single Parent	.24#	.06	.20#	.15#
Ethnicity	.21#	.67#	.50#	.47#
Residual Chi square	8.07	8.63	8.97	40.25#

* = the interaction between that variable and ethnicity.
\# Statistically significant at or beyond the .05 level of probability by the chi-square test.

the generality of the original hypothesis. It seems to apply only to some groups, but it is not apparent why the effect exhibits such selectivity.

The joint impact of ethnicity and central city residence follows much the same pattern as the main effects, but there are a few exceptions. For Norwegians and Mexicans, the direct effect is important, but the joint effect is not. This suggests that their ethnicity does not combine with place of residence to produce an unusually large impact; or put otherwise, ethnicity does not play a role in the relationship between place of residence and underclass membership. In contrast, place of residence per se is not important for Poles and Afro Americans, but when combined with ethnicity, the joint effect is important.

Gender. Among all groups, females are more likely to be in the underclass than males. However, these findings are not completely consistent with an assumption contained within the feminization of poverty perspective. The interaction between ethnicity and gender varies from group to group. Statistically, the interaction term is not significant for Germans, Irish, Italians, Norwegians, Swedes, Czechs, Poles, and Native Americans, but it is significant for all other groups. Thus, while women are more likely to be poorer than men (the main effect), ethnicity does make a difference for several groups (the interaction effect). This pattern implies that divisions of gender do not always supersede divisions of ethnicity.

Single Parenthood.   Single parenthood generally has the antici-pated effect. However, among four groups (Norwegians, Swedes, Czechs, and Russians), the measure does not significantly differ from zero. While all four groups are white, two are Western Euro-pean and two are Eastern European, and one (Russians) probably includes many Jews, a group subjected to much ethnic discrimina-tion. Seemingly, these groups have no common characteristic distin-guishing them from groups among whom single parenthood did have a significant impact. As with central city residence, the selec-tivity of the impact is difficult to explain. Also difficult to explain is the pattern of the interaction terms. The joint impact of ethnicity and single parenthood affects underclass membership among Ger-mans, Irish, Italians, Poles, Spanish, Mexicans, Asians, and Native Americans. While stereotypes might lead us to believe these groups possess strong family values that denigrate single parenthood, the same should hold true for Russians (Jews), among whom the inter-action was not significant. Even more puzzling, given Wilson's em-phasis, the joint impact of ethnicity and single parenthood is not significant for blacks.

Ethnicity.   There was no reason to believe that the ethnicity of Western Europeans would predispose them to be in the underclass, and the results generally confirm that expectation. Nevertheless, there were two exceptions. The first is the Irish, a group historically subjected to intense discrimination. The findings show that being Irish increases the likelihood of being in the underclass.[87] If we as-sume that anti-Irish prejudice is no longer a major force, this ethnic effect possibly represents the residual of past discrimination. Dis-proportionately large numbers of Irish may be in the underclass be-cause they have not managed to overcome the effects of past obstacles, even though the obstacles themselves have been disman-tled. An opposite finding emerges for the French: the negative co-efficient suggests that being French reduces the probability of being in the underclass. Why the French should be favored, compared to the British, is not evident. In neither the French nor the Irish case, though, should too great a weight be placed on those findings per se. Overall, Western European ethnicity does not influence under-class membership.

Among Eastern Europeans, the ethnic effect is important only for Poles. Like the Irish, Poles are a white ethnic group subjected to hostility and derision. And like the Irish, the impact of their ethnicity might reflect past inequality, as well as current discrimination. The lack of a significant ethnic effect for Russians comes as a mild surprise. If the Russian grouping is a surrogate measure for Jews, we would expect it to reduce the probability of being in the underclass. Apparently, though, it has no impact at all.

Ethnicity does have a significant effect among Italians, Spanish, Mexicans, Asians, blacks, and Native Americans. While these groups vary in race and subculture, they are currently, or have very recently been, minorities. As minorities, they have had disproportionately less power, prestige, and wealth, and have been the subject of intense and oftentimes violent discrimination. That these groups are disproportionately in the underclass, even after allowing for the impact of other independent variables, comes as no great surprise, and supports the initial prediction. Asians are the one exception. The Asian finding may be due to the heterogeneity of the category, but that is difficult to know for sure. Recent evidence indicates that certain Asian groups, such as the Vietnamese, have not met with much socioeconomic success and that many of them live in poverty.[88]

Residual.   The residual terms shown in the table represents the inadequacies of the model: random variations, measurement error, and omitted variables. A statistically significant residual chi-square thus implies that an alternative model should be sought; a non-significant value implies that the model is adequate. Except for the French, Germans, Irish, Italians, and Spanish, the residuals are not significant. For those five groups, the chi-squares suggest that other measures might improve the model—if they could be identified.

A further consideration in assessing the residuals is the distribution of the dependent variable. Underclass membership is highly skewed: no more than 19% of any group was in the underclass. The greater the skew of the dependent variable, the more difficult it is to explain. At the hypothetical extreme of skewness (100% in the underclass), we are attempting to explain something that does not vary, a goal impossible to achieve statistically.[89] While this point does not mean we should ignore the residuals, we should keep it in mind when coming to conclusions about the overall adequacy of the model.

Conclusions

The analysis has produced a welter of findings, some of which were theoretically anticipated, but several others which were not. Because sixteen groups were being analyzed, some of which have hardly been subjected to empirical scrutiny before, the mixed outcomes were to be expected. More attention was therefore placed on interpreting patterns of data, and several broad conclusions can be drawn.

The Nature of Socioeconomic Status

Socioeconomic status can be operationalized in several ways. With the present data, three obvious alternatives were available: occupation, income, and education. On both theoretical and empirical grounds, occupation was chosen. Theoretically, Weber's notions of class and status logically lead to using occupation as an indicator of socioeconomic status; and empirically, much past research indicates that the occupation is an empirically useful measure.

An equally important consideration in choosing occupation was the desire to analyze the underclass. Previous analysts have focused on it as a separate and distinct entity, most often measured by the federal government's poverty index. While appropriate for those purposes, a criterion based on poverty level cut-offs is difficult to adapt to the broader concept of socioeconomic status. One reason is that sociologists have not previously conceptualized socioeconomic status in that fashion, and so even if such a conceptualization could be developed, it would not be comparable to past research. Not only would that make generalization a problem, but it would be conceptually awkward. We would have to discuss socioeconomic status based on one set of criteria, and the underclass based on another. Clearly, a more appropriate tactic would be to include the underclass as part of an overall schema of socioeconomic status. This goal was served by using occupation.

Although occupation is well grounded in theory and research, the rankings of each occupation are not totally agreed upon. One question concerns how one determines which occupation represents which level of socioeconomic status. If we rank occupations solely by income, then the ranking is managerial, professional, craft, labor, technical, service, and the underclass. This ranking is, as the analysis showed, highly uniform across various ethnic groups, with a few exceptions. Among Asians and Italians, the professional category has a higher income than the managerial category, and among Czechs, labor has the highest median income of all. However, considering the number of ethnic groups in conjunction with the heterogeneous groupings designated "Other," these exceptions are rather minor.

An alternative, more truncated occupational ranking results from using education. It consists of the combined category of professional-managerial at the top, the underclass at the bottom, and all other occupations combined into a mid-range category. This is also uniform across ethnic groups.

In some respects, whether one prefers ranking based on education, income, or occupation is more a matter of personal preference than empirical outcome. Good cases can be made for each choice. Perhaps, though, the best solution is to recognize that even while the specific operationalization produces somewhat different socioeconomic categories, the basic hierarchical structure remains constant. An analogy is a book case. If the case represents socioeconomic status, then each shelf represents a specific socioeconomic level within it. The placement of a given shelf might be changed without radically altering the overall structure of the book case.

Socioeconomic Status and Ethnicity

The analysis of socioeconomic status by ethnic group provided many specific findings, but overall, it leads to one basic conclusion: the concept and operationalization of socioeconomic status is not ethnic group specific, or to put it otherwise, socioeconomic status applies across the board. When Milton Gordon proposed that ethnic groups develop socioeconomic structures paralleling that of the majority, one could question the empirical validity of the possibility. Now, however, we now know that ethnic groups manifest much the same socioeconomic structure as the majority.

Previous writings had suggested that while minority groups adopt a socioeconomic system similar to that of the majority, the relative numbers in the various strata would be very dissimilar. The data amply confirmed that suggestion. Once the sizes of the groups were taken into account, Western Europeans were clearly overrepresented in the upper strata and underrepresented in the lower ones. With a few exceptions, the opposite pattern was found for nonwhites.

Correlates of Socioeconomic Status

A common technique for conducting exploratory investigations of a subject is to ascertain if variables correlate with it as expected.

If they do, that increases one's confidence in the theory and methodology underlying the investigations. Here, four correlates were examined: multiple ancestry (intermarrige), place of birth, gender, and education. These were chosen because simple hypotheses could be declared about the correlations, and because they are among the most basic structural variables affecting socioeconomic status and ethnicity.

Multiple Ancestry and Place of Birth.   Because persons born in the United States are assimilated, almost by definition, both that measure and multiple ancestry can be interpreted along similar lines. Neither measure proved to be consistently related to socioeconomic status across the various ethnic groups. To be sure, a few exceptions to this statement existed, but they did not change the essentially negative conclusion.

Although negative, this conclusion is not inconsistent with Milton Gordon's notion of the ethclass. In fact, these data strongly support the notions advanced by Gordon. To recall, he said that ethnic groups could establish a socioeconomic hierarchy paralleling that of the majority without assimilation taking place. He called this structure the ethclass and cited intermarriage as the *sine qua non* of assimilation. Evidently, Gordon's analysis is basically correct. While the various ethnic groups have similar socioeconomic structures, the structures have no consistent relationship with assimilation.

To speculatively carry this conclusion one step farther, it means that socioeconomic equality can be achieved without cultural (structural) asssimilation taking place. Minorities could conceivably attain parity and still remain outside the social mainstream of American life. This is, of course, a variation on the theme of "separate but equal." However one feels about the ethical basis of the theme, Gordon's notion and these data indicate that "separate but equal" might well apply to socioeconomic status.

Gender.   Women were overrepresented in the professions, technical, service, and underclass while men were overrepresented in managerial, craft, and labor. The predominance of women in service and the underclass, and the preponderance of men in the labor and craft and managerial categories, could be anticipated. Less readily anticipated is the preponderance of women in the professional category. However, it should be noted that the percentage differences between males and females were small. Across the groups, the female percentages exceeded the male percentage by three points seven times. The largest difference was 7 points, and the mean difference was 1.2 points. These figures suggest that the female predominance in the professional category is slight. The presence of many females in professions such as teaching, nursing, and home economics probably accounts for this gender difference.

The large preponderance of women in the technical category might seem odd at first glance, but recall that the term "technical" is being used as a short-hand name for a category that includes sales and administrative support occupations. Many of these jobs have been aptly described as "pink collar," or dominated by females (for example, dental hygienists, sales counter clerks, cashiers, secretaries, stenographers, and typists).

Overall, these data show that no simple relationship between gender and socioeconomic status exists. Rather than saying that being male is positively related to higher socioeconomic status (and vice versa for females), a particular category must be specified.

Education. Socioeconomic status was straightforwardly related to education: higher education was associated with high socioeconomic status, lower education with low socioeconomic status. Interestingly, among all groups, some percentage of the college educated were in lower socioeconomic categories, including the underclass. Although the percentage was sometimes quite small, this finding demonstrates that education is not an absolute guarantee against underclass membership, nor for that matter, is being male, or native born, or of multiple ancestry. Some percentage of each of these categories were also in the underclass.

The Underclass and Ethnicity

On a purely descriptive basis, some proportion of every group was in the underclass. However, when group size was taken into account a much different picture emerged. Blacks were more overrepresented in the underclass than any other group, a fact that helps justify the emphasis placed on their plight. Nevertheless, that fact should not deflect attention from other groups. Mexicans, Spanish, and the miscellaneous categories of Anglo American, Other Hispanics, and Other Nonwhites were also overrepresented in the underclass. The issue clearly extends beyond blacks.

A basic model intended to explain underclass membership was developed and tested. Among Western Europeans, ethnicity was unimportant. That was expected because, historically, Western Europeans are the cultural core of the United States and a numerical majority. The findings for Poles and Italians rested on less firm grounds. They have been subjected to much discrimination, but their ethnicity may now be losing salience.[90] As it turned out the data imply that their ethnicity contributes to underclass membership.

That ethnicity had a significant effect among all groups classified as nonwhite (Spanish, Mexicans Asians, blacks and native Americans) reinforces the notion that color is still an important dividing line in American society. Even Asians, who have relatively high socioeconomic standing, are affected. For them, once the impact of other variables has been controlled, the net impact of being Asian increased the probability of being in the underclass.

According to the conventional statistical criteria, this model was adequate but not exceptionally strong. Of course, no statistical model can be better than the variables included in it, and, admittedly, the present model is crude. It consisted of variables derived from largely descriptive works rather than from a complete theory of the underclass. Still, the model is useful. It can serve as a first step toward a more complete explanation. Without a firm grounding in basic data, construction of more complex explanations will be more difficult, if not impossible.

This chapter has presented a large amount of data, both descriptive and analytical. The sheer volume might be distracting, preventing us from contemplating the broader issues at hand. Out of the welter of these numbers, what overall conclusion finally emerges? Most simply, yet reconditely, it is this: ethnicity and color still make a difference in America.

3

Ethnicity and Socioeconomic Gains

Virtually all theories of American ethnic inequality rest on two assumptions: that upward mobility is a good and shared goal, and that American society does not have enough resources to satisfy everyone. One group's success, therefore, must come at another group's expense. If these two assumptions are correct, or just partially correct, the fundamental ethnic question is simple: "Who gets up the socioeconomic ladder?"

At a broad level, the answer to this question is already known. Whites have gotten farther up the ladder than nonwhites, and among whites, Western Europeans have gotten the farthest. Even a hasty glance at the American ethnic scene or at American history will confirm this, as does the data shown in the previous chapters.

Of course, to say that whites have succeeded does not mean the situation has not changed or cannot change. Reynolds Farley showed that, over the years, blacks have been moving up the ladder. The income of black males was 61% of the white level in 1955, 68% in 1970, and 71% in 1982. The situation has improved, although these figures may imply more equality than actually exists. The gap between male black-white incomes decreased, in part, because of white losses rather than black gains. In contrast, black females have closed the gap by consistently gaining on white females.[1] These findings caused Farley to be generally optimistic about the future, but he did recognize that several decades of improvement must pass before blacks achieve complete economic parity with whites.[2]

Some Asian groups may have already achieved parity. Anecdotal evidence suggests as much, but the facts are more nebulous. One study showed that Asian Americans in Hawaii do not receive the same benefit from education as whites and that the similarity between the economic standing of Asians and whites results largely from the greater rate at which Asian females participate in the labor force.[3] Another study indicated that residential segregation among Asian groups in Honolulu is fairly high, implying that intergroup assimilation has not progressed at a rapid pace.[4]

Of nonwhites, Japanese Americans may be the only group to have achieved socioeconomic parity. Interestingly, even though Chinese and Korean Americans have as much or more education than whites, their incomes are less than that of whites. And one Asian group, the Vietnamese, is one of the most disadvantaged groups in the nation.[5]

Findings such as these confuse the ethnic scene. While gains have undeniably been made, many blacks, Hispanics, and Native Americans have yet to achieve socioeconomic parity. The Asian case, especially with regard to Japanese Americans, further implies that even if parity is achieved, that will not automatically lead to widespread integration in housing, marriage, or the disappearance of prejudice. American society clearly divides along ethnic lines, and even though vast amounts of research have tried to fathom why, major issues remain.

Explaining Ethnic Inequality

Several explanations have been offered for the persistence of ethnic inequality, ranging from the purely psychoanalytic to the purely rational-economic. Because it is neither feasible nor relevant to review the entire gamut of literature, here the discussion will consider only explanations alluding to the benefits that the majority gains from the presence of a subordinate minority.

Majority Gains

In a classic study, *Caste and Class in a Southern Town*, John Dollard pointed out that whites benefited from the subordination of blacks.[6] Although the benefits take the form of sex, prestige, and economic rewards, Dollard emphasized economic gains.

While he also recognized that the white middle class gained from the white lower class, he did not discuss that relationship, claiming that he did not know very much about it. He wrote the following:

> It is quite plain that the most active sources of antagonisms between Negroes and whites lie between the middle class white and the Negroes. In promoting their own interests the white middle class uses any means at hand to fight competi-

tors; this they do with whites and Negroes alike, of course, but in the case of Negroes the caste barrier and various other un-American methods of competition can also be used.[7]

Apparently, Dollard viewed the process of black subordination as primarily determined by economic or competitive interests, supplemented by caste and prejudice. These racially linked elements placed blacks in an especially weakened position vis-a-vis the white lower class.

Dollard described Southern race relations in a bygone era, but the kernel of the idea is still relevant. On a more general level, it suggests that the majority group benefits from the subordination of a minority group. Benefits can take many specific forms, with economic benefits having major importance. Assuming this reasoning to be correct, three scenarios can be developed showing how a majority derives economic gains from a minority.

1. In the case of recent immigrants, unfamiliarity with American culture and a lack of human capital applicable to the American workplace limits their employment opportunities. This forces minority workers to accept low wages, poor working conditions, and onerous jobs.

Although clearly detrimental to the minority, this situation benefits majority employers because the less desirable tasks are performed at relatively low wages. At the extreme, if the minority wage rate is substantially lower than that of majority workers, employers will hire the minority exclusively. However, the willingness to do that is mitigated by employer prejudice, and the possible repercussions from unions, consumers, politicians, public opinion, and other sources. Yet, even if minority workers are not actually hired, their mere presence opens the possibility they might be hired, thus dampening the demands of the majority work force. In a sense, a minority work force "sitting on the sidelines" constitutes a "reserve labor army."[8]

2. Another possible scenario is that competition for scarce resources, such as jobs, socioeconomic status, and mobility, forms a wedge between workers of different ethnic groups. Rather than mobilizing against employers, workers must divert energy to combat each other. A union, for instance, might reject members of certain groups. Thus, rather than growing larger and more powerful, the union limits its strength in the face of the majority employer.

Approaching the question of "who gains" from a different perspective, Gunnar Myrdal also discussed the ethnically fractured labor force. However, rather than starting his argument from an economic premise, Myrdal argued that the starting point was the prejudice of whites. The causal chain was thus: prejudice produces job restrictions against blacks, which produces black poverty, which produces further job restrictions. Myrdal wrote:

> When once the white workers' desire for social prestige becomes mobilized against the Negroes in this way, when they have come to look upon Negroes as differently from themselves and consequently do not feel a common labor solidarity with them, 'economic interests' also will back up discrimination. By excluding Negroes from competition for jobs, the white workers can decrease the supply of labor in the market, hold up wages and secure employment for themselves. To give white workers a monopoly on all promotions is, of course, to given them a vested interest in job segregation.[9]

Here, Myrdal states that when whites look upon blacks as different, *then* economic interests reinforce discrimination. Although the net result is that blacks are subordinate to whites, the basic causal argument differs from that of Dollard. He emphasized the causal role of economic variables while Myrdal emphasized prejudice and discrimination.

3.   According to still another scenario, if minority group A and majority group B are in the same labor pool and equally qualified in all respects, employers will not prefer one group over the other on economic grounds. Thus, to be hired, one group, say the minority, must accept lower wages. If the differential is sufficiently large, minority workers will be hired in place of majority workers, thus establishing a wage differential benefiting employers. Majority group B can counter by lowering its wage demands to a point where majority workers will once again be hired. Hence, as long as employers are willing to substitute the minority group for the majority group, they can bid down wages.

A possible example of this process, documented with historical data, was presented by Joan Moore and Harry Pachon.[10] They claimed that the border between Mexico and the United States has never been effectively policed, in large part, because a porous border permits illegal immigrants to enter the country. This benefits majority employers. Illegal immigrants, under the threat of deportation, will work for extremely low wages under harsh conditions.

Rather ironically, this scenario means that as long as employers are unprejudiced about hiring minority workers (that is, as long as they use economic considerations as their sole criteria), employers benefit from the prejudices of majority workers. However, if majority workers set aside their hostility toward the minority, and unite to present a common front to employers, the situation of all workers improves. According to Marxist logic, this will occur because the economic interests of majority workers will eventually supersede their antipathies towards the minority, and conversely, the minority will set aside its antipathies towards the majority.

Several studies based on census data have examined various aspects of the Marxian position. Michael Reich argued that while the white capitalist class profits from racism, one need not invoke a conspiracy theory to explain it.[11] Rather, the system itself works in such a way that white capitalists reap the benefits. Reich tested the hypothesis on forty-eight standard metropolitan statistical areas (SMSAs). The ratio of black to white median family income served as a measure of racism, a low ratio indicating high racism. Of particular interest for the present study is Reich's measure of income concentration: the percentage share of all white income received by the top one percent of white families. He found that the Pearson correlation between this percentage and the racism indicator was −.55. As the Marxist hypothesis suggests, the greater the racism, the higher the concentration of white income. A similar finding for states rather than SMSA's was reported by Bowles.[12]

Albert Syzamanski performed a related analysis using 1970 census data based on states.[13] Rather than restricting the study to blacks, he also included Spanish origin, American Indians, and Asians in a category he called "third world minority." The assumption was that these groups perform substitutable roles with regard to occupying less desirable jobs. One of his hypotheses was that because the minority is forced to take low paying jobs, whites will "pile up" in the higher paying jobs. This would produce an unequal distribution, which he operationalized with a Gini index based on white male earnings. (The index varies from 0, which indicates equality across the distribution, to 1, which indicates no equality. Syzamanski does not indicate how he calculated the index).

For states with a population at least 12 percent Third World, the Pearson correlation between the Gini index and the percentage of third world population was -.58. The value was not significantly affected by introducing statistical controls for the percentage of the state population that was urban, worked in manufacturing, or had a certain per capita income. Based on this and several other findings, Syzamanski concluded that whites do not economically gain from discrimination against a minority.

E. M. Beck performed a time series analysis for 1947–1975 census data, using similar measures.[14] He found no support for the hypothesis that white workers gain from discrimination, although some of his findings suggested that white workers do gain from having a nonwhite labor force at the periphery of the economy. This finding hints at the possibility that the minority serves as a "reserve labor army," but Beck did not expand upon the point.

While the foregoing studies refer directly to income, the same logic has implications for socioeconomic status as well. It is easy to visualize how income gains in the marketplace translate into socioeconomic gains in general. Wealth constitutes the basis for upper strata life styles, social status, political power, or more generally, high socioeconomic position. In addition, the process is self perpetuating. Because the majority occupies the higher socioeconomic niches, the majority controls the key positions in the economy, polity, and other institutions that enable the majority to further protect their position.[15]

Queuing

Working with historical census data, Stanley Lieberson proposed a "queuing" model.[16] He reasoned that if the minority group is as qualified as the majority with regard to job requisites, a rank ordering will result, such that the majority group piles up in the favored positions, leaving the less favored positions to the ethnic minority. Once established, the situation becomes partially self fulfilling. Those with the good jobs—that is, the majority—will grant benefits and favors to others like themselves, thus increasing the majority's dominance of the occupational hierarchy. Moreover, if workers outnumber available jobs, unemployment will fall hardest on the bottom of the job hierarchy, thus causing the minority to be more disadvantaged and further securing the position of the majority. Lieberson concedes that some exceptions to this scenario are possible, but argues that the overall aggregate structure of jobs will be queued in this way.

Lieberson provides a few illustrative scatterplots showing the relation between the percentage of blacks in the United States labor force and their percentage in selected occupations, circa 1900. Visually inspecting the graphs suggests that the relationship for the black percentage working as domestic servants is positive and curvilinear; for the black percentage in carpentry, it is positive and linear; for the black percentage in the clergy, it is also positive and linear; and for the black percentage in banking, there is no relation at all.[17] From these data, it is difficult to arrive at an overall conclusion.

Alexander Saxton makes a similar argument with historical evidence. He says that during the nineteenth century, the importation of Chinese workers for the transcontinental railroad had the dual effect of providing cheap labor and of upgrading the status of white workers.[18] As the Chinese filled less desirable jobs, whites moved into the more desirable ones and then reserved those positions for themselves. Phillips Cutright has called these "bonus jobs": jobs available to the majority because of a minority presence.[19] Even earlier, the same process had occurred when Chinese entered the California gold fields during the 1850s, first as menial laborers and then as miners purchasing poor producing mines from whites.

Other studies have examined the queuing notion with statistical data, although they do not use the queuing terminology, nor do they necessarily agree with Lieberson's viewpoint. With regard to blacks, Norval Glenn suggests that whites gain from a black labor force because blacks take the lower paying jobs in the economy, thus "freeing" white workers to move up to better jobs.[20] Alternatively, one can envision a process whereby blacks, by filling the lower ranking jobs, "push" the majority up the socioeconomic ladder. In either case, the net result will be beneficial to whites. Although Glenn does not mention it, white employers will also welcome the upward mobility of white workers, since they fill the better paying positions that must be filled anyway. That would be consistent with any employer and worker prejudices. Note that upward mobility achieved in the foregoing manner is conditioned on the existence of an opportunity structure that has openings in higher level positions. Otherwise, the majority would be blocked regardless of any minority presence. In sum, these considerations lead to the following hypothesis:

(1) The larger the minority, the larger the concentration of the majority in the upper echelons of the socioeconomic hierarchy.

Ethnic Heterogeneity

Although not much studied before, ethnic heterogeneity might also benefit the majority. In situations where a great many different ethnic groups exist, each group must compete with the majority as well as with other ethnic groups. Blacks, for instance, might be competing in the same labor market as Mexicans and whites. In order to secure employment, each group must underbid the other in wage demands, thus depressing the overall wage level for all groups, and hindering their opportunities for long-term socioeconomic advancement.

Marxian logic dictates that groups have more to gain than lose by uniting, but as an empirical matter, pan-ethnic unification has rarely occurred. Even minorities that superficially seem similar have not united. For example, Hispanic groups share certain elements of Latin culture, but they certainly do not share the same political, geographic, or economic histories.[21] They are, indeed, different, and to assume that all Hispanic groups are alike is a form of stereotyping. Thus, if the foregoing reasoning is correct, the following hypothesis follows:

(2)   The greater the ethnic diversity, the greater the concentration of the majority in the upper echelons of the socioeconomic system.

Labor Market and Dual Economy

In some ways, the terms "dual labor market" and "dual economy" are misnomers. The concept of a *labor market* actually refers to a classification of occupations (not a specific place) while *dual economy* refers to classification of industries (not to separate economic activities for the majority and minority). Although the dual labor market and dual economy are general concepts, they do have implications for inequality and socioeconomic status.

Dual Economy

According to this theory, the economy is divided into two sectors. The *core* consists of large industries that are capital intensive and deeply entrenched. A few large firms dominate these industries and while their earnings may be low at any given time, over the long run, they are generally profitable. Core industries also have internal labor markets, or career paths and jobs that are not much affected by changes in economic and political conditions.

The *periphery* presents a contrasting economic picture. It consists mainly of small firms and local enterprises. Entry into the periphery requires relatively modest capitalization, but competition is fierce and profits are, accordingly, difficult to achieve. Under this condition, emphasis shifts to short-term survival rather than long-term gains. Workers may easily enter periphery jobs, but wages and job security are low. Not surprisingly, minorities, the young, and women are to be found here in abundance.

Dual Labor Market

Michael Piore provided the major impetus for the concept of a dual labor market.[22] It divides occupations into two kinds. The *primary* market contains skilled and professional jobs that pay well, involve pleasant working conditions, and are accorded much prestige. These jobs also tend to be stable and provide long-term security. The *secondary* labor market contains jobs with the opposite characteristics. They require few skills, pay poorly, and are not well regarded. Moreover, the secondary labor market contains few safeguards to protect workers from changes in economic conditions or the capriciousness of employers. Historically, ethnic minorities and other powerless groups have gravitated into this labor market.

Economic Segments

The concepts of the dual labor market and the dual economy are not mutually exclusive. For example, day laborers might work within a core industry while conversely, lawyers might work for a peripheral business. It is therefore possible to generate a simple, fourfold classification scheme, as follows:

Economic Sector	Labor Market	Economic Segment
Core	Primary	A
Core	Secondary	B
Periphery	Primary	C
Periphery	Secondary	D

Let us call the combination of an economic sector and labor market a *segment* of the economy. Clearly, the most desirable segment is A, consisting of "good jobs" within "good industries," and the least desirable segment is D, which has the opposite characteristics. The relative desirability of segments B and C are unclear, but some research suggests that the labor market has a stronger impact on earnings than the economic sector.[23] If that is true, then segment C, which contains the primary labor market, would be preferable to segment D, which does not.

The foregoing considerations can be combined with elements of the Marxian logic discussed before. The notion that the majority benefits socioeconomically from a minority presence suggests that the majority will be disproportionately represented in the better places in the economy. To relegate the minority to lesser socioeconomic positions, in effect, relegates them to secondary labor markets, for that is where that type of occupation is located. Similarly, to relegate the minority to peripheral industries means that the minority will have less job security, less opportunity, and lower pay—all characteristics that contribute to lower socioeconomic status.

If the foregoing logic is correct, then the following hypotheses can be offered:

(3)　The larger or more diverse the minority, the greater the concentration of the majority in the primary labor market.

(4)　The larger or more diverse the minority, the greater the concentration of the majority in the primary sector of the economy.

(5)　The larger or more diverse the minority, the greater the concentration of the majority in the primary-core segment of the economy.

Procedures

Because the hypotheses call for aggregated data, the procedures followed here differed from those of the previous chapter. The major modifications were as follows:

1.　Past studies have been based on either states or metropolitan areas, the latter operationalized as Standard Metropolitan Statistical Areas.[24] In the present instances, however, the number of respondents per SMSA was too small (sometimes fewer than 100) to sustain much statistical analysis. Another unit of analysis was therefore sought, and states were the obvious alternative.

A total of 38 states met the criteria of having at least 5% of its population classified as a minority, and at least 500 respondents. Even with the second criterion, the data occasionally became somewhat sparse (as later indicated on the tables). Regarding the 5% minority criterion, the hypotheses imply that some minimum value must be established *a priori*. Obviously, if a state has zero percent minority, there is no minority to influence the majority; the percentage must be greater than that. Unfortunately, neither *a priori* theory nor past research specifies the precise minimum value, and so I chose 5%. I arrived at this value after examining the preliminary data, but the choice was somewhat arbitrary.

2. The ethnic groups were re-specified. No new groups were added, but some were combined into fewer categories. Groups such as Dutch or British became one generic category: Western European. This procedure was necessary to prevent data sparseness. If specific Western European groups had been used, the number of respondents in any given category of socioeconomic status would be unacceptably small. As before, Western Europeans were assumed to constitute the majority.

3. A "minority" was operationally defined as Hispanics, Native Americans, and all nonwhites. The category of Other Nonwhite was included on the assumption that they would be treated as a minority regardless of their specific race or ethnicity. The strong influence of color on socioeconomic status supports this assumption.[25] These specific groups were combined into one group, referred to in the tables as the "minority."

Note that the specific composition of the minority varied from state to state. For example, Mexicans are a politically and statistically important minority in Texas but not in Alabama. There, of course, blacks are the most numerous minority. The fact that different groups are unevenly distributed across states also means that region of the country should not be introduced as a control variable. To do so would, in effect, dilute the impact of minority group size, the key independent measure. While combining specific minorities into one group may seem to cloud the findings, it should be emphasized that, with regard to the hypotheses, the critical variable is not a specific ethnic group but the group's powerlessness in comparison to the majority.

4. Some hypotheses refer to ethnic group diversity, and for that purpose, the index of diversity was used:

$$D = 1 - [(a/z)^2 + (b/z)^2 \ldots (n/z)^2]$$

where D is the index of diversity, a is the number of ethnic group A, B is the number of ethnic group B, n is the number of ethnic group N, and z is the total of a through n.[26] The index was based on seven groups: Asians, Blacks, Mexicans, Native Americans, Spanish, Other Spanish, and Other Nonwhites. The index ranges from one to zero and has a simple interpretation. If only a single minority group is present in a state, then the index value is zero; if all seven groups are present, then the index approaches unity. Note that diversity partially overlaps the minority proportion, and in the extreme case where only one minority group is present, the two measures contain the same information. For that reason, the diversity index and the minority percentage were not included in the same statistical analysis. This operationalization should not be confused with differentiation based on a real location.[27] To be sure, the index is summarized by state, but it measures diversity among ethnic groups, not areal contiguity.

5. The dependent variables were operationalized as the percent of Western Europeans in these categories: primary labor market, core industry, the core-primary economic segment, and the categories of socioeconomic status used before, from underclass through professional.

Although the dichotomy between core and periphery encompasses most economic activities, two major segments are difficult to classify: the government and agriculture. The government is not a profit seeking entity. It has perpetual life, and the legal authority to command obedience. Similarly difficult to categorize is modern agriculture. While dominated by a few large firms, a politically important number of farms remain family enterprises representing a cultural ideal. It would have been possible to create separate categories for agriculture and government; however, rather than doing that, I placed government in the core and agriculture in the periphery. This practice is somewhat arbitrary but not uncommon. In the present instance, the major reason for following it was to help prevent data sparseness.

Model

In order to evaluate the hypotheses, a simple regression model was established:

$$Y = B_1 (X_1) + BX_2 (X_2) + e$$

where Y is a dependent measure, X_1 is the minority percentage in some equations or the index of diversity in others, X_2 is a control variable (discussed below), B_1 and B_2 are standardized regression coefficients, and e is a random error term.

This equation is presented in its general form. More specifically, ten equations were established, one for each dependent variable being evaluated. These were, as mentioned earlier, the percentage of Western Europeans in the following categories: primary labor market, core industry, the core-primary economic segment, and the seven categories of socioeconomic status, from the underclass through professional.

The control variable, (X_2), was state wealth, operationalized as per capita state income (the sum of the income of all persons in a state divided by the state population). This was included because large minority populations might be attracted to wealthy states, while at the same time, state wealth could also enhance the occupational and economic standing of Western Europeans. This was the only control variable included. Even though some analysts might prefer to include more, the small sample of states limits that number, while theoretical considerations do not suggest others critical to the hypotheses. On the other hand, some analysts might prefer to even exclude the one control variable that is included, feeling that per capita income and the dependent variables are so closely related conceptually that the one might be used as proxy measure for the other.

Results

The descriptive statistics are presented in Table 3.1. It shows that 18% of each state is a minority, but since that and all other figures are based on 38 states, they should not be generalized to the nation as a whole. It should be emphasized, however, that these 38 states do have a minority presence; hence, one could argue that they are the only states to which the hypotheses apply.

The mean of the diversity index, .58, is approximately midway between its theoretical high and low, but the standard deviation is relatively large, indicating that states vary substantially in ethnic diversity. The per capita income figure is approximately $7,000. As to places in the economy, 45% of Western Europeans are in the primary labor market, 42% are in the core sector, and 18% are in the core-primary economic segment. Across socioeconomic status, the Western European figure varies from 8% in the underclass to 28% in technical. The descriptive data provide background, but do not directly address the hypotheses. For that purpose, I turn to the multiple regression equations. The first set assesses the impact of ethnic diversity.

TABLE 3.1

Means and Standard Deviations of Model Variables*

Variable	Mean	Standard Deviation
Minority	18.2%	9.4%
Diversity index	.58	.17
Per capita income	$6,950	$923
Western European in:		
Primary labor market	44.9%	4.9%
Core industry	41.6	5.2
Core-primary segment	17.9	4.4
Professional	12.3%	2.4%
Managerial	10.6	3.1
Technical	27.9	4.2
Craft	15.6	3.4
Service	10.5	3.1
Labor	15.4	4.2
Underclass	7.7	3.8

*Based on 38 states.

Ethnic Diversity

Table 3.2 shows the equations that relate per capita income and the index of ethnic diversity to the Western European percentage in the various places in the economy. While the R^2 for the primary market equation reaches statistical significance, it is small, indicating a poor fit between model and data. The same is true of the R^2 for primary-core segment. Smaller still and not statistically significant is the R^2 for the core sector equation. However, in this equation, per capita income does affect the Western European percentages while in the labor market equation, ethnic diversity has a significant impact.[28]

Concerning socioeconomic status, Table 3.3 displays the seven multiple regression equations corresponding to the percentage of Western Europeans in each of seven socioeconomic categories. The R^2's are small, except for the managerial and underclass equations. Nevertheless, in no equation does the index of ethnic diversity have a significant impact on the Western European percentages.

In general, the equations relating ethnic diversity to the socioeconomic and economic position of the majority provide but little support for the original hypotheses. The assumption that ethnic

TABLE 3.2

Labor Market, Economy, Economic Segment and Ethnic Diversity:
Multiple Regression Model (Standardized Regression Coefficients)[a]

	Dependent Variable		
	Percent of Western Europeans in:		
Indendent Variable	Primary Market	Core Sector	Primary-Core Segment
Per capita income (logarithm)	−.02	.37*	.22
Index of ethnic diversity	.46*	−.05	.27
Squared multiple correlation	.20*	.12	.19*

[a]Based on 38 states.
*Statistically significant at or beyond the .05 level of probability.

groups compete with each other, and thereby hinder their own socioeconomic and economic mobility, is not supported by these data.

Minority Percentage

Turning to another set of equations, Table 3.4 displays the data
regarding the minority percentage. Although the R^2 for the primary

TABLE 3.3

Socioeconomic Status and Ethnic Diversity: Multiple Regression Model
(Standardized Regression Coefficients)[a]

	Dependent Variable						
	Percent of Western Europeans in:						
Independent Variable	P	M	T	C	S	L	U
Per capita income (logarithm)	−.04	.47*	.22	−.20	.25	.02	−.66*
Index of ethnic diversity	.31	.19	−.20	.04	.11	−.30	.07
Squared multiple correlation	.08	.35*	.04	.03	.10	.08	.39*

[a]Based on 38 states.
*Statistically significant at or beyond the .05 level of probability.
Legend: P: professional; M: managerial; T: technical; C: craft; S: service;
L: labor; U: underclass.

market equation is statistically significant, it is small in absolute size. Still, in that equation both percent minority and per capita income affect the Western European percentage. The only other statistically significant effect occurs for per capita income in the primary-core equation. However, the R^2 is small and not significant, implying a poor fit between model and data.

These data, like those for ethnic diversity, provide but meager support for the hypotheses. The size of a minority seems not to substantially affect the majority's position in the economy.

Minority Size and Majority Socioeconomic Status

In contrast to the previous findings, much stronger outcomes are found among the equations regarding the Western European percentages in the seven socioeconomic categories. The R^2's in Table 3.5 vary from small to moderately large. Moreover, all the R^2's, except that for the service equation, are statistically significant. In other words, for six out of the seven equations, the outcomes are consistent with *a priori* predictions.

In the equations for manager, technical, craft, and underclass, per capita income has a significant impact. However, in the technical and craft equations, the impact of per capita income is smaller than that of the minority percentage. This is in inconsistent pattern, making it difficult to arrive at an overall conclusion.

Regarding the minority percentage specifically, it has a relatively consistent impact, reaching statistical significance in five of

TABLE 3.4

Labor Market, Economy, Economic Segment, and Minority Percentage: Multiple Regression Model (Standardized Regression Coefficients)[a]

| | Dependent Variable | | |
| | Percent of Western Europeans in: | | |
Independent Variable	Primary Market	Core Sector	Primary-Core Segment
Per capita income (logarithm)	.35*	.32	.40*
Percent minority	.42*	−.08	.13
Squared multiple correlation	.21*	.12	.15

[a]Based on 38 states.
*Statistically significant at or beyond the .05 level of probability.

TABLE 3.5

Socioeconomic Status and Minority Percentage: Multiple Regression Model
(Standardized Regression Coefficients)[a]

Independent Variable	Dependent Variable Percent of Western Europeans in:						
	P	M	T	C	S	L	U
Per capita income (logarithm)	.28	.70*	.34*	−.35*	.23	−.28	−.69*
Percent minority	.52*	.44*	.72*	−.56*	−.25	−.49*	−.24
Squared multiple correlation	.25*	.50*	.48*	.31*	.15	.24*	.44*

[a]Based on 38 states.
*Statistically significant at or beyond the .05 level of probability.
Legend: P: professional; M: managerial; T: technical; C: craft; S: service;
L: labor; U: underclass.

the seven equations. Equally as important, the minority percentage positively affects the percentage of Western Europeans in the upper occupational categories (professional, manager, and technical), and negatively affects the lower categories (craft, service, labor, and the underclass). In two of these equations, the coefficient is not statistically significant, but the signs are in the hypothesized direction.

The findings indicate that craft may be the crossover point: in craft or socioeconomic categories below it, the minority percentage has a negative impact while the opposite holds for categories above it. Put otherwise, the greater the minority percentage, the more likely it is for Western Europeans to occupy high socioeconomic positions and the less likely it is for them to occupy low socioeconomic positions—high and low being operationalized as above or below the craft category. Whether craft itself should be considered high or low is not clear, however.

Other Models

Thus far, each dependent variable has been analyzed separately, and the findings indicated that the craft category is the "crossover" point between higher and lower ranking occupations. With this knowledge now at hand, a more compact, summary model may be examined. In order to do that, a single dependent variable was constructed: the percentage of Western Europeans in the categories above craft. That is, professional, managerial, and technical were combined into a single "higher" grouping. This grouping was chosen because the individual equations (Table 3.5) have indicated that the craft category is a dividing point in the occupational distribution. With these data, the following multiple regression equation resulted:

$$Y = .60 \ (X_1) + .77 \ (X_2)$$
$$R^2 = .69$$

where Y is the Western European percentage in higher socioeconomic categories, X_1 is per capita income, X_2 is the minority percentage, and R^2 is the squared multiple correlation coefficient. As the R^2 indicates, this is a strong model. Moreover, all coefficients are statistically significant.

The final model to be examined addresses the issue of socioeconomic differentiation. To assess the issue, a measure of occupational unevenness was constructed. It is based on the following logic: if randomness were the only factor at work, Western Europeans should be represented in any given occupational category in proportion to their number in each state. Even though the chi-square statistic is usually used as a test of statistical significance, it can also serve to measure the unevenness of an entire distribution. That is because the chi-square compares the observed frequencies against the frequencies expected based on randomness, summed across all categories (in this case, seven socioeconomic groupings). The larger the chi-square, the farther the distribution of Western Europeans departs from what one would expect from their population size. Table 3.6 shows these data in percentage form (the actual chi-squares were based on frequencies). The calculations clearly show that the preponderance of overrepresentation occurred in the technical category, which consists of sales, clerical, and other similar, middle-range, white collar jobs. Not surprisingly in light of the relatively large frequencies used, all chi-squares were statistically significant. In every state, the hypotheses that the distribution of Western Europeans across the socioeconomic categories is proportionate to their population size could be rejected well beyond the five percent level of significance.

The relationship between the chi-square and the two independent variables being studied was summarized by the following regression model:

$$Y = .42\ (X_1) + .46\ (X_2)$$
$$R^2 = .28$$

where Y is the chi-square based on the Western European percentages in the seven socioeconomic categories, X_1 is per capita income, X_2 is the minority percentage, and R^2 is the squared multiple correlation coefficient. This model is considerably weaker than the previous model, as indicated by the comparatively low R^2. Nevertheless, the model does reach statistical significance (five percent level), as do the two standardized regression coefficients. The larger the minority, the less proportionate is the distribution of Western Europe-

TABLE 3.6

Over- and Under-Representation in Socioeconomic Categories, and Chi-Square, for Western Europeans[a]

State	P	M	T	C	S	L	U	Chi-Square
Alabama	−3.1	−7.4	12.3	1.1	−7.4	5.4	−1.0	198
Arizona	−1.4	−2.1	17.5	−0.1	−4.3	−2.8	−6.8	199
Arkansas	−7.3	−8.2	16.2	3.1	−4.7	1.4	−0.4	167
California	0.5	−1.1	18.9	−0.3	−4.3	−4.4	−9.3	884
Colorado	3.6	−0.6	11.5	2.6	−3.8	−0.1	−13.2	227
Connect.	−0.2	1.8	19.9	−1.5	−8.9	−0.9	−10.3	307
Delaware	1.1	−2.8	12.6	1.1	1.1	−2.8	−10.4	26
Florida	−2.4	−2.2	19.9	−1.5	−3.2	−3.9	−6.7	776
Georgia	−2.9	0.8	18.6	−2.1	−9.0	0.8	−6.2	414
Idaho	−2.0	−2.0	8.8	5.7	−0.4	1.1	−11.2	56
Illinois	−3.7	−2.3	16.4	2.9	−5.1	1.8	−10.0	829
Indiana	−3.5	−7.1	13.1	0.1	−1.8	8.7	−9.6	513
Kansas	−2.2	−4.5	8.7	5.2	−2.2	3.0	−8.0	125
Kentucky	−2.5	−5.7	9.2	1.2	−3.6	3.4	−2.0	101
Louis.	−2.1	−3.7	19.0	3.7	−7.4	−6.4	−3.2	331
Maryland	−3.5	1.0	19.8	−3.1	−2.6	−2.2	−9.4	401
Mass.	−2.4	−3.2	16.7	−4.6	−1.8	1.6	−6.3	445
Michigan	−1.5	−3.9	13.5	−0.6	−3.3	4.0	−8.3	537
Miss.	−1.2	−9.4	16.9	3.8	−6.9	1.3	−4.4	195
Missouri	−3.2	−6.9	15.5	0.1	−2.9	1.4	−3.9	339
Montana	−3.9	10.1	6.6	10.7	4.5	−1.8	−6.0	56
Nevada	1.2	−0.5	6.4	−0.5	4.7	−5.7	−5.7	26
New Jersey	−2.1	−1.1	17.6	−0.1	−0.5	−2.8	−11.0	474
New Mexico	4.2	−1.3	17.2	−6.9	−3.2	−5.0	−5.0	80
New York	−0.5	−2.1	13.8	−2.1	−3.2	1.6	−7.5	589

TABLE 3.6

Continued

State	P	M	T	C	S	L	U	Chi-Square
N. Carolina	−2.6	−4.2	10.9	0.5	−7.7	7.4	−4.2	306
Ohio	−5.0	−2.8	11.2	2.1	−4.5	6.5	−7.4	621
Oklahoma	−0.1	−8.3	8.7	7.6	−2.3	1.0	−6.6	161
Oregon	−1.7	1.1	6.9	1.7	−5.7	5.1	−7.4	103
Penn.	−3.6	−8.4	10.7	1.4	−3.6	10.4	−7.1	808
S. Carolina	1.0	−4.5	15.2	−0.2	−6.9	3.5	−8.2	215
S. Dakota	−4.8	−6.7	10.2	6.5	−3.0	0.8	−3.0	43
Tenn.	−5.0	−6.2	13.5	0.8	−6.6	8.1	−4.6	342
Texas	−1.4	−1.3	15.9	2.6	−5.9	−1.4	−8.5	814
Virginia	1.2	−0.7	17.6	−2.4	−4.0	−3.3	−8.5	453
Washington	−2.8	−2.8	14.2	1.1	−5.2	3.5	−8.0	284
W. Virginia	−4.3	−4.3	5.7	4.6	−7.6	−2.1	7.9	68
Wisconsin	−3.8	−4.6	11.1	4.5	−2.1	4.2	−9.3	366

Legend: P: professional; M: managerial; T: technical; C: craft; S: service; L: labor; U: underclass.
[a]The percentage of Western Europeans in a category minus 14.28 percent, the percentage expected based on chance. A negative value indicates under-representation; a positive value indicates over-representation. Chi-square is based on the frequencies of Western Europeans in each category.

ans regardless of income. As previously mentioned, piling up occurs mainly in the technical category. Hence, these data suggest that the impact of a minority is to increase the Western European concentration in middle-range, white collar occupations.

Conclusions

In sum, the diversity of ethnic groups did not affect the percentage of Western Europeans in the various socioeconomic categories, core industries, or primary-core economic segment. By and large, these findings fail to support the original predictions.

Reasons for the failure are difficult to adduce. Possibly, the concepts were not properly operationalized, or possibly, merging the Marxian perspective with the perspectives of the dual labor market and dual economy is an inappropriate theoretical procedure. Another possibility concerns the boundaries between places in the economy. For example, unions and other internal labor markets may or may not discriminate, but that might be more a function of prevailing economic conditions and power relationships among management, government, and workers than of prejudice. If that is true, boundaries would not be especially responsive to the diversity of minority groups, or to their sizes.

In contrast to the preceding outcomes, both the index of minority diversity and the minority percentage affected the Western European percentage in primary labor markets. This supports the initial argument that diverse and large minority populations are funneled into poor jobs, thus boosting the job status of the majority. The finding also provides further evidence that, of the concepts of the dual labor market and the dual economy, the former plays the more decisive role for ethnic relations.

Another clear finding concerned socioeconomic status. The minority percentage had a consistent and major impact on the socioeconomic standing of Western Europeans. The larger the minority, the greater the percentage of Western Europeans in occupational positions above the craft category. Conversely, the larger the minority percentage, the lower the percentage of Western Europeans in the craft position and below it. In addition, the greater the minority percentage, the greater the piling up of Western Europeans in middle-range, white collar jobs. These patterns persisted controlling for income. Overall, the data lend support to the Marxist notion that the majority benefits from the presence of a minority. In this case, the benefits are socioeconomic standing.

Finally, it is worth noting, as Glenn says, that the benefits accruing to the majority may be offset by certain "costs" that are a necessary part of the situation.[29] For instance, the availability of cheap minority labor may slow the process of substituting efficient work processes for inefficient ones. In the long run, that cost might be extremely high to the economy as a whole. A poor minority population will also require resources in the form of higher transfer payments, medical costs, and police protection. Just as important, enforcing subordination may incur a heavy political cost. If the minority clamors for upward mobility and is denied, a terrible price might be extracted in terms of civil disobedience, social dislocation, and violence.

4

Demographic Potential and Socioeconomic Status

This chapter is concerned with the demography of ethnic group success. The basic idea is simple: demographic characteristics determine the success of the group. More specifically, the idea is that every ethnic group has a *demographic potential*, or demographic capacity that tends to heighten or lower the group's socioeconomic status.

Demography is often defined as the study of population, a serviceable, simple definition. However, it may be too simple for present purposes because it misses the link between demography and the concept of demographic potential. A better way to reveal the link is to consider demography not as a discipline with rigid boundaries, but as a discipline varying in breadth and emphasis. In the 1950s, Philip Hauser and Otis Dudley Duncan divided the discipline into two areas: demographic analysis and population studies.[1] The former concerns the components of population whereas the latter concerns the relationships between those components and non- demographic variables. This distinction still holds, although in what has become a standard reference work, Henry Shryock, Jacob Siegel, and associates proposed a somewhat more complex scheme.[2]

They say that, viewed narrowly, demography pertains to the size, distribution, structure, and change of a population. Size, for instance, refers to the number of persons, distribution to their geographic location, structure mainly to their sex and age characteristics, and change to variations over time. Frequently associated with this emphasis is an emphasis on analytical techniques, many of which are highly mathematical.[3] This view of demography is sometimes called "formal demography."[4]

A wider view incorporates other population characteristics, such as race, marital status, and social class. In addition, demographers sometimes engage in "differential analysis": the application of demography to subgroups of the population.[5] Combining both this view and differential analysis under one heading, we can refer to it as "social demography."

The widest view encompasses the relationships between demography—either formal or social—and other disciplines. For example, demographers have long studied immigration, income inequality, and residential segregation, topics that fall within the field of ethnic relations. When doing so, any sharp distinctions between the two fields largely vanish. The one folds into the other, and, following Hauser and Duncan, this view can be called "population studies."

Demographic Potential

The concept of demographic potential deals with the impact of demographic dimensions on socioeconomic attainment, thus falling between demography and ethnic relations. Or, to use the scheme outlined above, the concept is part of population studies.

Demographic Potential Defined

Thus far, the definition of demographic potential has remained implicit. An explicit definition is now offered: *The impact of demographic variables on socioeconomic attainment constitutes the demographic potential of the group.* Following the lead of formal demography, demographic dimensions are taken to be the size of an ethnic group, its location, and its age and sex composition. Other dimensions might be added, but for now the boundaries suggested by formal demography provide a logical and convenient rationale for reducing the scope of the inquiry to practicable proportions.

The concept of demographic potential asserts that certain population characteristics affect ethnic group attainment. This has been demonstrated before. For example, a study of California ethnic groups has shown that the mean age of a group strongly correlated with the group's per capita income.[6] Older groups earned substantially more than younger groups. Another example is the hypothesis that large groups have difficulty in being absorbed into the economy while small groups have difficulty in accumulating political power.[7] Yet another example is provided by William Wilson's concept of the black underclass. He identifies the black underclass by its youth, high fertility, low marriage rate, and high rates of single parenthood.[8] These characteristics fall within the purview of formal demography and population studies, and even though Wilson does not discuss them as such, they also constitute the demographic potential of the group. One reason the black underclass remains an underclass is its demographic composition, a causal factor often ignored in past research.

Although good empirical grounds exist for accepting the importance of demographic potential, conceptual grounds exist as well. To define an ethnic group means that some criteria must be invoked identifying the group's boundaries. Once identified, the group must then have a size (some people must be in it and others not), and size is a demographic dimension. In effect, the notion of size exists by virtue of identifying the group.

The concept of demographic potential also can be considered a generalization of an argument offered by George Easterlin: that the size of a generation affects the fortunes of the generation. Those born in the 1930s, a small birth cohort (generation), faced less competition for education, jobs, and seniority than those born in the baby boom following World War II. Facing different prospects, each cohort opted for different life styles and family structures, and even became involved in different kinds of deviance.[9] There were exceptions, naturally. Some individuals of the small cohort did not find abundant success while some individuals in the large cohort did. But to an important degree, the success or failure of the generation as a whole can be attributed to the demographic potential of the cohort.

Easterlin's basic point—that demography affects generational outcomes—can be modified to fit the topic being studied here. The unit of analysis becomes the ethnic group rather than the cohort; focus is restricted to a few demographic dimensions rather than a host of causes and consequences; and comparisons are made across groups rather than across time. Although these modifications may or may not be too simplistic, the essential point still remains: demographic variables affect ethnic group outcomes.

At least two major theoretical schools recognize this point. The *Annale* school of history views explanation as consisting of layers of causation—the deeper the layer, the more basic the cause. Among the deepest layers are economic and demographic forces.[10] Cultural Materialism, a broad theory of society, also relies on demographic causation. As proposed by Marvin Harris, demographic dimensions are embedded in the infrastructure of society; they belong to the "modes of production and reproduction." Within these modes, Harris places fertility, morality, age, and sex, and so accords demographic factors key roles in explaining society and culture.

Though brief, this review indicates that while the concept of demographic potential has not been emphasized before, it does have links to other research. Such a situation is not unusual. In the social sciences, supposedly new concepts frequently turn out to be variations on an older idea. Precursors almost invariably exist, and recognizing them helps place the "new" idea within a broader causal nexus. Thus, when applying the concept of demographic potential, we are simultaneously but indirectly applying that broader base of theory to which the concept is linked.[11]

Demographic Potential: Assumptions

The notion of demographic potential rests on two assumptions. The first is the causal importance of infrastructure. Marvin Harris named this assumption *infrastructural determinism*.

> The behavior modes of production and reproduction probabilistically determine the behavioral domestic and political economy, which in turn probabilistically determine the behavioral and mental superstructures. For brevity's sake, this principle can be referred to as the principle of infrastructural determinism.[12]

As this quotation mentions, probability underlies all causal relationships in science, a noncontroversial point.[13]

Harris also used two concepts not widely known in sociology: emic and etic. Both are types of understanding. The former places priority on understanding as seen through the eyes of those immersed in a situation whereas the latter relies on categories and data supplied by the researcher. Although nothing in the theory prevents the two forms from corresponding or being identical, in practice that would be rare because the principle of infrastructural determinism calls for a particular flow of causation. It goes from infrastructure to superstructure. This reverses the traditional way of thinking about ethnic relations because it gives priority to the structural and to the material, practical aspects of existence rather than to "ideas" and abstractions. In that respect, it is consistent with the concept of demographic potential.

The concept of demographic potential is etic in another sense. It relies on a logic and data not generally available to actors in the situation. For example, few members of an ethnic group are consciously aware that their fertility behavior affects group size, which may then affect the response of the majority toward the group, which may then affect the socioeconomic attainment of the group. Even if the typical individual knew about this causal sequence, it is too involved and too abstract to guide his or her behavior.

The second assumption is that a demographic dimension exists *sui generis*, that is, a dimension exists apart from the individuals composing it. Although individuals make up a given dimension, concepts such as size and central tendency refer to the dimension *qua* dimension. An individual, for instance, cannot compose a mean.[14] Similarly, the concept of demographic potential takes the ethnic group (not individual member) as its referent and also exists *sui generis*.

These two assumptions are important because they redirect the common and often implicit belief that ethnic relations can be explained by individual personality, prejudice, interpersonal discrimination, and other concepts linked to the individual. Although demographic potential does not contradict individual level explanation, it is located on a different causal plane.

Demographic Dimensions: Descriptive Findings

The concept of demographic potential asserts that demography affects the socioeconomic attainment of an ethnic group, but the concept makes no mention of specific variables. Those must be identified within the context of a given research situation. Once identified, however, the concept does not require that variables have the same impact on all ethnic groups. For some groups a given variable might have one effect, and for others it might have no effect or the reverse effect. Were a more fully developed theory available, these possibilities could be identified *a priori*, but as it stands, a combination of induction, deduction, and practicability must be used.

Here, the available data impose practicable constraints. The Census Bureau file being analyzed does not contain information from registries, so data on marriages, births, and deaths were not available. Fortunately, these omissions did not halt the research because alternative measures could sometimes be constructed. Table 4.1 displays the measures used. They are presented in tabular form and in one place for easy reference. However, because the arrangement of the table makes intergroup comparisons awkward, each measure is also portrayed graphically with discussion centering on the graph.

Sex Composition

Even though an individual's sex is biologically determined, mortality and migration can cause the proportion of males and females to vary among groups. Sojourning provides an example. Young males have usually been the ones seeking their fortunes abroad, and as a consequence, some immigrant groups have contained disproportionately few females. This demographic factor slows the rate of family formation and childbearing, and possibly increases the prevalence of male-oriented deviance, such as prostitution, drinking, and gambling. This line of reasoning has been used to explain the historical situation of Chinese in California, and with modification, it might apply to Mexicans today.[15] The steady

TABLE 4.1

Selected Demographic Measures

Ethnic Group	Sex Ratio	Fertility Ratio	Dependency Ratio	Age Squeeze Ratio	U. S. Born Percentage
Dutch	96.0	134.1	58.9	52.3	96.4
British	93.4	124.0	57.3	58.1	97.8
French	84.6	128.1	54.4	77.2	95.6
German	101.0	121.1	58.0	65.1	97.6
Irish	91.5	138.9	53.2	60.1	98.3
Italian	93.9	115.2	54.3	61.7	90.9
Norwegian	85.0	126.5	55.0	52.5	96.4
Swede	115.3	117.4	56.5	69.4	97.0
Czech	89.5	67.6	53.6	52.9	92.3
Pole	100.0	114.1	52.2	60.5	93.0
Russian	93.6	116.7	43.2	46.2	87.3
Anglo American	97.3	129.2	75.6	77.0	99.8
Other White	99.3	124.4	54.4	56.2	82.8
Mexican	116.0	178.2	68.7	110.4	71.1
Spanish	85.4	146.0	59.7	81.4	76.9
Other Hispanic	94.3	135.1	57.9	72.8	57.3
Asian	96.5	131.6	57.5	72.6	38.0
Afro American	90.6	166.5	75.7	86.8	99.0
Native American	84.3	142.5	56.5	94.1	99.8
Other Nonwhite	95.2	150.2	71.7	80.4	84.7

(sometimes illegal) stream of Mexican workers undoubtedly favors males. Expecting to return home, married sojourners will be inclined to leave their families behind, and single males will be less motivated to establish families in the United States. Of course, events do not always correspond to expectations, and many sojourners remain in this country.

To quantify sex composition, the sex ratio (SR) was computed for each of the twenty groups being considered:

$$SR = (\text{number of males/number of female}) \times 100$$

This ratio indicates the number of males per 100 females in the group. A value greater than 100 indicates more males, a value less than 100 indicates more females, and 100 indicates an equal number of males and females (see Figure 4.1). The mean and standard deviation shown on the figure (and on all subsequent figures)

TABLE 4.1

Continued

Ethnic Group	Child Percentage	Youth Percentage	Mature Percentage	Older Percentage	Mean Age
Dutch	24.2	21.6	41.3	12.9	35.8
British	23.6	23.4	40.2	12.9	35.7
French	25.0	28.2	36.5	10.2	32.8
German	26.1	25.0	38.3	10.6	33.3
Irish	23.1	24.5	40.8	11.6	35.3
Italian	23.4	24.7	40.1	11.8	35.0
Norwegian	23.1	22.2	42.3	12.4	36.0
Swede	21.1	26.2	37.7	15.0	36.5
Czech	19.8	22.5	42.6	15.1	39.2
Pole	22.9	24.8	40.9	11.4	35.3
Russian	13.4	22.1	47.8	16.7	41.2
Anglo American	32.2	24.8	32.2	10.9	31.0
Other White	21.3	23.3	41.5	13.9	36.7
Mexican	36.6	31.1	28.2	4.1	25.6
Spanish	31.2	28.1	34.5	6.2	29.1
Other Hispanic	33.0	26.7	36.7	3.6	27.4
Asian	30.7	26.7	36.8	5.8	28.6
Afro American	35.6	26.5	30.5	7.4	28.5
Native American	31.1	31.0	32.9	5.0	27.4
Other Nonwhite	34.8	26.0	32.3	6.9	28.5

FIGURE 4.1

Sex Ratio

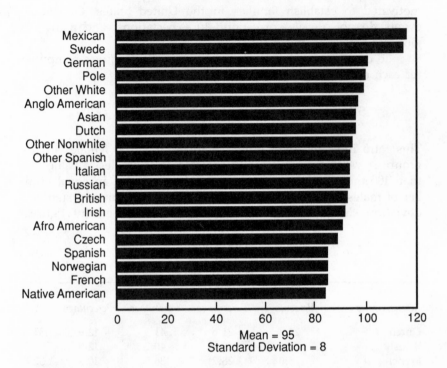

Mean = 95
Standard Deviation = 8

were calculated from the twenty group means; that is, they are the mean and standard deviation of means. On average, the groups have 95 males for every 100 females. Only among Poles are the proportions equal.

The preponderance of females in most groups comes as no surprise. For several social reasons, females live longer than males, greatly altering the sex composition of a group in the long run. Apparently, though, these social factors do not affect all groups equally. The sex ratios do vary, as indicated by the standard deviation of eight points.

What value constitutes a significant departure from the average is open to question, but some perspective can be gained by considering the standard deviation. Values above or below one standard deviation from the mean (below 87 or above 103) can be considered noteworthy. By that criterion, Mexicans and Swedes have high sex ratios, whereas Spanish, Norwegians, French, and Native Americans have low ratios. Ratios of less than 100 are to be expected for mature populations, but an explanation for the low ratios among these *particular* groups is not readily forthcoming. They seemingly have little in common: two are Western European, one is Native American, and the other is Spanish. Regarding the other extreme, the high value for Swedes is puzzling, but the value for Mexicans is not. Even though a substantial proportion of the Mexican population is now native born, the effects of past and present sojourning have possibly produced the male predominance evident in the data.

The pattern of sex ratios holds no obvious relationship with socioeconomic success. We already know that Mexicans, who have a high ratio, rank low in socioeconomic status. Although Swedes rank considerably higher in socioeconomic status, they have virtually the same sex ratio as Mexicans. Norwegians and French, two groups with high socioeconomic standing, have much the same sex ratios as the Spanish and Native Americans, groups with much lower standing. Perhaps a refined statistical analysis will reveal a causal pattern in these data, but at this point, none can be discerned.

Fertility Ratio

Fertility is important to socioeconomic attainment because groups with many children must devote proportionately more resources to child support and socialization than groups with fewer children. In effect, a low fertility group can direct its resources away from child rearing to acquiring upward mobility.

A long-held theory asserts that upwardly striving individuals or groups reduce their fertility to acquire a higher life style.[16] In the parlance of economics, the upwardly mobile "consume" life style rather than children; they trade off the one for the other. Variations on this idea have been applied to several ethnic groups, including Jews and Japanese Americans. The data generally support the idea, although it is far from proven.[17]

Here, fertility is measured by the fertility ratio (FR):

FR = (number children ever born/number of fecund women) × 1000

The age span 15–44 presumably covers the childbearing period of female life, and the resulting ratio thus indicates the number of births per 1,000 fecund women. The distinction between marital and nonmarital fertility can be important for some purposes, but with regard to ethnic group resources, children must be supported regardless of the parents' marital status. If that is correct, then the overall fertility ratio shown above would be an appropriate measure (see Figure 4.2). The typical group ratio is 130.4, but considerable variation exists, as indicated by the standard deviation of 21.8. Assuming that a ratio above 150 is "high" (approximately one standard deviation above the mean), then Mexicans, Afro Americans, and Other Nonwhites have high fertility. Although fertility is sometimes explained by religion—Mexicans are largely Roman Catholic—that explanation does not hold true for blacks. Moreover, if Catholicism is the major explanatory variable, then it is difficult to explain why

FIGURE 4.2

Fertility Ratio

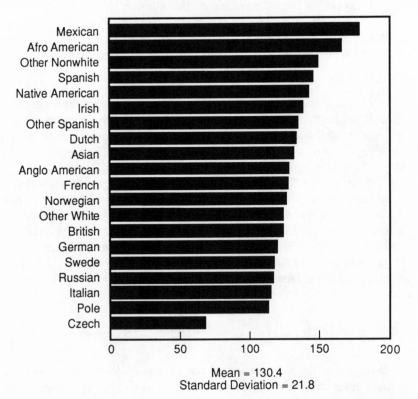

Mean = 130.4
Standard Deviation = 21.8

other predominantly Catholic groups, such as the Irish and Italians, have considerably lower fertility than Mexicans.

At the other end of the continuum, Czechs have a fertility ratio less than 70, far lower than any other group. After a considerable gap are Poles, Italians, Russians, and Swedes, all with ratios of between 110 and 120. These groups rank higher socioeconomically than groups with large fertility ratios, a result consistent with expectation. However, the extremely low ratio for Czechs has no obvious explanation.

Age Structure

One of the most fundamental demographic features of a society is its age structure. Universally, different age groups have different responsibilities allocated to them, a phenomenon called *age grading*. In the United States, children are expected to play but are not expected to work, to participate in government, or even to be responsible for their own conduct. The elderly, to take the other extreme, also have reduced responsibilities for work. Nevertheless, they are expected to fulfill civic duties and to bear the legal responsibility for their behavior, a responsibility sometimes "winked at" (for example, the elderly may be excused for causing a disturbance in public places). Between these two extremes lies the bulk of the American population. This group has the primary responsibility for producing income, socializing and supporting the young, governing the society, and, when necessary, contributing to the welfare of the elderly.

In addition to organizing society, age grading also implies a distribution of resources. Although on different ends of the age continuum, both children and the elderly absorb resources from the society while not directly contributing to it. To be sure, retirement funds support many of the elderly, who have thus already, in a sense, "earned their keep." Children, on the other hand, must be directly supported by the working population.

Having a large dependent population has implications for socioeconomic status. A group with many dependents must direct resources to support functions (such as schools) while a group with few dependents can allocate resources to functions directly related to socioeconomic attainment (such as businesses and work).

The age structure of a group may be measured with several statistics, of which the mean is the most basic (see Figure 4.3). Mean age is 33 years with moderate variance, as indicated by the

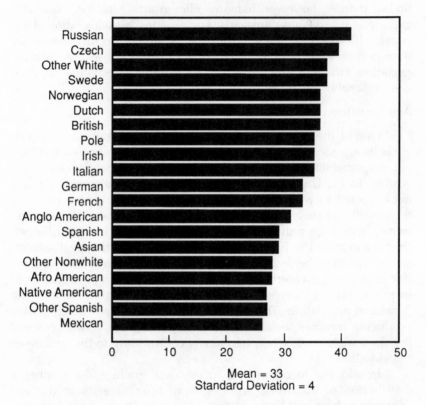

FIGURE 4.3

Mean Age

Mean = 33
Standard Deviation = 4

standard deviation of 4 years. Using one standard deviation as a criterion, any group falling outside the range 29–37 years is noteworthy. Czechs and Russians are thus "old," whereas Native Americans, Asian, Afro Americans and Mexicans are "young." The relatively low Asian mean is inconsistent with past research, but the heterogeneity of the Asian grouping possibly accounts for the finding, especially since the grouping includes Vietnamese, who, on average, are very young.[18]

In general, mean age correlates with the socioeconomic standing of the groups. Russians and Czechs have high socioeconomic standing and have high mean ages while Native Americans, Afro Americans and Mexicans have low standing and low mean ages. These findings are consistent with previous research.[19]

Age structure can be further specified by dividing a population into age groups. While that would be a relatively straightforward task if dealing with just one group, when dealing with several groups, problems of comparability arise. The precise cut-off ages separating say, children from adults, might vary among groups. For example, within one group, a person might begin supporting him- or herself at approximately age 16, while within another group those same obligations might not be incurred until several years later. If that is true, then comparing the two groups using the same age cut-offs would be misleading. Thus, the empirical task is to identify the age cut-offs that correspond to social categories. Unfortunately in the present case, that can not be done in much detail. No one knows the precise age cut-offs that would be appropriate for each category within each of the groups being studied.

If the foregoing were the only considerations, inter-ethnic age comparisons might be impossible. Fortunately, though, reasons exist to believe that American ethnic groups use approximately the same age cut-offs. Perhaps the most basic is biology. Physical and mental development follows somewhat the same course regardless of ethnicity. Because of physique, very young children cannot perform the same physical labor as adults, nor are children on the same intellectual plane as adults. All societies recognize this fact and, presumably, it is the reason that children are not given much responsibility.

Another factor leading to comparability of age cut-offs is assimilation. As groups assimilate, they adopt the culture of the broader society, including its age-grading patterns and age cutoffs. Standardization at the societal level also dampens interethnic variations. To illustrate, the legal age for driving, drinking, signing contracts, leaving school, marriage, and a host of other activities is the same for all groups living within a given legal jurisdiction. Furthermore, some age criteria apply nationwide (for instance, voting, registering for the draft, and collecting Social Security benefits). Hence, whatever subcultural variations in age grading exist, the necessity to comply with these legally imposed age criteria forces the group to at least partially adopt the age grading of the broader society.

These considerations suggest that age grading, and the associated age cut-offs, will be fairly uniform across ethnic groups—perhaps not perfectly uniform, but sufficiently uniform to render inter-ethnic comparisons meaningful. Operationally, I used fairly standard age cut-offs to create four age categories:

Child: Aged 16 or younger
Youth: Aged 17 through 30
Mature: Aged 31 through 64
Elderly: Aged 65 or older

The percentage of each group within each category is shown in Table 4.1. However, with four categories and twenty ethnic groups, a cell by cell discussion would be tedious at best. Fortunately, the "dependency ratio" (DR) can be used to summarize the relationships among the four age categories into a single number. It is defined as follows:

$$DR = (\text{children} + \text{elderly}) / (\text{youth} + \text{mature}) \times 100$$

This ratio shows the number of dependents (children and elderly) per 100 active persons (youth and mature). The higher the number, the greater the dependency found within the group (see Figure 4.4). On average, an ethnic group has 59 dependents for every 100 active persons in its population. Put otherwise, every 100 active persons must support 59 other people. Whether that figure is high or low is a matter of judgment, but again, the standard deviation can serve as an approximate criterion. Accordingly, ratios beyond 67 or below 51 are considered extreme. Excluding the two groups that are heterogeneous and therefore difficult to interpret (Anglo American and Other Nonwhite), Afro Americans and Mexicans have the highest dependency ratios by a considerable margin. On the low side, also by a considerable margin, are Russians, the only group falling below the criterion established by the standard deviation. Note, however, that both the Irish and Poles have relatively low ratios.

The low and the high dependency ratios correspond to groups known to rank low and high on socioeconomic status. The effect is not especially strong, though, because several groups with intermediate dependency ratios also have high socioeconomic standing (for example, Dutch and Germans).

Age Squeeze

Age structure also affects work and income. Young people usually take entry-level positions, earn low wages, and undergo on-the-job training. As they gain experience, they rise in the occupational hierarchy, acquiring more responsibility and larger incomes. In essence, the young are expected to "work their way up."

FIGURE 4.4

Dependency Ratio

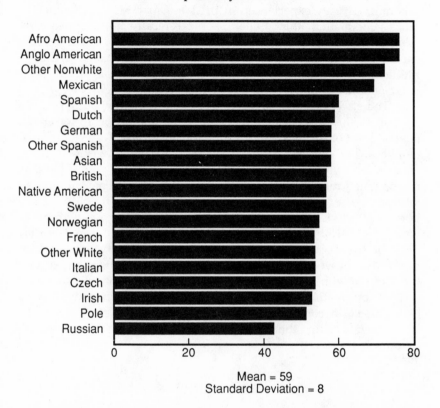

Mean = 59
Standard Deviation = 8

Of course, this scenario assumes that openings exist in upper-level positions, but they might not. Older workers may be already occupying them, blocking the upward mobility of younger workers. This places younger workers in a precarious position. Occupying the lower job levels, they are most vulnerable to being laid off should conditions change.

When the foregoing argument is specified for ethnic groups, an additional factor must be taken into account. Groups that work predominantly within an ethnic economy, as perhaps Asians might, will find the group's age structure relevant. Groups that work in the broader economy must compete with many other groups, including the majority, and the age structure of those groups will be the relevant ones. Although no one knows what proportion of each group works in which economy, the present data can still provide hints about the work potential of each group.

The age squeeze has been discussed in terms of work because it is most directly experienced in the labor market, but the effect is more general than that. Older people typically hold higher positions in all realms of life, such as political office, school boards, church memberships, and other community functions, as well as in the family and peer group. Moreover, in some ethnic subcultures, older people are deferred to and their opinions sought.

The effect of a tight age squeeze (that is, many young persons relative to the number of mature persons) should be to lower the general level of socioeconomic status for the group. That would happen because older persons block the mobility of younger persons. It would also happen because the presence of many young persons means that a relatively large proportion of the group has but limited job experience, seniority, and training. A more subtle but still important effect would also come about indirectly. A group with many young people might lack a layer of older, well established leadership, or the disproportion might lead to conflicts over leadership rights. As the young seek more responsibility in all realms of life, they collide with the older segment of the population. A prolonged conflict, by creating generalized ethnic group disorganization, could lower the socioeconomic achievements of the group as a whole.

Operationally, the *age squeeze* ratio (AS) was calculated as follows:[20]

$$AS = (\text{youths} / \text{mature}) \times 100$$

This ratio shows the number of youths per 100 mature persons. The higher the ratio, the tighter the age squeeze (see Figure 4.5). The mean of the group ratios indicates that there are 69 youths per 100 mature persons. Based on the standard deviation of 16, ratios greater than 85 and less than 53 are considered extreme. Accordingly, three groups (black, Native American, and Mexicans) have high ratios, with the Mexican ratio being the highest by a considerable amount (16 points). At the other end of the range, four groups have low ratios (Czech, Norwegian, Dutch, and Russian). The low and high ratios are 46 and 110, suggesting that Mexican youths face over twice the competition faced by Russian youths. That is too literal an interpretation of the age squeeze ratio, but it does draw attention to the problems brought about by the groups' age structure.

FIGURE 4.5

Age Squeeze Ratio

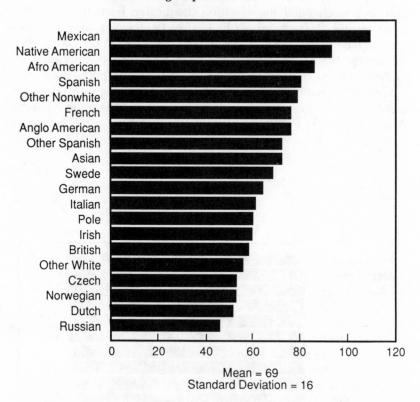

Mean = 69
Standard Deviation = 16

A crude correlation exists between the age squeeze ratios and socioeconomic standing. Groups with high ratios have lower standings than groups with low ratios. This is especially apparent when comparing the extremes. Mexicans, Native Americans, and Afro Americans have high age squeeze ratios and low socioeconomic status, whereas the opposite holds for Czechs, Norwegians, Dutch, and Russians. Impressionistically at least, the greater the age squeeze, the lower the socioeconomic status.

United States Born

The percentage of persons born in the United States varies considerably across ethnic groups. In the past, laws limited immigration of Eastern Europeans and barred Asians and most nonwhites outright. Being isolated, these groups could increase in size only through natural growth and, concomitantly, the proportion of the native born within them increased. Even though the 1965 immigration law changed the situation drastically, by that time a firm demographic infrastructure had already formed around many groups (see Figure 4.6). Typically, 88% of each group was born in the United States. The high value (100%) for Native Americans was to be expected because they are an indigenous population. Also having 100% native born is the Anglo American group. The exact identity of this group is unknown, but their declaration as Anglo Americans implies that they consider themselves to be indigenous Americans, which would explain the 100% value. Although not

FIGURE 4.6

U. S. Born

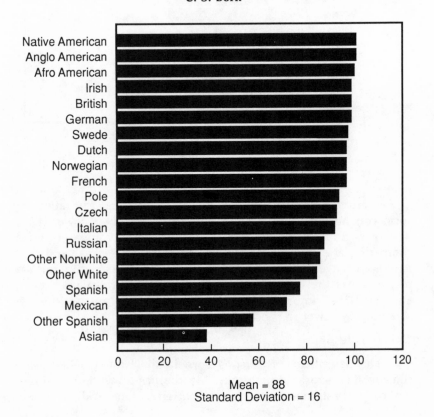

Mean = 88
Standard Deviation = 16

100% native born, several other groups are very close. Afro Americans, Irish, British, and Germans are 98% or higher while Swedes, Dutch, Norwegians, and French are 96% or higher. The lowest percentage is for Asians. This undoubtedly reflects the liberalization of immigration policies after 1965, the refugees of the Vietnam war, and the increased commerce with Pacific rim nations. The value for Other Hispanic is also low, probably due to Cubans. Even though a second generation is now emerging, the bulk of the American Cuban population arrived in the United States as political refugees.

A confused situation exists with regard to socioeconomic status. Groups with the highest percentages of native born (Native American and Afro American) have low socioeconomic status, whereas other groups with virtually the same percentages of native born have high status (for example, Irish, British, and German). Asians generally rank high in socioeconomic status but have a low percentage of native born; Mexicans and Spanish have higher percentages but rank lower in socioeconomic status. At this point in the analysis, therefore, percent native born and socioeconomic status appear to be unrelated.

When considering all the data presented above, an overall relationship emerges: groups with mature age structures have high socioeconomic status. This makes sense in light of what we know about education, seniority, income, and employment. Still, we can hardly say that the relationship was proved. For one thing, the analysis was impressionistic; and for another, it was univariate. No attempt was made to ascertain the simultaneous net impact of each demographic dimension on socioeconomic status. That requires a more complex statistical analysis based on a multivariate model.

Modeling Demographic Potential and Socioeconomic Attainment

The notion of demographic potential asserts that a group's demographic structure affects its socioeconomic attainment. This can be stated as a formal model:

$$Y = f(X_i)$$

where Y is the measure the socioeconomic status used in previous chapters (seven occupational categories ranging from professional to the underclass), the X_1 are various demographic dimensions, and the units of analysis are the twenty ethnic groups. The model can be operationalized as a multiple regression equation, but because the dependent variable consists of seven socioeconomic categories, a decision on how to incorporate it into the equation was required. A summary measure (such as the percent in the upper categories) is one possibility, and that is discussed later. Another possibility is a measure of central tendency (such as mean socioeconomic status), but that might over-summarize the information, obscuring important details. Consequently, an intermediate strategy was used: the percentage of each group in each socioeconomic category was calculated and analyzed separately, as follows:

$$Y_1 = B_1(X_1) \cdots B_n(X_n)$$
$$\cdot$$
$$\cdot$$
$$\cdot$$
$$Y_7 = B_1(X_1) \cdots B_n(X_n)$$

where Y_j is the percentage of each group in each category of socioeconomic status, and B_i is a standardized regression coefficient showing the net impact of X_i. To illustrate, the percentage of each ethnic group in the professional category was regressed against the independent variables, and then the percentage in the managerial category was regressed against the same variables, and so on for each of the seven socioeconomic levels. This approach assesses the impact of the various demographic dimensions on each category of socioeconomic status, revealing for example, whether variables that affect higher categories have the same effect on lower categories. Given the complexity of the socioeconomic system, this specification could prove important.

Variables and Hypotheses

Operationally, each independent variable in the model represents a specific hypothesis, the confirmation of which would strengthen the case for the overarching concept of demographic potential. These hypotheses are listed below.

United States Born. The percentage of each group born in the United States (native born) was included to account for the possible impact of generation. By virtue of birth, persons born in the United States typically speak English, attend American schools, and receive thousands of subtle and unconscious cultural inputs from the media, peers, family, and other channels of everyday life. Being better socialized into American culture, the native born might attain higher socioeconomic standing. Once they have higher standing, they can help launch the group upward, an effect that would impact the group as a whole regardless of birth place.

The preceding hypothesis is reasonable, but another equally reasonable prediction can be made. The 1965 immigration law gave preference to immigrants with scarce occupational skills. If the law has attracted disproportionately large numbers of professional and skilled immigrants, then the foreign born of a group may have higher socioeconomic status than the native born of that group. This could affect the socioeconomic attainment of the entire group. Arriving with high-level occupational status, the foreign born might attain gatekeeper positions rather quickly. They then might open the way for the entire group. On the other hand, if foreign born gatekeepers discriminate against the native born, as anecdotal evidence suggests they sometimes do, the overall standing of the group could actually decrease even while the proportion of high-standing immigrants increases.

These possibilities lead to opposite conclusions, yet considered *a priori*, they all have merit. Therefore, choosing among them in the absence of data is difficult, perhaps inappropriate. These circumstances dictate another, more conservative strategy: to simply hypothesize that the percent of group that is native born affects the group's socioeconomic status.

Sex Composition. Due to past and present immigration, some groups may have an imbalanced sex ratio; that is, there may be proportionately more males than females (or vice versa) in the group. This could have an indirect impact on the group's socioeconomic status. Regardless of ethnicity, males may encounter less job discrimination than females and thus earn more and have higher socioeconomic status in general. Once ensconced in higher level positions, they can then provide openings for the entire group regardless of gender. If this reasoning is correct, then the higher the sex ratio (that is, the greater the relative number of males), the higher the proportion of the group in upper level socioeconomic categories.

Group Size. To identify an ethnic group, certain criteria must be established. Once established, those persons meeting the criteria are members of the group and their number is the size of the group. This means that size exists because the group exists, making size one of the most fundamental of demographic dimensions.

Undoubtedly, the best known demographic hypothesis in ethnic relations is Blalock's contention that large ethnic groups face
more discrimination that small ones. That is because large groups
pose more threats to the majority. The minority competes for jobs,
absorbs more resources, and more easily imposes its subculture on
the majority. Faced with this threat, the majority responds with discrimination, thereby reserving the best jobs, housing, schools, and
other benefits for themselves.[21] For example, one study suggests
group size might lie behind the contrasting socioeconomic paths of
Asians and blacks. Both groups initially experienced intense hostility, but Asians, being the much smaller group, have garnered
greater acceptance than blacks.[22] Data showing that Asian intermarriage rates are higher than black rates, and that Asian levels of residential segregation are lower than black levels, support this
contention.[23] Although more research needs to be done before accepting this particular application of the size-discrimination hypothesis, it has been documented in other contexts as well.[24]

Applied to socioeconomic status, the size-discrimination hypothesis implies that the larger the ethnic group, the lower its status. Or stated with regard to specific socioeconomic categories, the
larger the group, the lower the percentage of the group in higher-
level occupations and the larger the percentage in lower-level ones.

The foregoing hypothesis reflects the weight of theory and
data and for those reasons cannot be readily dismissed. Nevertheless, an alternative line of reasoning is worth considering. Large
groups have (or potentially have) more resources at their disposal
than small groups. For example, a large group can muster many
voters, forcing politicians to pay heed to their ethnic demands, especially at the local and state levels where the group may constitute
an especially large proportion of a political jurisdiction. Assuming
that ethnic political power translates into ethnic socioeconomic
gains, then it follows that the larger the group, the larger the percentage in higher socioeconomic categories and the lower the percentage in low categories. This may be called the "size-power
hypothesis."

A third outcome is also possible. If large groups engender
more discrimination than small groups, and if large groups also
have more political power, then the two processes may work against
each other. As group size increases, its power increases but so
does the discrimination against it. Consequently, (a) if the size-
discrimination factor is the stronger, as the data suggests it is, then
size will lower the group's socioeconomic status. But (b) if the size-

power factor is the stronger, then size will raise the group's socio-economic status. And (c) if the two forces are of equal strength, then size will have no net effect.

The third possibility produces a theoretical impasse, for now all possible outcomes have been specified. No matter how the data fall, they *must* be consistent with one of them, a situation obviously untenable on grounds of scientific logic. The impasse cannot be here resolved on theoretical-empirical grounds; nevertheless, some decision must be made in order for this research to proceed.[25] I therefore opt for the most conservative hypothesis, which is simply that group size affects the group's socioeconomic status.

Age Potential: Youthfulness. Previous research has argued that as groups mature, they acquire greater seniority on the job, higher occupational standing, and possibly, assets that generate further income (such as interest from savings, or tax deductions from home ownership). On average, therefore, older groups should have greater income. Data on eight racial groups in California strongly supported this hypothesis. The group's mean age and per capita income were strongly correlated.[26]

The same essential argument applies here. However, rather than focusing solely on mean age, the procedure was expanded to include several age-related measures, and consequently, multiple lines of reasoning.

As the findings shown in the appendix to this chapter document, the four measures already examined—mean age, the fertility, dependency, and job squeeze ratios—are highly correlated. That is, young groups tend to have high fertility, which in turn means there are many young people in the population, and that in turn means high dependency and age squeeze ratios. The correlations between these measures present no problems when analyzing each variable separately, but in a multiple regression equation, certain problems do arise. Highly correlated independent variables might produce a "partialing error": each variable cancels the other, making it appear that each is unimportant.[27]

To circumvent the problem, the four measures were combined into a single scale called "youthfulness." The resulting youthfulness scale was a broad global measure, and it reflected the concept of a group's age potential—a global idea—better than any single variable composing it. (The scaling technique, principle components, requires an extended discussion along with ancillary statistics. See the appendix to this chapter).

I use the term *age potential* to simply mean the summary impact of age-related variables on socioeconomic achievement. *Positive* age potential means that the group's age advances their achievement; *negative* age potential means it retards their achievement.

More specifically, the prediction is that the more youthful a group, the greater the percentage of the group in lower socioeconomic categories. Conversely, taking *maturity* to be the opposite of *youthfulness*, the more nature a group, the greater the percentage of the group in upper-level socioeconomic categories.

Findings

The seven regression equations that relate socioeconomic attainment to the various demographic dimensions are displayed on Table 4.2. To facilitate the comparison of one variable with another, standardized regression coefficients are shown. Since each equation contains the same independent variables, the regression coefficients are always standardized on the same means and variances. This

TABLE 4.2

Socioeconomic Status and Demographic Potential:
Multiple Regression Model[a]

	Dependent Variable Percent of the Ethnic Group in:						
	P	M	T	C	S	L	U
U. S. born	−.37	−.13	.10	.50*	−.13	.00	−.16
Sex ratio	.06	.29*	−.10	.44	−.18	−.29*	−.13
Group size	.18	−.05	−.02	−.15	−.02	−.09	−.09
Youthfulness	−.88*	−.90*	−.85*	.36	.77*	.85*	.76*
Multiple correlation squared	.68*	.88*	.82*	.40	.64*	.72*	.65*

[a]Based on 20 ethnic groups
Standardized regression coefficients are shown.
Sex ratio: males per 100 females.
Group size: natural log of the number of persons in the group.
Youthfulness: scale combining mean age, the fertility ratio, the dependency ratio, and the age squeeze ratio.
*Statistically significant at or beyond the .05 level of probability.
Legend: P: professional; M: managerial; T: technical; C: craft; S: service; L: labor; U: underclass.

simplifies comparison across equations. The equations fit the data extremely well, as indicated by the large squared multiple correlations (R^2s). For the professional, service, and underclass equations, they are over .60; for labor, slightly over .70; and for managerial and technical, over .80. All are statistically significant, but more important, they are high in absolute terms. The only equation with a relatively low and nonsignificant R^2 is craft.[28]

As to individual variables, the percentage of the group born in the United States has a statistically significant coefficient only in the craft equation. That is, only one out of seven equations supports the initial prediction, which is weak support at best.

Data on the sex ratio are also inconclusive. The coefficient has a statistically important effect in the managerial and labor equations but in no others. Managerial and labor jobs, while disparate in terms of socioeconomic status, might disproportionately select males into them. Given the intense discrimination that historically prevented women from assuming administrative and managerial positions, the finding might have been anticipated. Similarly, women have been largely excluded from many (possibly most) jobs requiring heavy manual labor. While the data prevent us from pursuing this reasoning further, the negative findings do indicate that the sex ratio does not have an important consequence for most socioeconomic categories.

In sharp contrast to native birth and the sex ratio, group size and the youthfulness scale have consistent, but opposite, effects across socioeconomic status. In every equation, the regression coefficient for the size measure is comparatively small, and in no equation does it reach statistical significance. Evidently, size has no effect on the proportion of a group in any given category of socioeconomic status.

Given considerable research relating ethnic group size to inequality, this finding is quite surprising. Although it was mentioned that the political power associated with group size could offset majority discrimination, that was not the hypothesis. Nevertheless, these negative findings are consistent with that possibility. At this point, however, the interpretation comes after-the-fact, and would obviously require much more new data and direct measures of power and discrimination, to be sustained.

The youthfulness scale has a statistically significant effect in all equations except craft, but recall that equation was weak to begin with. Specifically, youthfulness negatively influences the proportion of the ethnic group in the professional, managerial, and technical categories, and positively influences the proportion in the service, labor, and underclass. The more youthful a group is, the smaller the proportion in higher socioeconomic categories and the higher the proportion in lower categories. As in Chapter 3, a shift in direction occurs above and below craft, indicating that craft constitutes the dividing line between high and low socioeconomic status.

In short, United States birth, the sex ratio, and group size do not have the anticipated effects across all seven socioeconomic categories, whereas the opposite holds for youthfulness. Under these circumstances, an appropriate tactic is to reduce the model. That is, eliminate all measures but youthfulness from the equations and recompute the statistics. The results are shown in Table 4.3. Simplicity is the advantage of a reduced model. Simplifying the interpretation even more, youthfulness has a consistent effect across all but one socioeconomic category. The squared correlation coefficients range from a high of .79 to a low of .08. In general, correlations based on aggregated data (such as ethnic groups) are higher than those based on individual level data, but even so, the correlations shown in the table exceed those usually found in sociological research.

The only equation not statistically significant is craft. This outcome has appeared before, suggesting that craft category is a "cross-over" point between "higher" and "lower" socioeconomic status. Because of that, the craft equation will not be discussed further (although the findings will be shown for completeness).

TABLE 4.3

Socioeconomic Status and Demographic Potential: Regression Model[a]

| | Dependent Variable Percent of the Ethnic Group in: | | | | | | |
	P	M	T	C	S	L	U
Youthfulness	−.75*	−.89*	−.89*	−.29	.77*	.79*	.79*
Correlation Squared	.56*	.79*	.79*	.08	.59*	.62*	.62*

[a]Based on 20 ethnic groups.
Standardized regression coefficients are shown.
Youthfulness: scale combining mean age, the fertility ratio, the dependency ratio, and the age squeeze ratio.
*Statistically significant at or beyond the .05 level of probability.
Legend: P: professional; M: managerial; T: technical; C: craft; S: service; L: labor; U: underclass.

With one independent variable in the equation, the relationship between youthfulness and each dependent variable can be easily portrayed graphically, and provides insights not easily derived from the equations. In the following figures, the regression line (indicated by *'s) depicts the relationship between the two variables and the scatter of points shows the position of each ethnic group. Insofar as possible, each point is represented by the letter denoting the group's name (for example, M stands for Mexican), but that was not possible in all cases (for example, O stands for Afro American).

Groups constituting "leverage points" are underlined. In this context, a leverage point is an ethnic group that disproportionately influences the regression outcomes. To identify groups as leverage points, two standard related procedures were used. The first assesses the group's impact on the regression coefficient, and the second assesses the impact on the fit between data and equation. On the one hand, a leverage point indicates the adequacy of the model, but on the other hand, a leverage point represents a failure of the model—the model does not apply to that particular group.[29] Something more than age potential must therefore be considered.[30] This strategy (but not the specific methodology) often goes under the name "deviant case analysis." The appendix contains more details on these procedures, but note that because leverage points take into account the variance, they cannot be identified by visually inspecting the graphs.

The graphs for higher socioeconomic categories are shown first (Figures 4.7A, 4.7B, and 4.7C). First, consider the relation between youthfulness (or its converse, maturity) and the percentage in the professions. Czechs, Russians, and Asians constitute leverage points (Figure 4.7A). For example, note the position of Russians above the regression line. Given their maturity, Russians are disproportionately overrepresented in the professional category. The same holds for Asians. Even though they are more youthful than both Czechs and Russians, the Asian percentage in the professional category is higher than it 'should' be (should is enclosed in single quotation marks to emphasize that this is a statistical statement, not a normative one). The opposite applies to Czechs. Although they rank relatively high in socioeconomic status, they 'should' rank even higher given their age potential. Czechs also appear as a leverage point in the managerial equation and again 'should' have a higher proportion in that category given their age (Figure 4.7B). In the same equation, Swedes and Mexicans are also leverage points. A

FIGURE 4.7A

Professional and Youthfulness

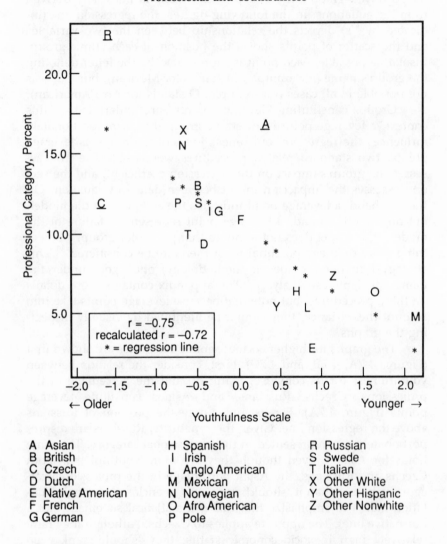

A Asian   H Spanish   R Russian
B British   I Irish   S Swede
C Czech   L Anglo American   T Italian
D Dutch   M Mexican   X Other White
E Native American   N Norwegian   Y Other Hispanic
F French   O Afro American   Z Other Nonwhite
G German   P Pole

relatively large percentage of Swedes are in managerial jobs, but
that percentage is still disproportionately high for their maturity.
On the other hand, Mexicans have a low managerial percentage,
but that is high relative to their youthfulness. Mexicans 'should'
rank lower. In the technical equation (Figure 4.7C), Czechs again are

FIGURE 4.7B

Managerial and Youthfulness

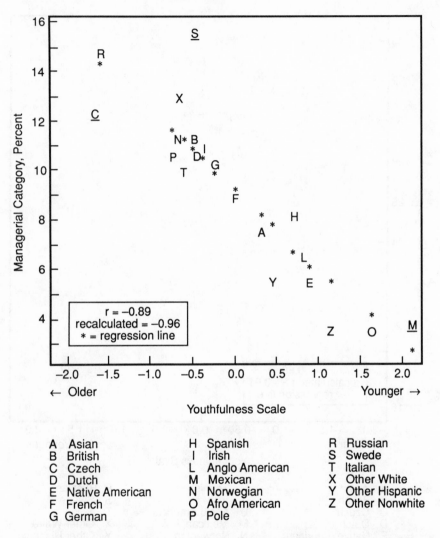

A	Asian	H	Spanish	R	Russian
B	British	I	Irish	S	Swede
C	Czech	L	Anglo American	T	Italian
D	Dutch	M	Mexican	X	Other White
E	Native American	N	Norwegian	Y	Other Hispanic
F	French	O	Afro American	Z	Other Nonwhite
G	German	P	Pole		

a leverage point. Allowing for their youthfulness, a disproportion-ately small percentage is in technical occupations. Since Czechs are the only leverage point on the graph, we can say that the equation applies to all groups except one, a relatively straightforward find-ing. The relationships among the lower-ranking socioeconomic cat-

FIGURE 4.7C

Technical and Youthfulness

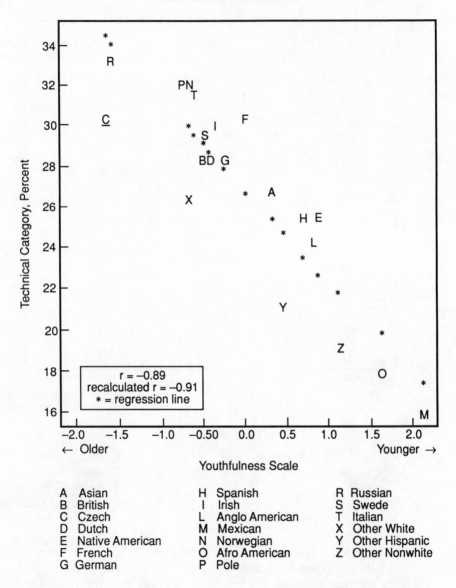

egories are reversed from the higher-ranking ones. Now, the greater the youthfulness, the greater the percentage of the group in the oc-cupation (the craft equation, Figure 4.7D, is shown but not dis-

FIGURE 4.7D

Craft and Youthfulness

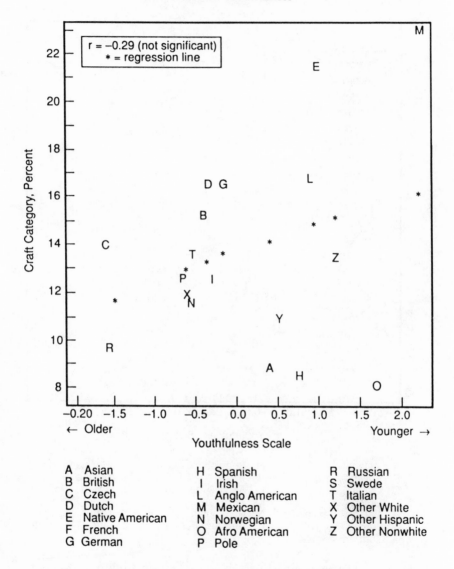

A Asian   H Spanish   R Russian
B British   I Irish   S Swede
C Czech   L Anglo American   T Italian
D Dutch   M Mexican   X Other White
E Native American N Norwegian   Y Other Hispanic
F French   O Afro American   Z Other Nonwhite
G German   P Pole

cussed). For the service category, Mexicans 'should' have a higher percentage but blacks should have a lower one (Figure 4.7E). The Spanish also appear as a leverage point, and, like blacks, 'should' have a lower percentage in that category. Concerning labor (Figure

FIGURE 4.7E

Service and Youthfulness

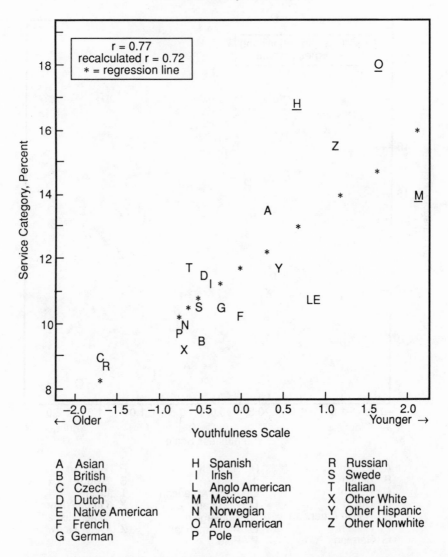

A Asian
B British
C Czech
D Dutch
E Native American
F French
G German

H Spanish
I   Irish
L Anglo American
M Mexican
N Norwegian
O Afro American
P Pole

R Russian
S Swede
T Italian
X Other White
Y Other Hispanic
Z Other Nonwhite

4.7F), both Mexicans and Russian are relatively underrepresented even though they differ substantially as to their youthfulness. Czechs, who are virtually as youthful as Russians, 'should' have a lower percentage in the labor category.

FIGURE 4.7F

Labor and Youthfulness

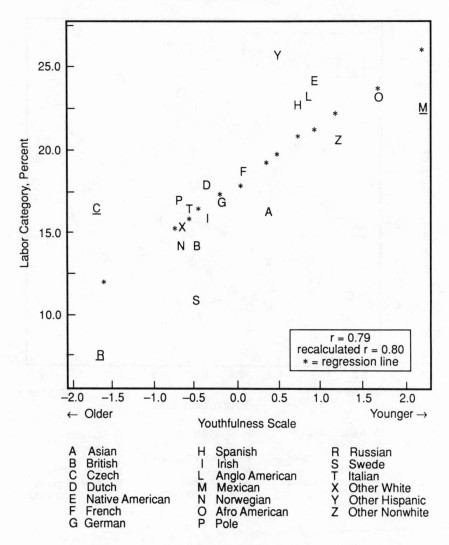

A   Asian
B   British
C   Czech
D   Dutch
E   Native American
F   French
G   German

H   Spanish
I   Irish
L   Anglo American
M   Mexican
N   Norwegian
O   Afro American
P   Pole

R   Russian
S   Swede
T   Italian
X   Other White
Y   Other Hispanic
Z   Other Nonwhite

In the underclass equation, several groups constitute leverage points (Figure 4.7G). Blacks and Mexicans are leverage points but with different implications. Mexicans are underrepresented in that underclass relative to their youthfulness, whereas blacks are over-

FIGURE 4.7G

Underclass and Youthfulness

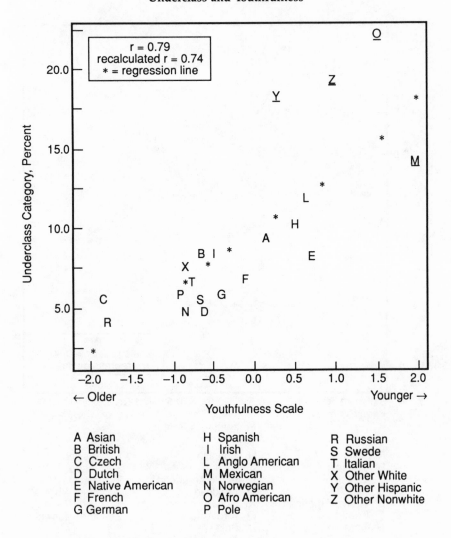

A Asian
B British
C Czech
D Dutch
E Native American
F French
G German

H Spanish
I Irish
L Anglo American
M Mexican
N Norwegian
O Afro American
P Pole

R Russian
S Swede
T Italian
X Other White
Y Other Hispanic
Z Other Nonwhite

represented. Also overrepresented are Other Hispanic and Other Nonwhites, two groups difficult to substantively interpret due to their heterogeneity. However, all the groups mentioned do share one attribute: they are nonwhite.

To summarize the data on age potential, we have seen that it affects the percentage of the group in a given socioeconomic category, except craft, and that the effect generally applies to all ethnic groups. Possible exceptions (leverage points) were Czech, Russians, Swedes, Asians, Blacks, Mexicans, Other Hispanic, Other Nonwhites, and Spanish. In any given equation, the number of leverage points varied from one (technical) to four (underclass). Although the number of leverage points may seem large, they were spread across seven equations and twenty ethnic groups. Cases that fit a particular equation far outnumbered those that did not.

Conclusions

Several conclusions emerge from this analysis, some anticipated by theoretical considerations and others not. One conclusion not readily anticipated was the reemphasis on separating the Hispanic groups. The Mexican data did not behave the same way as the data for the Spanish and Other Hispanic. Although researchers may lump these groups together because they all speak the same language, Mexicans, Puerto Ricans, Cubans, and South and Central Americans have different cultural and racial backgrounds, factors that may divide them more than their common language unites them. How much in common do Mariel Cubans have with Hispanos, for instance, or Puerto Ricans with Chileans? Except for language and some other residual roots to Spanish history, these groups are separated by a great gulf of culture and history. Furthermore, these groups do not necessarily speak the same Spanish. Variations in pronunciation, grammar, and vocabulary are easily recognized and further solidify the boundaries between the groups. While past research has acknowledged differences among Hispanic groups, most has assumed that the category was homogeneous enough for statistical purposes. In contrast, the present data suggest that this assumption ought to be carefully examined. In some cases, the assumption might be appropriate or necessary, but in other cases it might not.[31]

Conclusions also emerged from considering sets of commonalities among the leverage points. One set concerns Europeans. Czechs have high socioeconomic status, but their representation 'should' be greater in the upper categories and less in the lower ones. Unfortunately, it is difficult to place this finding in a broader theoretical context because Czechs have not been studied very much. One possible explanation concerns the nature of the youthfulness scale. On it, low fertility and high age translated into a low score (indicating less youthfulness, or maturity). As we know (from Figures 4.2 and 4.3), Czechs have extremely low fertility and high mean age, characteristics making them unusually mature on the scale.

In addition to the scaling technique, historical factors might also be involved. Czechs established an American presence during the nineteenth century, but the quota system of 1924 prevented the community from being continually replenished with fresh immigrants. That changed somewhat when, in 1948 and again in 1968, Czech political refugees fled to the United States. Many were skilled workers and professionals.[32] Some downward mobility probably occurred, but the selectivity of the immigration may have skewed the socioeconomic standing of the American Czech population in relation to its age potential. Considering how often Czechs have appeared as exceptions throughout the present monograph, they clearly warrant more study than they have heretofore received.

In some respects, Russians are the opposite of Czechs. Even allowing for the Russian age potential, they are still overrepresented in upper socioeconomic categories and underrepresented in labor. This finding can be interpreted in terms of religion. To the extent that the Russian category represents the American Jewish population, we would expect it to have relatively high socioeconomic status.[33] In addition, many current immigrants from the Soviet Union are Jews with professional backgrounds, which further contributes to the high socioeconomic standing of the Russian category.

Swedes were the only other European group constituting a leverage point. An unusually high percentage were in managerial jobs relative to their maturity. This finding was not predicted and remains puzzling; but because Swedes appeared in just one equation out of seven, perhaps not too much should be made of it. It might represent nothing more than a perturbation in the data.

With regard to nonwhites, disproportionately large percentages of blacks, Other Hispanics, and Other Nonwhites were in the underclass. While this outcome would seem to reinforce the case for color discrimination, it does not apply to Mexicans or Asians.

The Asian case might be explained by the high selectivity of recent immigration that favors the well educated professional, the prevalence of Asian sojourners in the form of businessmen and their families who do a tour here and then return home, and the long history of the Asian American population in the United States, a history dating back to the nineteenth century.

The Mexican case is more difficult to explain. In the past, a culture of poverty argument has been applied to Hispanics.[34] However, before the argument can be applied to these data, substantial modification must be made to it. Mexicans are actually underrepresented in the underclass, implying that some subcultural elements are propelling them upward to a greater extent than their age potential suggests 'should' be the case. Mexicans have always been stereotyped as "lazy" and as having a "mañana attitude." Perhaps that stereotype has wormed its way deeper into sociological and anthropological explanations than realized (more will be said about this argument in the next chapter).

Afro Americans constitute leverage points in both the service and underclass equations, where their percentages are higher than they 'should' be relative to their age potential. Those findings come as no surprise. A greater surprise, however, is the fact that blacks do not always constitute leverage points in the equations for the higher socioeconomic categories. There blacks are approximately where they 'should' be relative to their age potential.

Although these data apparently contradict conventional sociological wisdom, note that when analysts discuss socioeconomic parity, they usual mean the absolute levels. The percentages of blacks in upper-level occupations are, in fact, small relative to other groups. However, that fact does preclude a relationship between youthfulness and socioeconomic status. The one is quite distinct from the other.

Mexicans are another group highlighted by the analysis. Like blacks, they are a young population, but they exert the opposite leverage. Mexicans are underrepresented in service, labor, and the underclass. Moreover, Mexicans are overrepresented in the managerial category. These findings imply that the present picture of Mexican Americans is both accurate and misleading. It is accurate in that Mexicans have not done well socioeconomically. It is misleading in that Mexicans have done well despite their youthfulness.

The model fits neither blacks nor Mexicans, but for different reasons, a situation leading to theoretical difficulties. If the most commonly cited explanatory variable, discrimination, is the cause, then the situation is far more complicated than previously thought. Both Mexicans and blacks are targets of discrimination, yet the one group does better than its age potential indicates 'should' be the case, while the other group does worse. A similar difficulty appears when contrasting Russians to Czechs. If the Russian grouping is a surrogate for Jews, then they have overachieved (relative to their age potential) despite anti-Semitism while Czechs have under-achieved in the absence of blatant hostility.

Attempts to explain situations such as these invoke several considerations, among them history, culture, economics, and politics. No two groups share an identical mix of such factors; hence each group is partially unique and not completely comparable to any other group. The lack of comparability—or what is the same thing, the group's uniqueness—can then account for its particular socioeconomic situation. An example of this are the numerous accounts of American slavery, and the lasting impact that it has had on Afro Americans. (I will return to this broad issue in the last chapter).

In some ways, groups constituting leverage points are the most interesting, for they indicate exceptions and suggestions for further research. Nevertheless, we should not allow the exceptions to distract us from the basic model that originally prompted the analysis. It received considerable support, suggesting that age potential is far more important than realized before.

At a broad level, the support is consistent with the perspectives of the *Annale* school of history and with cultural materialism, both of which emphasize infrastructural causes, such as demography. At a more specific level, William Wilson has discussed selected aspects of age, pointing out that disproportionate numbers of young females, may of whom are single parents, are to be found in the lowest stratum of the black population. To restate Wilson's point from the perspective being used here, the black underclass has low age potential.

In the past, demographic considerations have not been the center of ethnic studies. Concepts such as culture, prejudice, and inequality have been usually studied from non-demographic viewpoints. However, age potential is a deeply layered causal factor, providing the foundation for specific developments, many of which may not be visible for a generation or more. The theory and data presented here point to the importance of deep causes. To a greater extent than has been realized before, these causes can propel an ethnic group along a course over which it has virtually no control.

Appendix to Chapter 4
Procedures

Scaling the Age-Related Measures

Four of the demographic dimensions considered reflect some aspect of a group's age structure. These were mean age and the fertility, dependency, and age squeeze ratios. Mean age measures central tendency and so is a direct measure of age structure. A high fertility ratio indicates that a group has many children, which depresses mean age and contributes to the dependency and age squeeze ratios. Because the latter two measures compare different segments of the age distribution to the same age category (mature), they partially overlap each other. For these reasons, we would expect these measures to be correlated, and they are (see Table 4.4, Panel A). The correlations vary from .60 to -.89 and can be de-

TABLE 4.4

Youthfulness: Age Related Demgraphic Dimensions

	Panel A: Correlations[a]		
	Age Squeeze	Dependency Ratio	Fertility Ratio
Mean age	−.89	−.67	−.75
Age squeeze		.65	.73
Dependency ratio			.60

	Panel B: Principal Components Analysis Number of Eigenvalues:			
	1	2	3	4
Eigen Value	3.16	.43	.30	.11

One component retained (1.0 or greater):
Factor Pattern Matrix

Mean age	−.94
Age squeeze ratio	.93
Dependency ratio	.81
Fertility ratio	.87

[a]Pearson correlation coefficients.
Based on 20 ethnic groups. All correlations are statistically significant at the .05 level.

scribed as moderate to large. The higher the mean age, the lower the three ratios. At the same time, the various ratios are correlated with each other. The higher the age squeeze ratio, the higher the dependency and fertility ratios; and the higher dependency ratio, the higher the fertility ratio. These correlations were anticipated on theoretical and methodological grounds; nevertheless, they can cause problems.

To place each measure in a multiple regression equation would undoubtedly produce a problem of "multicollinearity."[35] That is because in a regression equation, the higher the intercorrelation among independent variables, the smaller the regression coefficients and the larger the associated standard errors. Each variable might thus appear unimportant by itself, whereas the total set of variables might be quite important. Sometimes, this phenomenon is also called a "partialing error."

To circumvent the problem, the four measures were combined into a single summary scale using the method of principal components. The first step in this procedure is to ascertain the number of dimensions contained in the four measures. This is done by extracting the eigenvalues from the correlation matrix (see Table 4.4, Panel B). Only one eigenvalue exceeded the usual criterion of 1.0 and by a substantial amount. Clearly, only one basic dimension exists in the data.

The eigenvector ("factor pattern" or "loadings") indicate the importance of each measure to the dimension.[36] These weights are high, suggesting that each measure makes a substantial contribution to the dimension. Note that mean age has a negative impact on the dimension while the other measures have a positive impact. In other words, this dimension (or principal component) can be characterized as consisting of low mean age and high age squeeze, dependency, and fertility ratios. In light of these findings, I called the dimension "youthfulness."

The final step in constructing the scale was to use the weights in conjunction with the raw data to construct a single score for each ethnic group. Following custom, the scores were scaled to have a mean of zero and a standard deviation of unity. These scores were then used in the multiple regression equations.

Leverage Points: Influential Groups

Leverage points, or groups exerting substantial influence on the regression analysis, were identified with two statistics: DFBETA and DFFITS. These can be explained by considering a data file consisting of r rows, with each row representing a case, and c columns, with each column representing a variable. A regression equation relates one column (dependent variable) to one or more other columns (independent variables). DFBETA indicates the change in the regression coefficient that results from deleting a row (case) from the analysis, the change being standardized to the variance of the regression coefficient. To illustrate, the regression coefficient is calculated using all the cases (rows) in the data set; then the first case is deleted and the coefficient recalculated; then that case is returned to the data set, the second case deleted, and the coefficient recalculated; and so on until the cases are exhausted. In this manner, changes in the coefficients can be tracked as cases are eliminated. Large changes indicate the importance of the case to the equation.

The statistic DFFITS indicates the change in the fit of the equation to the data. The same procedure described above is followed. However, rather than focussing on the regression coefficient, the predicted value of the regression equation is calculated as cases are eliminated and replaced. The resulting differences are then scaled to the variance of the fit, taking sample size into account.

The two statistics, DFFITS and DFBETA, usually identified the same groups as leverage points and thus complemented each other. In those few instances when different cases were identified, all cases were accepted as leverage points. Note that both DFFITS and DFBETA are standardized measures, so identifying leverage points by visually inspecting the graphs is difficult, if not impossible.

As far as I know, these procedures have not been much used in sociology, perhaps because sociologists typically deal with large samples, and the utility of these criteria decreases as the sample size increases. In a small sample, any single observation is potentially more important than any single observation in a large sample. David Belsley and associates show the mathematical basis for these statistics and discuss their interpretation.

5

Explaining Ethnic Inequality

The goal of this chapter is to conceptually expand upon the relationship between ethnicity and socioeconomic status. To do this, the chapter begins by reviewing several theories that were only briefly discussed before, or not discussed at all. Culture is examined first, but the emphasis then turns to economic and quasieconomic theories. Particular attention is paid to the concept of competition and the impact it has on ethnic relations. Second, a framework for interpreting ethnicity and socioeconomic status is suggested. This framework is based on the commonalities found in the literature and data under review.

At some point, all theories of ethnic relations address inequality because it is a dominant social concern. Although inequality can take many forms—political, cultural, or psychological—for sociologists, the major form is socioeconomic status. Put abstractly, any society has only a finite supply of resources and rewards, and the central political issue reduces to how they will be distributed. People who receive a given quantity form one grouping whereas people who receive another quantity form another grouping, and so on. In this way, resources and rewards—the *good things* of life—become the basis for organizing society. The fundamental issue can thus be reduced to a simple question: *who* gets *how much* of *the good things*, and *why?*

The question is simple but the answer is not, and a huge literature on the topic exists. To make the following literature review more manageable, only highly *selected* theories pertaining to ethnic relations are included, and they are further categorized as cultural and economic. As with most categorizations, this one does not always sharply distinguish among all theories, but it is heuristically useful.

Cultural Theories

I use the term culture in a very basic sense: the totality of a group's sentiments, norms, values, and most generally, learning (for example, folklore and language). When this totality coheres around a given group and differs significantly from that of another group, it is an ethnic culture. The lines between ethnic culture and concepts such as general culture, structure, social organization, and ethnicity itself, are difficult to draw. Nevertheless, several theories directly or indirectly use ethnic culture as an explanatory variable.

A notable example is Herbert Gan's study of an Italian community in Boston. He concluded that the class divisions found in that ethnic community reflected American society as a whole. However, he further found that middle-class Italians distinguished themselves from working-class Italians, not by education or income, but by how closely they adhered to cultural values stressing loyalty to the group, sacrifice, and strict morality.[1] This is an interesting observation. Gans might not have intended to make the argument, but his observation implies that the basis for forming ethnic class categories are cultural rather than socioeconomic.

Culture of Poverty

Oscar Lewis carries the cultural argument to, perhaps, its extreme. First developed in conjunction with ethnographic studies of Puerto Ricans, Lewis said that a culture of poverty is characterized by low wages, social isolation, compaction in slums, consensual marriages, and households headed by females. Individuals immersed in this culture demand immediate gratification for their wants and have feelings of marginality, helplessness, dependency, and inferiority. Moreover, Lewis wrote that ". . . the culture of poverty transcends regional, rural-urban, and national differences" because it is ". . . both an adaptation and a reaction of the poor to their marginal position in a class-stratified, highly individuated, capitalistic society."[2]

By an early age, perhaps six or seven, children will have absorbed the culture of poverty and ". . . are not psychologically geared to take full advantage of the changing conditions or increased opportunities that may occur in their lifetime."[3] By impacting children, poverty perpetuates itself. It gets passed from one generation to the next, trapping the poor in an endless cycle. Although Lewis did state that the potential for class cohesion, creativity, individualism, and spontaneity also existed within a culture of poverty, those characteristics have never been emphasized in subsequent discussions of his thesis.[4]

In many respects, William Wilson's description of the black underclass resembles Lewis's culture of poverty. Wilson's theory, however, is implicit and scattered throughout *The Truly Disadvantaged*, and so the details must be pieced together.[5] Apparently, it is a loose collection of what he calls "social dislocations," such as long-term poverty, female headed households, out-of-wedlock births, welfare dependency, and crime. These characteristics do not differ much from those Lewis used to define the culture of poverty.[6] About the possible differences, Wilson simply says the following:

> [social dislocations] . . . cannot be accounted for simply in terms of racial discrimination or in terms of a culture of poverty. Rather, they must be seen as having complex sociological antecedents that range from demographic changes to problems of economic organization.[7]

To a certain extent, Wilson's statement echoes Lewis's: "I would agree that the main reasons for the persistence of the subculture [of poverty] are no doubt the pressures that the larger society exerts over its members and the structure of the larger society itself."[8]

The culture of poverty thesis has been roundly criticized ever since it first appeared, which may be the reason Wilson disassociates his theory from it. The major criticism is tinged with ideology, centering on the imputation of blame. If we accept the culture of poverty, the criticism goes, then the poor must be held responsible for their plight, not the broader society. And if we do that, then solutions will be misdirected toward changing the poor rather than toward the real cause, society. Although one may or may not agree with this criticism, in all fairness to Lewis, he did write the following:

> There is nothing in the concept that puts the onus of poverty on the character of the poor. Nor does the concept in any way play down the exploitation and neglect suffered by the poor. Indeed, the subculture of poverty is part of the larger culture of capitalism, whose social and economic system channels wealth into the hands of relatively small group and thereby makes for the growth of sharp class distinctions.[9]

The controversy over the culture of poverty began almost thirty years ago, and in retrospect, the ideological criticism is less forceful than it used to be.

Culture of Success

If blaming the poor for their socioeconomic failure is misdirected, then crediting the rich for their success is equally misdirected. Yet, in the field of ethnic relations, the latter is often done without protest. That line of reasoning can be called the *culture of success*.

To illustrate, consider Japanese Americans, one of the few (possibly, the only) nonwhite groups to have achieved socioeconomic parity with the majority. The expression "six times down, seven times up" characterizes their overall value system, which in addition, stresses education, study, hard work, deferred gratification, patience, perseverance, group unity, family, obedience, conformity, and stoicism in the face of adversity. The Japanese American community is also highly structured. Clubs promote various ethnic features, such as flower arranging, martial arts, and language, and some also furnish monetary capital.[10] By all accounts, this is the opposite of the culture of poverty, and it provides an easy explanation for Japanese American success. Following a similar approach, other ethnic groups might be explained. The Chinese, Poles, and Irish—to name just three—have communities structured along clear ethnic lines, and possess a culture with elements that would seemingly promote upward mobility.

Qualifications

Cultural arguments have a strong appeal. They seem logical and are consistent with the importance that social scientists attribute to culture. Nevertheless, a problem does exist. Do not cultural arguments, whether about poverty or success, place the "cart before the horse," the effect before the cause? Analysts already know about Japanese American success, and with that knowledge in hand, they begin examining their culture. Because culture is so broad and amenable to manifold interpretations, it is easy to find elements bespeaking success.

Japanese Americans are a case in point. Their success can be explained by their culture, but hypothetically, suppose that they had failed. Then, would not other features of their culture be emphasized, or the same features reinterpreted? For example, we could argue that the high value placed on obedience and conformity saps creativity and entrepreneurship, or reinterpret patience as pas-sivity, group unity as a resistance to change, and the stress on edu-cation as nonfunctional. In other words, knowing that a group has failed, we can easily interpret the group's culture to fit that fact.

On the surface, proceeding in this way seems logical. We are explaining a known fact based on information about the group. We are piecing together elements of the cultural puzzle to form an in-terpretable whole. This is valuable, clearly, but it is a description of the group, not a scientific explanation. The scientifically valid pro-cedure would be to interpret the group's culture first, and based on that interpretation, next predict group outcomes. That is, knowl-edge of the independent variable leads to a prediction about the dependent variable. Unfortunately, following such a sequence is difficult, or impossible, because the outcomes are already known.[11]

Although the foregoing criticism amounts to an admittedly overly strict application of scientific procedure, the criticism does serve as a cautionary reminder. Observers of the American ethnic scene already know the general standing of the various groups, so they cannot very easily put that knowledge out of their minds when trying to explain the socioeconomic status of those groups. To be sure, an objective picture of a group's culture might be drawn, and then that picture used to generate a hypothesis that is then as-sessed with independent data. I do not argue that this cannot be done. I only argue that when interpreting existing American ethnic groups, it would be very difficult, and to my knowledge, has not been done yet.

Economic and Quasi-Economic Theories

By economic theories I simply mean models that use competi-tion and self-interest as the primary dynamics generating ethnic in-equality. Because models vary in how closely they adhere to strictly economic variables, the modifier "quasi" is used to mean models that stress economic dynamics but also include non-economic fac-tors. Several models proposed by sociologists can be classified "quasi economic" whereas models proposed by economists are typ-ically "economic." The clearest illustration of the strict economic approach is the neoclassical analysis of racial inequality.

Neoclassical Economic Model of Discrimination

Gary S. Becker proposed what has become the most widely followed neoclassical theory of discrimination. Although his analysis could apply to almost any group, Becker described it with specific reference to American blacks and whites, and it will be so described here.[12]

He begins by making all of the neoclassical assumptions, including those of a free market and full employment. He then postulates a prevailing wage rate of W, and the existence of wage discrimination against blacks, as reflected in the discrimination coefficient, d_i. Employers must therefore pay a net wage of $W(1 + d_i.)$ If d_i is positive, then the employer likes or favors blacks; if d_i is negative, then the employer dislikes or discriminates against blacks. Thus, the net wage rate for the favored group is $(W + d_i)$ and for the unfavored group it is $(W - d_i)$. The difference between these two terms represents the wage differential due to discrimination. For the marketplace as a whole, discrimination is $[(W_w - W_b)/Wb]$, where W_w is the equilibrium rate for whites and W_b is the equilibrium rate for blacks.

This model has important implications. Discrimination exists to the extent that $W_w - W_b$ is not zero. If the difference between white and black market rates is not equal to the monetary value imputed to discrimination, then employers will prefer either black or white workers exclusively. However, if $W_b < W_w$, and $d_i = 0$, employers will turn to black workers because their wage rate is lower. That, in turn, would encourage white workers to lower their wage demands in order to be hired. In the long run, therefore, $W_b = W_w$. That is, racial inequality in wages will cease to exist.

While the internal logic of the neoclassical argument is widely accepted as correct, other criticism can be leveled against it. In a review piece, Ray Marshall lists several. One is that the theory concerns anti-black discrimination, but ignores blacks—a curious omission. Another criticism concerns the conceptualization of discrimination. Marshall argues that Becker views discrimination as the desire of whites to avoid close personal contact with blacks. If that is so, then how does one explain discrimination by people who have little contact with blacks, especially management? Still another criticism is that the neoclassical model does not constitute a theory of discrimination. Rather, it is a theory of wages in which race discrimination distorts the free play of market forces. In reformulating the neoclassical position, Kenneth Arrow recognized this shortcoming and suggested that cognitive-dissonance theory might serve as the explanation for discrimination.

Although the neoclassical model can be criticized, as Marshall has done, that does not necessarily invalidate the approach. For example, the criticism that it is a model of wages rather than discrimination does not mean that wages are unimportant. Indeed, one might argue that wages are among the most important components of equality, for they determine life style and are a social and economic index of personal worth. In addition, and arguably more important, the neoclassical model provides an unobstructed view of how economic forces can determine ethnic inequality. Discrimination exists to the extent that market imperfections exist.[13] This conclusion means that if we could somehow correct market imperfections, we would simultaneously get rid of racial inequality in wages.

From a sociological perspective, a major weakness of the neoclassical model is the treatment of discrimination. As Marshall implied, it is treated as an exogenous variable. That is, the model explains the impact of discrimination on wages, but offers no explanation of discrimination itself. Becker suggests that this problem could be resolved by integrating economic and other types of variables into a single explanation.[14]

Although the economic perspective (whether the one above or an alternative) has much to offer, sociologists seldom use it—at least not directly. Indirectly, though, the several economic ideas are embed in sociological theory, particularly the concept of competition.

The Nature of Competition

Sociologists often treat competition as a "primitive term," or one left undefined because everyone presumably know its meaning. That is undoubtedly true to a large extent; nevertheless, a few comments on definition are appropriate.

Competition is the process wherein two or more parties strive to achieve scarce goals within a normative framework. As Michael Banton writes, "It can be said that competition begins when two individuals or groups both want the same thing and strive for it within a market."[15] Zero-sum competition exists when the achievement of the goal by one party means that the other party cannot achieve it; there is no sharing of the prize. Many discussions implicitly assume this type of competition, although with regard to ethnic relations, non-zero sum competition is more common. The majority seldom achieves so total a victory that the minority receives nothing. More typically, the resulting competitive balance allocates some portion of the resources and rewards, even if small, to the losing group.[16]

Competition, to be competition, must take place within a normative framework. It establishes the implicit and explicit norms, values, rules, and laws that govern the striving. Without the framework, the striving would too easily degenerate into conflict and, possibly, violence. In an economic context, the term *marketplace* describes the framework and the terms *society, culture,* or *structure* describe the broader framework of which the market is a part.

When competition works in "dog eat dog" manner, it is called *greed*. However, in a neutral context, *greed* is just a logical extension of self interest and profit maximization. Although relabeling competition as greed implies rapacity, it does not change the underlying process; it is still competition.[17]

Competition and Sociological Theory

Whereas sociology is not economics, that does not mean that sociology has ignored the fundamental economic concept of competition. It is implicit in functional, conflict, and exchange theories, and explicit in ecological theory. It was a key dynamic in Marx's theory of class, and in sociological theories inspired by Darwinian thought, such as those of Herbert Spencer and William Graham Sumner.

The basic notion of social Darwinism rests on the underlying dynamic of competition. Charles Cooley wrote, "Competition is the term in social theory which associates the fact of struggle with the function of order. It is the key word in an account . . . of how rivalry for prestige and income, for power and wealth, comes to promote organization."[18] In the first sociology textbook, Robert Park and Ernest Burgess wrote, "Of the four great types of interaction—competition, conflict, accommodation, and assimilation—*competition is the elementary, universal and fundamental form.*"[19] Some sociologists would disagree with these statements, but that is not the point here; rather, the point is simply that competition has deep roots in sociological thought.

Amos Hawley *(Human Ecology)* has outlined a process through which competition leads to order: (1) Competition begins when demand exceeds the supply of whatever is sought, whether it be "food, raw materials, . . . or position in any type of social system."[20] (2) Because all competitors adopt similar strategies to gain the best returns, they become increasingly homogeneous. (3) With the elimination of noncompetitive units, supply comes into equilibrium with demand, at which point the competition ends. (4) With the end of competition, differentiation among competitors and former competitors sets in. Losers may take new jobs or positions or ". . . take up ancillary roles in which they became dependent on but noncompetitive with those who have gained command over the supply."[21]

Hawley's abstract language is appropriate because his theory is abstract. Competition nevertheless has direct human consequences. For instance, competition helps explain the cruel treatment of Native Americans on the frontier. Resources and rewards were scarce, sheer physical survival was sometimes problematic, and the prospects for economic and social prosperity were grim. Under these conditions, competition for resources and rewards would be intense, and the wholesale categorization and subordination of Native Americans would be predicted. A similar logic applies to the original Mexican populations of the Southwest. After the war with Mexico, the disenfranchisement of the Californios and Hispanos took place with brutal thoroughness and quickness, transforming them from a power elite to an impoverished minority within a generation.

In practice, competing groups often develop pejorative and hostile attitudes towards one another, but that need not be the case. In principle, competition does not involve hostility, nor does it necessarily involve conscious choice. For example, anthropologists have documented instances of "silent trade," wherein one party leaves its goods in a specified place and later returns to fetch the goods left by the other party.[22] In this exchange, the two parties never come into direct contact and know little, if anything, about each other. Another example is the modern marketplace. Consumers purchasing lettuce may not know, or care, that their behavior affects ethnic relations in the produce fields where Mexican stoop laborers work. If consumers just follow the dictates of the marketplace, they will be involved in the competitive process.

In short, competition can be an impersonal process. Involved parties need not be aware of competition, nor of its consequences. It is sufficient that they serve their self-interest, and behave in accordance with the dictates of the marketplace and abide by the strictures of the broader culture.

Competition and Theories of Ethnic Relations

Quasi-economic models are common in sociology, and especially with regard to ethnic relations. Discussed below (in approximately the order they were proposed) are several theories that use competition as an important dynamic generating ethnic inequality.

Competition and Concentric Zones

An early application of competition to sociological processes is Robert Park's and Ernest Burgess's classic *concentric zone* model.

This model postulates that urban immigrants initially resided near the center of city in order to be near their places of work. As these groups assimilated and achieved upward mobility, they relocated to more desirable housing in the outer rings. Blacks were an exception. Even if they could afford to move, discrimination prevented it. Ghettos formed and eventually acquired unique structural and institutional features, such as churches, businesses, and local leadership.[23] These areas became, to a large degree, isolated and somewhat self-contained communities. Park and Burgess did not present any statistical evidence for their hypothesis, but the black ghetto obviously exists.

Years later, Karl and Alma Taeuber provided a comprehensive statistical study of residential segregation. Ever since their *Negroes in Cities* appeared over twenty-five years ago, we have known that in most cities, blacks are segregated in excess of 90%. Although this level fluctuates over time and place, it has never fallen to a value remotely close to zero. In addition, studies of Asians living in various metropolitan areas of California showed their segregation levels usually exceeded 50%, while in Honolulu, supposedly a paradise of inter-racial harmony, Asians are approximately 40% segregated from other Asians.[24] In general, high residential segregation is the rule.

Ghettoization has consequences for ethnic relations that stem from physical location. Ghetto residents must make long journeys to work, especially if the ghetto is in the central city while jobs are in the urban periphery. Ghetto land values are low in absolute terms, decreasing property tax revenues and possibly leading to fewer city services and poorer schools. Health care is substandard. Few hospitals are located in ghettos, and few physicians practice there. Racism is another by-product of residential segregation. The minority does not have not much contact with the majority and therefore has little opportunity to enter majority networks. This isolation, in turn, promotes stereotypes and myths, reinforcing a sense of "us" against "them."

Residential segregation is also an important part of William Wilson's theory of dislocations. He argues that in the past, the black middle class lived in the ghetto and provided the community with its leadership and conventional role models, thus dampening crime and deviance. But this is no longer true. As discrimination has declined, the black middle class has moved out, leaving behind the most unstable and disorganized portion of the black population.[25] It is surely ironic that decreases in antiblack discrimination have contributed to the development of the black underclass.

If Wilson is correct in his contention that the black middle class has left the ghetto, the size of the black underclass should be correlated with ghettoization. The greater the ghettoization, the larger the underclass. Moreover, socioeconomic status within the ghetto should be homogeneously low and certain communal aspects should be moribund while other aspects should be increasing. The black church may be losing membership while street gangs may be flourishing. Both represent community, but at different ends of the "moral" spectrum.

Competition and Group Size

Most analysts agree that larger ethnic groups encounter more hostility than smaller groups. Numerous studies show that group size correlates, for example, with minority poverty, poor health, residential segregation, interracial violence, and even lynchings. Regarding socioeconomic status, the data in Chapter 3 showed that minority size correlated with the percentage of Western Europeans in both upper socioeconomic categories and the percentage in primary labor markets. In contrast, minorities were concentrated in lower socioeconomic positions and in secondary labor markets.

Although quantitative studies have consistently supported the group size argument, historical studies present a more complex picture. For instance, how do we explain the extraordinary hostility encountered by the Chinese and Japanese, two tiny groups?

One possible explanation is politics. In California, where the majority of Chinese and Japanese on the mainland resided, virtually all politicians, supported by labor unions and the press, seized upon anti-Asianism as a vote-getting issue. The courts also had an impact, ruling that the alien land laws, and the prohibitions against Asians from acquiring citizenship, were legal.

The anti-Chinese movement died quickly because it succeeded quickly. Once exclusion was in place, the Chinese retreated into urban ghettos and segregated occupations, thereby withdrawing from direct competition with white labor. The Japanese followed a different course. They went into agriculture, first as workers and then as farmers who rented land, or in some cases owned it. The major weapons in the anti-Japanism campaign were laws prohibiting them from owning farm land. Contrary to expectation, these laws were not particularly effective, for two reasons. First, many Japanese placed their land titles in the names of their native born offsprings, who, being United States citizens by birth, could legally own land. Second, the land laws were not rigorously enforced in the first place, mainly because white farmers could make high profits from selling their marginal lands to the Japanese while secondary agricultural enterprises (such as banks) profited from Japanese patronage. In a sense, Japanese farmers moved into an agricultural arena abandoned by whites and, therefore, despite the anti-Japanist political rhetoric, were not competing with white farmers over land.[26]

While an extensive historical analysis of the Chines and Japanese experiences in the United States is beyond the scope of this monograph, the two cases do suggest that the operative variable is not size per se, but the competitive threat posed by the group.[27] This can be clarified by considering a simple heuristic diagram. In this diagram, the numbers 1 through 4 in the cells represent the majority discriminatory response, with 1 representing strong discrimination through 4 representing weak or no discrimination. The diagram illustrates the lack of a one-for-one correlation between group size and competition. The majority responds most strongly to large groups posing large competitive threats and least strongly to small groups posing small competitive threats. That much is straightforward, but the responses to the other possibilities ("high threat, small group" and "large group, low threat") are not clear. If competitive threat is the more powerful variable, then the majority will respond strongly to the "high threat, small size" situation—but no data exist with regard to this prediction.

These considerations, though heuristic, help clarify the apparent inconsistency between quantitative studies that overwhelmingly support the size hypothesis and the exceptions found in historical analysis. In quantitative studies, the two variables are not independently measured—group size is used as surrogate for threat. In historical studies, however, threat can be separated from group size,

TABLE 5.1

Relation between Group Size and Competitive Threat[a]

| | Ethnic Group Size | |
Competitive Threat	Large	Small
High	1	2
Low	3	4

[a]1: High anti-ethnic response by the majority; 2 and 3: intermediate anti-ethnic responses by the majority; 4: no anti-ethnic response by the majority

and when that is done, threat turns out to be the stronger variable. Viewed this way, historical and quantitative studies do not necessarily contradict each other. Both suggest that competitive threat is the key variable, but for methodological reasons, they follow much different research strategies.

A complicating factor with regard to size is public ignorance of demography. Few people know the size of the American population, much less the size of specific ethnic groups in specific places. Consequently, perception of size may affect the majority response as much as actual size. Behind the misperception lie several factors. Residential segregation, by compacting like people in a small place, makes the group appear larger than it is. The group's homeland is also a factor. China is well-known for being a huge country, and that reputation probably spills over to the Chinese community in the United States.[28] Finally, groups with reputations (either accurate or not) for high fertility might be perceived as being large and as having many young people. Although no one knows the correlation between perceived and actual size, a reasonable first hypothesis would be that the correlation is positive but small.

Competition and Split Labor Markets

Edna Bonacich has proposed that ethnic inequality results from racial divisions in the labor market. The minority group earns less than the majority even though both groups do exactly the same work. Carried to the extreme—that is, a situation where the inputs to the job, and the job itself, are precisely identical but the wage rates still differ according to race—the split labor markets represents "pure wage discrimination."

In a split labor market, racial differences in wages result from the interplay among three competing parties: (1) high priced labor, usually consisting of the majority group; (2) cheap labor, usually consisting of the minority group; and (3) employers, who could either be of the majority or minority, but who are most often of the majority. Assuming that employers are rational profit seekers, they will hire workers who proffer their services for the lowest wages.

Cheap labor thus threatens the wage demands of majority labor. As long as the minority works at a lower wage, majority labor must reduces its wage demands, or not be hired. To counteract this threat, majority labor may adopt two tactics. One is to exclude the minority, either from immigrating into the country, or if that is not feasible, by enforcing legal and normative restrictions against hiring the minority. Another is to reserve the better jobs for the majority. Bonacich has cited historical examples where both tactics have been used.

Bonacich feels that the split labor market differs from the more usual Marxian approach. The latter assumes that in a divide and conquer strategy, management actively promotes racial divisiveness within the labor force.[29] This makes no sense, according to Bonacich. If management actually did that, they would have to pay the majority a higher wage than necessary.[30] Of course, the counter-argument is that management does not forge a division among the labor force to hire the expensive majority worker, but to drive down all wages and then hire the least costly group.

Note that the conflict between the majority and minority exists only when the supply of labor exceeds the demand. When there is a labor shortage, the minority does not threaten the majority since everyone can find a job. In addition, the minority will fare better when economic prosperity prevails because prosperity means higher wages in general, and full employment.

In several respects, split labor market theory resembles the neoclassical theory of wages. Both theories assume that employers seek maximum profit and so are eager to hire cheap labor. In a notation similar to that used before, let W_{min} = the wage rate of the minority, W_{maj} = the wage rate of the majority, and d_i = the value imputed to discrimination. If $(W_{maj} - W_{min})$ exceeds d_i, the minority will be hired. This implies that even if prejudice exists, the minority will lower its wage demands enough to offset the prejudice.

The split labor market has an ironic implication that has not been emphasized by sociologists: namely, that when $W_{maj} = W_{min}$, pure wage discrimination can take place. That is because once rational economic considerations have been satisfied, as they are when the wage rates are equal, employers are free to express their personal prejudices. If they dislike the minority for any non-economic reason whatsoever, they can refuse to hire them and still not have to pay a higher wage rate.

Competition and Ethnic Enclave Theory

Alejandro Portes and associates argue that some groups are highly entrepreneurial, possess capital, and so develop ethnic economies consisting of many small businesses, some of which interface with the majority economy. Within this enclave economy, ethnic workers gain a commensurate return on their education, experience, and other human capital. They also can climb the socioeconomic ladder free of majority discrimination.[31] Although Portes argues that the enclave concept does not necessarily entail ghettoization, studies have focused mainly on the Cuban community in Florida, a highly ghettoized group.

The enclave model assumes that a continual supply of ethnic workers exists, and that they fill in the bottom of the socioeconomic pyramid: "The organization of an immigrant enclave economy typically requires recent arrivals to take a tour of duty at the worst jobs."[32] In reality, the "tour of duty" is far from benign. A review of Peter Kwong's, *The New Chinatown*, describes the tour with regard the Chinese enclave:

> Those who work for the prosperous Chinese form a pool of cheap labor. Waiters and shop clerks work six days a week more than 10 hours a day, with no compensation for overtime, no holidays and no sick leave. A shop clerk gets about $600 a month for a 60-hour week. . . . Because of language problems and lack of job skills, [they] have little chance of leaving the old Chinatowns . . . and joining such suburban communities as . . . Monterey Park in Los Angeles.[33]

The phrase "tour of duty" does not convey the reality of this situation. It is exploitation, and even though members of the group impose it on other members, that does not make it less exploitative. As long as most immigrants do not know English or local customs and have difficulty finding work in the majority economy, the enclave labor force will be large relative to the number of enclave jobs, and employers can easily bid down wages.

To the extent that workers rely on enclave employment, their income, and by implication their socioeconomic standing, will be suppressed. But on the other hand, suppressing the income of workers raises the income (and socioeconomic standing) of ethnic employers. When this process takes place within the competitive milieu of the ethnic economy, high degrees of socioeconomic differentiation will be the outcome.

Competition and Ethnic Hegemony

The theory of ethnic hegemony stresses the ethnic domination of certain economic activities. Hegemony has not been studied as much as many other theories; hence it must be considered more speculative.

According to the theory, an ethnic group's upward mobility results from the conjoining of several labor force and labor market
characteristics. Very briefly, these are as follows:[34]

1.　Ethnic members control decision-making positions in a labor market, monopolizing the authority to hire, fire, and promote
subordinates. Once inside this labor market, group members do
not encounter ethnic prejudice and discrimination, obstacles to upward mobility.

2.　This labor market is within an economic arena, or segment, that the ethnic group vertically integrates. That is, the group
controls key positions in production, distribution, and retailing,
thus forming an ethnically linked economic system. This frees the
group from dependence on the majority, thus reducing the impact
of prejudice and discrimination while increasing the economic and
political influence of the group.

3.　An economic interface with the majority exists. The interface means that wealth flows from the majority to the minority.
With sufficient wealth, socioeconomic mobility can take place.

When these three features are present, then the group has
achieved *ethnic hegemony.*

This model has been applied to the Japanese of California. Despite discrimination that would seemingly cripple their mobility,
they achieved socioeconomic parity with the majority over the course
of some forty years. In part, they did so by hegemonizing a narrow
segment of agriculture. Japanese produce farmers dealt with Japanese truckers and Japanese wholesalers, who dealt with Japanese
retailers. Later, supermarket chains replaced the Japanese retailers,
but by that time, the Japanese were strongly entrenched in farming,
transportation, and wholesaling. Business was generally good and
demand steady, supplying enough wealth to promote mobility. Even
the incarceration during World War II did not halt the upward climb,
as the Japanese reentered agriculture after the war. In a remarkably
short period, they managed to take up where they had left off.

Although the hegemony model does not specify how socioeconomic status will develop, several suppositions can be added.
Within an ethnically hegemonized arena, ethnic discrimination
does not influence decisions about pay and promotion. That alone
provides greater freedom to achieve mobility. In addition, the
wealth generated by the arena remains within the ethnic group.
Provided the amount is sufficient, median wealth will rise, and as it

does, the number of socioeconomic categories within the group will increase. Initially, the socioeconomic system may consist of just two tiers: a few wealthy persons, mostly owners of businesses and a few professionals, and many workers. However, as wealth flows into the group from the interface with the majority, some of it should flow downward, transforming the broad worker category into finer categories that eventually solidify as socioeconomic levels.

The descriptions of both enclave and hegemony theory, though admittedly brief, indicate how little is known about socioeconomic differentiation within an ethnic group. Nevertheless, one point is clear: ethnic group wealth will not necessarily result in an ethnic socioeconomic structure identical to the majority. That is because wealth enters the ethnic economy through selected portals and is redistributed from there. Both the amount of wealth and the process of redistribution determine the formation of socioeconomic levels within the group—but little is known about that process.

Competition and Ethnic Boundaries

Social reality is a matter of definition, not in any metaphysical or subjective sense, but in the sense that ethnicity is determined by the cultural meanings attached to distinctions. For example, Geschwender points out that the group we now call Italians did not originally exist. Not until arrival in this country did immigrants from different regions in Italy coalesce around a single ethnic identity, mainly because the majority defined them that way.

If we accept that ethnicity is socially defined, then our interest naturally turns to how the definitions arise. One possibility is racism, but, as one textbook states, ". . . there is some danger that *institutional racism*, or simply *racism*, will be used as an explanatory term when in fact it designates only a mode of behavior that itself requires explanation."[35] Geschwender makes a similar point, saying that racism is a catalyst but not a prime cause.[36] This is an important point, and to help analyze it, let us adopt the terms *exogenous* and *endogenous* and accept that the former means a variable that is the starting point of a causal argument and the latter means a variable that depends on the exogenous variable. We can thus call racism an endogenous variable, inequality a dependent variable, and proceed to search for the exogenous variables. In terms of a heuristic diagram, the proposition is as follows:

exogenous variable→racism→inequality

This view of the argument shows that racism produces ethnic inequality, but racism is unexplained because the exogenous variable is
unknown. This view also shows that inequality could arise without
racism:

$$\text{exogenous variable} \rightarrow \text{inequality}$$

Here, the unknown exogenous variable determines inequality, completely bypassing racism. This might occur, for instance, if the minority is entrenched in an economic niche, but demand for its
products and services vanishes. The resulting inequality would be
due to changes in the exogenous variable, economic demand, independent of any changes in racism. How often this happens, of
course, is an empirical matter.

Whether or not the endogenous variable is part of the causal
sequence, the diagram emphasizes the importance of identifying
the exogenous variable, for that is the starting point of the explanation. Recently, sociologist Michael Banton has attempted this task by
using the framework of rational choice.

Competition and Rational Choice

Banton stresses how ethnic groups come into existence, writing "a theory of racial relations must therefore, in the first, place, be
a theory about the creation, maintenance and change of [social]
boundaries."[37] To explain the boundaries, Banton relies on assumptions derived from economic theory, most basically, that individuals
maximize their own advantage, and that competition ultimately determines group boundaries. This approach is sometimes referred to
as "rational choice theory."[38]

Competition occurs on two levels, individual and group.
Paradoxically, individual competition reduces ethnic boundaries,
whereas group competition strengthens them. He writes:

> If they [individuals seeking their own advantage] compete
> with one another on an individual basis this will tend to dis-
> solve group boundaries. If they compete as a group, their
> shared interest will lead them to reinforce those boundaries;
> the whole life and culture of the privileged group will be ori-
> ented to defending their exclusive boundary, while the life of
> the subordinate group will be directed towards the cultivation
> of their inclusive bonds so as to mobilize strength for the at-
> tack upon the practices which exclude them from privilege.[39]

With regard to competition, Banton's argument resembles those made by Stanley Lieberson and Hubert Blalock. They both recognize that intergroup competition leads to intergroup hostility, and that observers often mistake surface manifestations, such as stereotyping, for the underlying cause.[40]

Banton classifies boundaries as either *hard* or *soft*. Hard boundaries are difficult to cross, and the more privileges a group possesses, the harder the boundary it will erect around itself. Conversely, groups with few privileges will erect soft boundaries and attempt to expand. As a case in point, Banton cites the racial categories that existed in the Deep South during the 1930s.[41] The region was not economically well-off and whites were often a statistical minority in certain towns and counties. Still, whites accumulated most of the privileges, and race became a hard boundary. Banton does not mention it, but the definition of race commonly used at the time illustrates the hardness of the boundary. If a person had a single black progenitor in his or her genealogy, the person was considered black; or as it was sometimes put, "a single drop of black blood" made a person black. Such people could either attempt to pass, thus secretly crossing the race boundary, or remain black and forego the privileges accumulated by whites.

Banton's argument also helps explain a related aspect of boundary maintenance in the South *circa* the 1930s and 1940s: Gunar Myrdal's well-known "rank order of discrimination." In *An American Dilemma*, Myrdal said that whites had clearly defined spheres of discrimination, and that the spheres could be ranked in order of importance, as follows:

MOST IMPORTANT: Bars against miscegenation involving black men and white women.
Etiquettes concerning personal relations, such as interracial dancing.
Use of public facilities.
Political disenfranchisement.
Access to courts, police, and public services.
LEAST IMPORTANT: Means of earning a living.

Myrdal further said that blacks had the opposite rank order; that is, they most objected to discrimination in jobs, wages, credit, and other means of earning a living, and cared least about interracial sex.[42]

The white concern with miscegenation and other interpersonal contacts with sexual overtones (such as dancing) may seem irrational, or explicable only in terms of sexual motivation. However, if we consider competition to be an exogenous variable, then both the white and black rank orders make sense.

For whites, the emphasis on preventing sexual contacts reinforced the hard boundary. If miscegenation were commonplace, then the race criterion would soften. This possibility helps explain the single-drop criterion. It freed a privileged group, white males, to engage in sex with black females without softening the race boundary. That was because the offspring of such unions became part of the black category.

For blacks, the situation was entirely different. They had few privileges to guard, so the race criterion was unimportant. They were most interested in gaining economic equality, so economic discrimination—which interferes with fair competition—was of primary importance.

Although race often forms a harder boundary than ethnicity, that does not mean that ethnic boundaries are soft in an absolute sense. For example, during the nineteenth century, white immigrants repeatedly encountered hard boundaries based on ethnicity. These boundaries softened over time, and by now, some may have vanished. Race, of course, cannot vanish as long as anti-miscegenation is the rule, which it is. And even if no obviously visible boundary markers exist, Amos Hawley indicated they can be invented: "It is of interest that certain Hindu castes which lack visible racial markings, substitute artificial an differential, such as an insignia painted on the foreheads, peculiar modes of haircutting, or distinctive dress."[43] We should not, in short, confuse the boundary markers with the underlying division itself.

Ethnic Socioeconomic Status

In ethnic studies, most attention falls on comparisons among different groups because intergroup differences constitute the major political concern. In contrast, within-group differences have drawn relatively little attention. This is unfortunate, for what transpires within a group can significantly affect the course of group success. We do know from Chapter 2 that every group has some members in every socioeconomic strata. Not unexpectedly, nonwhites (except Asians) are heavily overrepresented in the lower categories, with blacks being especially overrepresented in the underclass. Beyond descriptive facts, however, we know relatively little about the socioeconomic differentiation within ethnic groups.

This deficit in knowledge has long been recognized. John Dollard, as noted before, said he knew little about the black upper class and therefore could not adequately discuss it.[44] Perhaps this knowledge deficit is a reason that studies such as *Black Metropolis* have had such an enduring impact.[45] Though old, they are the only sources addressing the problem.

Myrdal's work does contain a hypothesis, however. He said that because the black lower class was large and the black upper class was tiny, membership in the upper class was highly desired. He further said that black socioeconomic status was divided into many fine categories, and correspondingly, minute distinctions assumed great importance.[46] If correct, these comments mean that the greater the distance between the minority and majority, the greater the number of socioeconomic distinctions within the minority.

Myrdal did not explicitly discuss it, but this hypothesis helps to explain the "cult of cloth," and the world of "make believe" described and criticized by E. Franklin Frazier, and St. Claire Drake and Horace Cayton.[47] These trappings assumed great importance because they reflected the many small distinctions that existed among black socioeconomic categories, and the categories existed because the distance between blacks and whites was so great.

Myrdal also wrote as follows:

Our hypothesis is that in a society where there are broad social classes and, in addition, more minute distinctions and splits in the lower strata, the lower class groups will, to a great extent, take care of keeping each other subdued, thus relieving, to that extent, the higher classes of this otherwise painful task necessary to the monopolization of the power and the advantages.

There is nothing unusual about Myrdal's point that the class system within the minority relieves the majority of the "otherwise painful tasks" of monopolizing power and advantages, but it is worth bearing in mind.

We can only wish that Myrdal had carried these arguments further, but he did not. He did, however, explicitly recognize that his ideas contradicted Marxian theory, particularly the Marxian notion that the lower classes will eventually unite in the face of their oppressors. According to Myrdal, unity did not exist among the lower classes of either the majority or minority.[48]

Ethnicity and World Systems

James Geschwender has stated that capitalism is the source of ethnicity.[49] This is not an entirely new idea (as he recognizes), but it does suggest that explaining the race situation requires an economic model of some type. He opts for the *world systems model*, wherein *peripheral* countries supply labor and raw materials to *core* countries that are the centers of technology and industrialization. Because the United States is an important part of the world system, events occurring in distant places can affect American ethnic groups.

As an illustration, consider how oil has affected Mexican Americans during the mid-1980s. Over-production by Arab nations caused oil prices to collapse, thereby devastating an already weak Mexican economy. This prompted more emigration to the United States, which then prompted political responses from the American government. Among them was an amnesty program for illegal aliens. Although the full effects of the program have not been realized at this writing, one effect will surely be to increase the size of the Mexican population in the United States, if only because formerly illegal residents will now come forward and be counted by the Census Bureau. Once outside the shadow economy, these people will then compete with the Anglo majority on a different basis than before. In effect, the manifest size of a group has increased, affecting the competitive position of Mexican Americans *vis a vis* the majority.

This scenario is oversimplified, of course. However, the point is that in a world system, causal networks are far-flung, fragile, complex, and indirect. Under such circumstances, slight perturbations in one part of the system might have a large impact far down the causal chain, and accurate predictions about ethnic relations (or anything else) are therefore difficult to make.

Regarding socioeconomic status, Geschwender argues that ethnic groups develop classes based on combinations of race and socioeconomic characteristics. He calls them *nation-classes*, a ". . . social collectivity comprised of persons who are simultaneously members of the same class and the same race. This social grouping possesses the maximum combination of shared interests."[50] Diagrammatically, the relationships are shown in Table 5.2, using blacks and whites as illustrations.

This diagram suggests several hypotheses about class-race alignments. If race interests predominate, then black capitalists and the black proletariat will unite against white capitalists and the

TABLE 5.2

Relation between Race and Class[a]

Class	White	Black
Capitalist	white capitalist	black capitalist
Proletariat	white proletariat	black proletariat

[a]Geschwender, 1978.

white proletariat. This is likely to occur with civil rights issues. On the other hand, if economic interests predominate, then all capitalists will unite against all proletariat, regardless of race. An example would be tax laws favoring the capitalists. Other combinations are also possible: white capitalists uniting with the black proletariat, which might occur if white capitalists were in heavy competition with black capitalists. The converse—black capitalists uniting with the white proletariat—is also possible and for the converse reason.

As it stands, Geschwender's model does not predict which of the preceding combinations will emerge. He states:

> Which alliance will actually be formed at any given time and place will be a function of external conditions affecting consciousness formation, perceptions of probable success for particular lines of struggle, and the willingness of all parties to form such alliances. . . . The position that immigrant populations come to occupy in core countries and the probability of their evolving into self conscious ethnic groups is a function of the opportunity structure existing at the time of first immigration.[51]

Class and Ethnic Resources

Ivan Light distinguishes between *class resources* and *ethnic resources*, and further subdivides them into *material* and *nonmaterial*.[52] This classification is diagrammed in Table 5.3. The diagram highlights several relationships. For example, Light cites Cubans and Koreans as groups who have translated substantial class resources, abetted by smaller ethnic resources, into entrepreneurship in the United States.

Light did not directly discuss competition, but his categorization does have implications for competitive outcomes. One is that

TABLE 5.3

Resources and Ethnicity[a]

	Class Resources
Material e.g.	*Nonmaterial e.g.*
property	bourgeois values
wealth	attitudes
capital	skills
	Ethnic Resources
Material e.g.	*Nonmaterial e.g.*
credit association	thrift
ethnic organizations	kinship
specialized knowledge	work ethic

[a]Light, 1985.

groups with substantial class resources pose a greater threat to the majority than other groups. That is because class resources permit the group to compete at the higher reaches of socioeconomic status. Immigrant physicians, engineers, and other professionals, for instance, compete with the majority in socioeconomic arenas that produce great rewards and, hence, are hotly contested. We would therefore expect that tight job markets in those professions will result in strong efforts to exclude the minority. A case in point are immigrant physicians. Some claim that even after meeting all the requirements to practice in this country, they still have great difficulty getting good residencies because strong preference is given the native born. In comparison, immigrant laborers sometimes work in economic arenas that have been abandoned by the majority and that produce relatively little wealth. There, competition, and hence job discrimination, are slight.

Interestingly, by focusing on ethnic resources, the explanation begins coming full circle. Many ethnic resources *are* elements of ethnic culture. And just as the culture of poverty and the culture of success sought explanations in the characteristics of the group itself, so does the argument of ethnic resources.

The Competitive Framework of Ethnic Relations

Although I have endeavored to limit the review, the discussion has been admittedly discursive. Still, underlying commonalities can be adduced, and when summarized, can serve as a framework for analyzing ethnic relations. The framework is as follows:

1. *Racism and Culture are Endogenous Variables.* Although racism and culture are far different concepts, they can be treated similarly with regard to their status in the framework. Both are endogenous variables: they influence inter-group relations but themselves require explanation.

2. *The Majority Gains from the Minority.* If an overabundance of resources and rewards existed, then the issue of allocation would not arise. But society is not that way. Scarcity is a fact, and consequently, the demands of all people cannot be satisfied at all times. Of the many mechanisms that could be invoked to allocate resources and rewards, competition is used in American society to determine the "winners and losers in the race for the good life."[53] This competition need not be morally fair or personal. That it takes place is sufficient.

With regard to ethnic relations, the outcomes of the competition are broadly known. The majority—most frequently operationalized as whites—has won consistently. For instance, the analysis presented earlier showed that the various white groups obtain a disproportionately large share of the socioeconomic pie and, moreover, that a large minority presence actually increased the proportion of whites in high socioeconomic positions and decreased their proportion in low positions. In short, the majority gains from the minority.

The implications of this conclusion are basic and simple. It means that the majority has a vested interest in maintaining ethnic inequality, and because the majority holds the bulk of power, it also means that inequality will be a feature of American life for a long time.

3. *Competition Produces Ethnicity.* Neither racial nor ethnic characteristics are important unless meaning is attached to them. This statement specifies a fundamental and widely held premise, but when we accept it, we ought to next inquire as to how the meanings develop. And further, if we accept the fundamental importance of competition, then competition must be involved in the inquiry.

The framework under development assumes that competition allocates resources and rewards, and that the greater the competition, the more likely ethnicity will become its focal point. When resources and rewards are scarce and competition high, the social

meaning of ethnic tags will rapidly crystallize, forming hard boundaries. The consequent rejection of people on the basis of ethnicity
amounts to excluding them from the competitive process, or to reducing and deflecting their competitive threat. In this sense, competition leads to ethnicity.

4. *Competition Produces Ethnic Socioeconomic Differentiation.*
Competition not only leads to ethnicity, but it also produces socioeconomic differentiation along ethnic lines. The result is a stratification pyramid with the minority disproportionately clustered at the
base and the majority clustered at the top. These two outcomes—
ethnicity and socioeconomic status—can be separated for purposes
of discussion, but in reality, they occur together.

The analysis presented in Chapter 2 showed that the correlates
of socioeconomic status are much the same regardless of ethnicity.
Education and gender, to illustrate, are highly and consistently correlated with socioeconomic status. These findings, and others like
it, suggest that the underlying causal processes are the same for all
groups. Thus, the structure of socioeconomic status will be the
same, but the distribution of individuals across the categories will
differ.

It is important to recognize that socioeconomic differentiation
occurs even without majority-minority competition. In ethnically
homogeneous societies, status differences are the rule, not the exception. Hence, ethnic competition should be regarded as *one* mechanism leading to a particular form of socioeconomic status in a
particular class of societies. Other forms and other mechanisms are
possible, but they are not discussed here.

5. *Competition Affects Demographic Potential.* The last factor included in the framework is the demography of a group. Although
not much emphasized in past research, ethnic competition affects
several demographic outcomes, the most obvious being group size.
This occurs because competition leads to boundary formation. In
situations where resources and rewards are plentiful, competition is
less intense and ethnic boundaries will be soft or, conceivably, not
exist at all. Without a boundary, group size is either infinitely small
or infinitely large, but in either case, not a factor in ethnic relationships. Other demographic variables may be similarly affected. For
example, dependency will continue to affect socioeconomic attainment, but in the absence of competition, its specification in terms of
ethnicity will be unimportant.

In the case of group size and threat, the actual number of persons in a group may have less to do with demography than with

perception. If W. I. Thomas's dictum is true—things that are defined as real are real in their consequences—then a group defined as large will be perceived as a threat by the majority and that will lead to discriminatory responses far out of proportion to their actual number.[54]

Although the foregoing is a summary of the competitive framework, it can be summarized still further:

Scarcity leads to competition; competition leads to ethnicity; ethnicity leads to inequality; and inequality *is* socioeconomic status.

A final point concerns the emergent nature of the competitive framework. It does not require that individuals be consciously aware of engaging in competitive processes, nor must they know the causes and consequences of their actions. If they just look after their own interests and follow the dictates of society and the marketplace, they will affect the course of inter-group relations. In other words, individual level behavior explains behavior at the group level.

Ethnic Consciousness

We can reasonably assume that individuals know of their ethnicity and of the boundaries surrounding their group. However, if that is all they know, then they are more like an aggregation than a social group. They recognize common traits and boundaries, and so have those in common, but little else. In contrast, if these individuals develop a consciousness of kind, a feeling that each is inextricably bound with the other, and that the fate of one is the fate of all, *ethnic consciousness* has formed.

In recent times, political events have created or intensified the ethnic consciousness of many minorities, as well as women. For example, during the 1960s, racial and ethnic issues were prominent national issues, and civil rights groups emerged to serve political ends. Violence was common and lesser forms of protest even more common. In such an atmosphere, ethnic consciousness is likely to arise or intensify, setting the stage for further political action, which then further intensifies ethnic consciousness, and so on.

Ethnic consciousness and the issues that it spins off are dramatic and important, but nevertheless, ethnic consciousness is not an integral part of the competitive framework. Nothing in the framework precludes it, but nothing requires it, either.

The important point, though, is not about ethnic consciousness per se, but about the relationship with the competitive framework. As long as we consider ethnic consciousness to be an endogenous variable, there is no contradiction between the framework and the concept. Ethnic consciousness results from competition, not the reverse.[55]

Ethnic consciousness calls to mind the Marxian notion of *class consciousness*, but despite the similarity of terms, the two concepts are fundamentally different. Within the Marxian perspective, social class is the major division within society, and if ethnic divisions are important, they are encompassed within class divisions. A simple, heuristic diagram illustrates this (Table 5.4).

TABLE 5.4

Illustrating the Marxian Relation between Class and
Ethnic Group Divisions

Upper Class		*Middle Class*		*Lower Class*	
group a	group b	group a	group b	group a	group b

In other words, ethnic groups are subgroups of class groupings.[56] Obviously, the order can be reversed, as shown by an alternative heuristic diagram (Table 5.5).

TABLE 5.5

Illustrating a Non-Marxian Relation between Class and
Ethnic Group Divisions

Group A	*Group B*	*Group A*	*Group B*	*Group A*	*Group B*
UC MC LC	UC MC LC	UC MC LC	UC MC LC	UC MC LC	UC MC LC

UC: upper class
MC: middle class
LC: lower class.

Ethnic groupings and ethnic consciousness now take precedence over class groupings and class consciousness. Milton Gordon implicitly assumed as much with his well-known concept of the ethclass. He postulated that ethnic groups have class structures paralleling the majority's, which means that ethnic divisions stand apart from class divisions.

Geschwender's analysis of the South during the Reconstruction period provides an interesting illustration of the idea. After the Civil War, the South retained its highly structured class divisions, and white planters soon amassed most resources and rewards, forming an upper-class gentry. At approximately the same time, a populist political movement began emerging, stressing grass roots equality. The movement, in effect, subsumed race divisions under class divisions, placing lower-class whites in the same social category as lower-class blacks (Table 5.4). This constituted a formidable threat to the white gentry. Had the situation remained that way, the social history of the South would have been much different, but the situation changed. Race divisions quickly superseded class divisions (Table 5.5). The interests of all whites came to be defined as contrary to the interests of all blacks, thus splitting the populist class grouping and diffusing the threat to the white gentry.

Implications of the Framework

The competitive framework has great potential for organizing statistical data and interpreting historical and cross-cultural events. It is not, however, a framework with sanguine implications. It rests on the premise of scarcity, which, if correct, means there will always be competition, and some groups will win and others will lose. Therefore, inequality will always exist, and to a substantial degree, harden along ethnic and racial lines. That does not suggest a bright, harmonious world.

The framework has another disturbing implication. If the minority climbs the socioeconomic ladder, the minority will come into greater competition with the majority. This is because at the higher rungs of socioeconomic status, resources and rewards are greater, and so competition is greater, and anti-minority responses will be higher. The comparison of immigrant physicians and laborers mentioned earlier illustrates this phenomenon, and the aphorism, "They should stay in their place," reflects it.

An alternative sequence is possible, however. If the minority attains success, its interests might then coincide with those of the majority, thus promoting cooperation between majority and minority. But reaching this cooperative stage might require a great deal of intermediate struggle. The history of the Irish, Italians, and Asians, for instance, speaks to such struggles. In a sense, only after the majority "loses" and the minority acquires a substantial share of resources and rewards, will the two groups join together in common cause.

Although the competitive framework has disturbing implications, it also implies a solution to ethnic inequality: reduce scarcity and thereby reduce competition. This can occur in two ways.

First, if everyone agrees to their proper place in the socioeconomic scheme of things, competition would be irrelevant because no one would aspire to have more resources and rewards than they have. Indeed, if we stretch the point, religious systems emphasizing fatalism, deferred gratification, and caste encourage people to be satisfied with their present lot, thereby weakening the relationship between scarcity and competition. Put otherwise, if the boundaries between socioeconomic positions and ethnic groups are accepted as impassable, then the current distribution of resources and rewards must do.

Second, a decrease in scarcity will also decrease competition. This would occur if the population rapidly declined while the supply of resources and rewards remained constant. In effect, the pie could be cut into fewer slices, and so each slice could be larger. For example, the Black Death ravaged Europe during the twelfth and thirteenth centuries, killing perhaps a third of the population. Those who survived found their economic position greatly improved because per capita scarcity had decreased.

Another, happier way to decrease scarcity is to increase the supply of resources and rewards. If the pie could be made larger, then intergroup competition would decline and, concomitantly, so would ethnic hostility. The solution is simple: get richer.

Obviously, that is facile, but it is also partially correct. The growing wealth of the United States has undoubtedly deflected many ethnic antagonisms. Consider one of Geschwender's analyses. He divides black history into four stages: (1) slavery, which expanded due to the demand for cotton; (2) emancipation, which freed blacks legally but did not end their economic dependence on whites; (3) World War I, which increased the demand for black labor at the same time European immigration was being curtailed; and (4) World War II and after, which maintained black gains as economic prosperity remained high. We can ask, would the gains in civil rights and socioeconomic equality, begun after the Civil War and continued to this day, have occurred if American wealth had not expanded? Surely not—or at minimum, the gains would have been far less than those actually achieved.

The American pie may not be big enough to satisfy all demands all the time, but it *is* big, and even though all Americans cannot be wealthy, it does not follow that most Americans must be poor. If the demand for resources and rewards increases at a substantially faster rate than supply, or if the demand remains constant while supply decreases, then ethnic antagonisms will increase, hardly a pleasant prediction. But, the obverse is equally logical. If supply expands faster than demand, ethnic relations will improve. These improvements will not follow a smooth path. History shows there will be surges forward followed by setbacks, but overall, the trend will be toward a better ethnic future.

Notes

Chapter 1

1. Marvin Harris, *Cultural Materialism: The Struggle for the Science of Culture* (New York: Vintage, 1979).

2. Robert Darnton, *The Great Cat Massacre and Other Episodes in French Cultural History* (New York: Basic Books, Inc., Publishers, 1984), Chapter 7.

3. Edward O. Wilson, *On Human Nature* (Cambridge, Massachusetts: Harvard University Press, 1978), 19; italics added.

4. Wilson, 33.

5. Philip Kitcher provides an anti-sociobiology critique while Wilson himself is the best source of the pro-sociobiology viewpoint. Philip Kitcher, *Vaulting Ambition: Sociobiology and the Quest for Human Nature* (Cambridge, Massachusetts: The MIT Press, 1985).

6. For a succinct review of this issue, see George Eaton Simpson and Milton J. Yinger, *Racial and Cultural Minorities: An Analysis of Prejudice and Discrimination*, Fifth Edition (New York: Plenum Press, 1985), 36–39.

7. Simpson and Yinger, Chapter 2.

8. For a critique, see Susan L. Farber, *Identical Twins Reared Apart: A Reanalysis* (New York: Basic Books, Inc., 1981).

9. Stephen Jay Gould, *The Mismeasure of Man* (New York: W. W. Norton & Company, 1981), 156.

10. Marshall Sahlins, *Culture and Practical Reason* (Chicago: University of Chicago Press, 1976).

11. Robert E. Park and Ernest W. Burgess, *Introduction to the Science of Sociology*, Third Edition, revised (Chicago: University of Chicago Press, 1969), 737; originally published 1921.

12. Stephen Thernstrom, (ed.), *Harvard Encyclopedia of American Ethnic Groups* (Cambridge, Massachusetts: The Belknap Press of Harvard University Press, 1980), *vi*.

13. William Petersen, *Japanese Americans: Oppression and Success* (New York: Random House, 1971), Chapter 10; Pierre L. Van den Berghe, *Race and Racism* (New York: John Wiley, 1967), 10.

14. William Petersen, "The Classification of Subnations in Hawaii: An Essay in the Sociology of Knowledge," *American Sociological Review* 34 (December 1969), 863–76.

15. Robert M. Jiobu, *Ethnicity and Assimilation*. (Albany, New York: State University Press of New York, 1988), Chapter 2.

16. John Gross, review of *St. John De Crevecoeur: The Life of an American Farmer*, by Gay Wilson and Roger Asselineau (New York: Viking, 1987), in "Books of the Times," *New York Times*, September 18, 1987, Y 29.

17. Edward Alsworth Ross, *The Changing Chinese: The Conflict of Oriental and Western Cultures in China* (New York: The Century Co., 1911); *The Old World in the New: The Significance of Past and Present Immigration to the American People* (New York: The Century Co., 1914); Robert E. Park, "Our Racial Frontier on the Pacific," reprinted in *Race and Culture: Essays in the Sociology of Contemporary Man* (New York: The Free Press, 1950), 150–51; Jesse Frederick Steiner, *The Japanese Invasion: A Study in the Psychology of Inter-Racial Contacts* (Chicago: A. C. McClurg & Co., 1917).

18. Horace M. Kallen, *Culture and Democracy in the United States: Studies in the Group Psychology of the American Peoples* (New York: Boni and Liveright, Publishers, 1924).

19. Robert Blauner, "Internal Colonialism and Ghetto Revolt," *Social Problems* (Spring 1969), 393–408.

20. For example, Michael Hechter, *Internal Colonialism: The Celtic Fringe in British National Development, 1536–1966* (Berkeley, California: University of California Press, 1977).

21. Jiobu, 1988.

22. Robert M. Jiobu and Harvey H. Marshall, Jr., "Urban Structure and the Differentiation Between Blacks and Whites," *American Sociological Review* 36 (August 1971), 638–649.

23. A term such as *ethnic identity* might be more appropriate for such cases. Ethnic identity is the extent to which an individual partakes of an ethnically defined role.

24. U.S. Bureau of the Census, *Census of Population and Housing, 1980: Public Use Microdata Samples, Technical Documentation* (Washington, D.C.: U.S. Government Printing Office, 1983), K–65; abbreviation in the original.

25. This does not mean, of course, that the distinction is unimportant among Umbrians.

26. Frances Leon Quintana, "Spanish," in *Harvard Encyclopedia of American Ethnic Groups*, ed. Stephan Thernstrom (Cambridge, Massachusetts: The Belknap Press of Harvard University Press, 1980), 951.

27. The converse is not necessarily true, of course.

28. U.S. Bureau of the Census, *Ancestry and Language in the United States: November, 1979* (Washington, D.C.: U.S. Government Printing Office, March, 1982), Table 1.

29. Sampling variation could have accounted for the differences, but I checked and then rejected that possibility after calculating the percentages based on the entire Microdata file.

30. For example, see Richard D. Alba, *Italian Americans: Into the Twilight of Ethnicity* (Englewood Cliffs, New Jersey: Prentice-Hall, Inc. 1985).

31. Karen Johnson Freeze, "Czechs," in *Harvard Encyclopedia of American Ethnic Groups*, ed. Stephan Thernstrom (Cambridge, Massachusetts: The Belknap Press of Harvard University Press, 1980), 261–72.

Chapter 2

1. Erik Olin Wright, Cynthia Costello, David Hachen, and Joe Sprague, "The American Class Structure," *American Sociological Review* 47 (December 1982), 709.

2. Erik Olin Wright, *Classes* (London: Verson, 1985), Chapter 1.

3. H. H. Gerth and C. Wright Mills, eds. and trans., *From Max Weber: Essays in Sociology* (New York: Oxford University Press, 1958), 181.

4. Gerth and Mills, 180.

5. Gerth and Mills, 181; also see Erik Olin Wright, *Class Structure and Income Determination* (New York: Academic Press, 1979), 9.

6. Gerth and Mills, 186–87, italics in original.

7. Gerth and Mills, 187.

8. Gerth and Mills, 189.

9. Gerth and Mills, 193.

10. Wright, *Class Structure and Income Determination*, 2, note 2.

11. Compare with Judah Matras, *Social Inequality, Stratification, and Mobility*, 2nd ed. (Englewood Cliffs, New Jersey: Prentice-Hall); 5–6.

12. John Dollard, *Caste and Class in a Southern Town*, third edition (Garden City, New York: Doubleday Anchor Books, 1957); originally published in 1937 by Harper & Brothers.

13. Dollard, 89.

14. Dollard, Chapter 5.

15. St. Clair Drake and Horace R. Cayton, *Black Metropolis: A Study of Negro Life in a Northern City*, Volume II (New York: Harper & Row, Publishers, 1962), 521; originally published in 1945 by Harcourt, Brace & Company.

16. Drake and Cayton, 522–26.

17. Gunnar Myrdal, *An American Dilemma: The Negro Problem and Modern Democracy*, Volume II (New York: Pantheon Books, 1972), 704–505; originally published by in 1944 by Harper and Row.

18. Myrdal, 694.

19. Myrdal, 700.

20. Myrdal, 704.

21. E. Franklin Frazier, "The Negro Middle Class and Desegregation," in *E. Franklin Frazier, On Race Relations* (Chicago: The University of Chicago Press, 1968), 292–308; originally published in *Social Problems* 4 (April 1957), 291–301.

22. Frazier, 306.

23. Drake and Clayton, xxiii.

24. William Petersen, *Population*, Third Edition (New York: Macmillan Publishing Company, Inc., 1975), 528–46.

25. Lloyd W. Warner and Leo Srole, *The Social Systems of American Ethnic Groups* (New Haven, Connecticut: Yale University Press, 1945).

26. Warner and Srole, 57.

27. Warner and Srole, 60.

28. Warner and Srole, 67.

29. Herbert J. Gans, *The Urban Villagers: Group and Class in the Life of Italian-Americans*, updated and expanded edition (New York: The Free Press, 1982); originally published in 1962 by the Free Press of Glencoe.

30. Gans, 24–25. At this point in the book, the ethnicity of the respondents is not clear. I assume that most were Italian, although several other groups also lived in the neighborhood (see Gans, 8–10).

31. Gans, 26–27.

32. Gans, 241–242.

33. Gans, 24, italics added. This definition is brief, but Gans never expands upon it very much despite his statements in note 15 to Chapter 2.

34. Milton M. Gordon, *Assimilation in American Life: The Role of Race, Religion, and National Origins* (New York: Oxford University Press, 1964), 51.

35. Gordon, 49.

36. Gordon, 162.

37. Gordon, 162.

38. Gordon, and several other authors, include religion as part of ethnicity, but that is not possible with census data.

39. Harry H. L. Kitano, *Japanese Americans: The Evolution of a Subculture,* Second Edition (Engelwood Cliffs, New Jersey: Prentice-Hall, Inc., 1976), 4–6.

40. See Chapter 1.

41. William Julius Wilson, *The Declining Significance of Race: Blacks and Changing American Institutions,* Second Edition (Chicago: University of Chicago Press, 1980), 144.

42. Wilson, 1980, Chapter 8; William Julius Wilson, *The Truly Disadvantaged: The Inner City, the Underclass, and Public Policy* (Chicago: The University of Chicago Press, 1987).

43. Wilson, 1980, p. 156.

44. Wilson, 1980, p. *ix*.

45. Wilson, 1980, p. 156.

46. Joseph A. Kahl and James A. Davis, "A Comparison of Indexes of Social-Economic Status," *American Sociological Review* 20 (June 1955), 317–25.

47. Peter M. Blau and Otis Dudley Duncan, *The American Occupational Structure* (New York: John Wiley & Sons, Inc., 1967), 118–21.

48. Blau and Duncan, 121.

49. Dennis Gilbert and Joseph A. Kahl, *The American Class Structure: A New Synthesis* (Homewood, Illinois: The Dorsey Press, 1982), 69.

50. National Opinion Research Center, *General Social Surveys, 1972–1984: Cumulative Codebook* (Chicago: University of Chicago, 1984), Appendix G.

51. Gilbert and Kahl, 70.

52. Delbert C. Miller, *Handbook of Research Design and Social Measurement*, Second Edition (New York: McKay, 1970), 169.

53. Clement Cottingham, "Conclusion: The Political Economy of Urban Poverty," in *Race, Poverty, and the Urban Underclass*, Clement Cottingham (ed.), (Lexington, Massachusetts: Lexington Books, 1982), 179–208; also see David M. Gordon, *Theories of Poverty and Underemployment: Orthodox, Radical, and Dual Labor Market Perspectives* (Lexington, Massachusetts: D. C. Heath and Company, 1972), 5.

54. U.S. Bureau of the Census, *Census of Population and Housing, 1980: Public Use Microdata Samples, Technical Documentation* (Washington, D.C.: U.S. Government Printing Office, 1983), K–35.

55. This clearly is not a ratio scale, so a true zero does not exist for it. At times, the Edwards scale is treated as an interval measure.

56. U.S. Department of Health, Education, and Welfare, *The Measure of Poverty: A Report to Congress as Mandated by the Education Amendment of 1974* (Washington, D.C.: U.S. Government Printing Office, April, 1976).

57. See Gilbert and Kahl, 1982, Table 3–4.

58. Gilbert and Kahl, 69.

59. Robert W. Hodges, Donald J. Treiman, and Peter H. Rossi, *Class, Status and Power* (New York: Free Press, 1966), 424–25.

60. R. Easterlin, "Does Money Buy Happiness," *Public Interest* 30 (1973), 3–10.

61. Robert M. Jiobu, *Ethnicity and Assimilation* (Albany, New York: State University Press of New York, 1988), Chapter 3.

62. Blau and Duncan, 1967; Jiobu, 1988.

63. Jiobu.

64. The precise proportion of Jews in the Russian category is unknown, but studies have indicated that it might be as high as 75%. Even if substantially lower, the statement stands. Erich Rosenthal, "The Equivalence of United States Census Data for Persons of Russian Stock or Descent with American Jews: An Evaluation," *Demography* 12 (May 1975), 275–90; Frances E. Kobrin, "National Data on American Jewry, 1970–1971: A Comparative Evaluation of the Census Yiddish Mother Tongue Subpopulation and the National Jewish Population Survey," in *Papers in Jewish Demography: Proceedings of the Demographic Session held at the 8th World Congress of Jewish*

Studies, eds. U. O. Schmelz, P. Glikson, and S. DellaPergola (Jerusalem, Israel: Institute of Contemporary Jewry: The Hebrew University of Jerusalem, 1983), 129–43.

65. This is the logic used in chi-square. The formal mathematical notation for this calculation is surprisingly involved. However, it amounts to multiplying the row marginal times the column marginal and dividing that product by the total number in the table. For an example, see Hubert M. Blalock, Jr., *Social Statistics*, Second Edition (New York: McGraw-Hill Book Company, 1972), Chapter 15; or almost any statistics textbook.

66. Asians are an exception.

67. Jiobu, Chapter 6.

68. Leo Grebler, Joan W. Moore, and Ralph C. Guzman, *The Mexican-American People: The Nation's Second Largest Minority* (New York: The Free Press, A Division of the Macmillan Company, 1970), 411.

69. Jiobu, Chapter 6.

70. Barbara Tomaskovic-Dewey and Donald Tomaskovic-Dewey, "The Social Structural Determinants of Ethnic Group Behavior: Single Ancestry Rates Among Four White American Ethnic Groups," *American Sociological Review* 53 (August, 1988), 650–59.

71. U.S. Bureau of the Census, *Statistical Abstract of the United States, 1984* (Washington, D.C.: U.S. Government Printing Office, 1983), 407.

72. See Wilson, 1987.

73. Miller, Section 4A.

74. Robert E. Park, "The City: Suggestions for the Investigation of Human Behavior in the Urban Environment," in Robert E. Park and Ernest W. Burgess, *The City* (Chicago: University of Chicago Press, 1967), 1–46; originally published by the University of Chicago Press, 1925.

75. Wilson, 1987, pp. 7–8.

76. Wilson, 1987, p. 61.

77. Oscar Lewis, "The Culture of Poverty," in *On Understanding Poverty: Perspectives from the Social Sciences*, ed. Daniel Patrick Moynihan (New York: Basic Books, 1968), 187–200.

78. Amos Hawley, "Dispersion versus Segregation: Apropos of a Solution of Race Problems," *Papers of the Michigan Academy of Sciences, Arts, and Letters*, 30, pp. 667–74. For other discussions building on Hawley, see Robert M. Jiobu and Harvey H. Marshall, Jr., "Urban Structure and the Differentiation Between Blacks and Whites," *American Sociological Review* 36

(August, 1971), 638–49; Harvey H. Marshall, Jr. and Robert M. Jiobu, "Residential Segregation in United States Cities: A Causal Analysis," *Social Forces* 53 (March 1975), 449–60.

79. U.S. Bureau of the Census, 1983, K–45.

80. Terry Dennis Lundgren, *Comparative Study of All Negro Ghettos in the United States*, Ph.D. Dissertation (Columbus, Ohio: Department of Sociology, The Ohio State University, 1976).

81. Jiobu, 1988; Robert Bibb and William H. Form, "The Effects of Industrial, Occupational, and Sex Stratification on Wages in Blue-Collar Markets," *Social Forces* 55 (June 1977), 974–96.

82. Diana Pearce, "The Feminization of Poverty: Women, Work, and Welfare," *Urban and Social Change Review* 2 (1978), 28–36.

83. George Eaton Simpson and Milton J. Yinger, *Racial and Cultural Minorities: An Analysis of Prejudice and Discrimination*, Fifth Edition (New York: Plenum Press, 1985), 199.

84. Recall that the British grouping also includes English-speaking Candians and Australians.

85. *SAS User's Guide: Statistics*, Version 5 Edition (Cary, North Carolina: SAS Institute, Inc., 1985), 205–206. An arbitrarily small number, .5, was added to each cell frequency to permit logarithmic transformations.

86. More formally, that differ from zero at the 5% level of probability.

87. Perhaps, I should remind the reader that the phrase "being Irish" (or any other ethnic grouping), is a convenience. The full phrase is "being Irish as contrasted to being British."

88. Jiobu, 1988.

89. The maximum variance would occur if 50% of the sample were in the underclass and 50% were not.

90. Richard D. Alba, *Italian Americans: Into the Twilight of Ethnicity* (Englewood Cliffs, New Jersey: Prentice-Hall, Inc., 1985); Victor Greene, "Poles," in *Harvard Encyclopedia of American Ethnic Groups*, ed. Stephan Thernstrom (Cambridge, Massachusetts: The Belknap Press of Harvard University Press, 1980), 801.

Chapter 3

1. Reynolds Farley, *Blacks and Whites: Narrowing the Gap?* (Cambridge, Massachusetts: Harvard University Press, 1984), 60.

2. Farley, p. 202.

3. James A. Geschwender and Rita Carol Seguin, "Exploring the Asian-American Success Myth," unpublished paper, 1988.

4. Robert M. Jiobu, and Linda Nishigaya, "Residential Segregation Among Asians in Honolulu," presented at the Annual Meeting of the North Central Sociological Association, 1985.

5. Robert M. Jiobu, *Ethnicity and Assimilation* (Albany, New York: State University of New York Press, 1988), Chapter 8; Robert M. Jiobu, "Earnings Differentials Between Whites and Ethnic Minorities: The Cases of Asian Americans, Blacks, and Chicanos," *Sociology and Social Research* 61 (October 1976), 24–38.

6. John Dollard, *Caste and Class in a Southern Town*, Third Edition (Garden City, New York: Doubleday and Co., 1957), Chapter 6; originally published in 1937 by Harper Brothers.

7. Dollard, 128.

8. Harold M. Baron and Bennett Hymer, "Racial Dualism in an Urban Labor Market," 188–195, in *Problems in Political Economy: An Urban Perspective*, Second Edition, ed. David M. Gordon (Lexington, Massachusetts: D. C. Heath and Company, 1977).

9. Gunnar Myrdal, *An American Dilemma* (New York: Harper and Row, 1944), 391.

10. Joan Moore and Harry Pachon, *Hispanics in the United States* (Englewood Cliffs, New Jersey: Prentice-Hall, 1985), 25.

11. Michael Reich, "The Economics of Racism," 107–113 in *Problems in Political Economy: An Urban Perspective*, ed. David M. Gordon (Lexington, Massachusetts: D. C. Heath and Company, 1971).

12. Reported in Reich, 1971.

13. Alber Szymanski, "Racial Discrimination and White Gain," *American Sociological Review* 41 (June 1976), 403–414.

14. E. M. Beck, "Discrimination and White Economic Loss: A Times Series Examination of the Radical Model," *Social Forces* 58 (September 1980), 148–68.

15. Several studies have examined the relationship between black population size and the occupational differentiation between blacks and white (for example, Blalock 1956; 1957; Jiobu and Marshall 1972). However, black-white differentiation does not directly address the issue being studied here.

16. Stanley Lieberson, *A Piece of the Pie: Blacks and White Immigrants Since 1880* (Berkeley, California: University of California Press, 1980), Chapters 10 and 11.

17. Lieberson, 301–303.

18. Alexander Saxton, *The Indispensable Enemy: Labor and the Anti-Chinese Movement in California* (Berkeley, California: University of California Press, 1971).

19. Phillip Cutright, "Negro Subordination and White Gains," *American Journal of Sociology* 30 (February 1965), 110–112.

20. Norval Glenn, "White Gains from Negro Subordination," *Social Problems* 14 (Fall 1966), 159–78; Norval Glenn, "Occupational Benefits to Whites from Subordination of Negroes," *American Sociological Review* 28 (June 1963), 443–48.

21. Several current examples are given in *Time*, June 13, 1983, pp. 18–25.

22. Michael J. Piore, *Birds of Passage: Migrant Labor and Industrial Societies* (Cambridge, Great Britain: Cambridge University Press, 1979).

23. Jiobu, 1988, Chapter 7.

24. A Standard Metropolitan Statistical Area consists of a central city of at least 50,000 persons and all the surrounding area that is socially and economically integrated with it. Once an area is so designated, the entire county becomes part of the SMSA. See: U.S. Bureau of the Census, *Census of Population and Housing, 1980: Public Use Microdata Samples, Technical Documentation*. Washington, D.C.: U.S. Government Printing Office, 1983, K–45.

25. See Chapter 2.

26. Joseph H. Greenberg, "The Measurement of Linguistic Diversity," *Language* 32 (1956), 109–115; Stanley Lieberson, "An Extension of Greenberg's Linguistic Diversity Measure," *Language* 40 (October-December 1964), 526–31; Roger Finke and Rodney Stark, "Religious Economies and Sacred Canopies: Religious Mobilization in American Cities, 1906," *American Sociological Review* 53 (February 1988), 41–49.

27. See the review in Jiobu 1988, Chapter 7.

28. When the multiple correlation is not significant, the regression coefficients are usually not significant either, although in some few cases that does not hold.

29. Glenn, 1963; 1966.

Chapter 4

1. Philip M. Hauser and Otis Dudley Duncan, "Overview and Conclusions," in *The Study of Population*, ed. Philip M. Hauser and Otis Dudley Duncan (Chicago: University of Chicago Press, 1959), 2–3.

2. Henry S. Shryock, Jacob S. Siegel, and associates, *The Methods and Materials of Demography*, Volume 1 (Washington, D.C.: U.S. Government Printing Office, 1973), 2.

3. William Petersen, *Population*, Third Edition (New York: Macmillan Publishing Company, Inc., 1975), 2–4.

4. Hauser and Duncan, 2–3.

5. For example, see Calvin Goldscheider, *Population, Modernization, and Social Structure* (Boston: Little, Brown and Company, 1971).

6. Robert M. Jiobu, *Ethnicity and Assimilation* (Albany, New York: State University of New York Press), Chapter 3.

7. For example, see Stanley Lieberson, *A Piece of the Pie: Blacks and White Immigrants Since 1880* (Berkeley, California: University of California Press, 1980).

8. William Julius Wilson, *The Truly Disadvantaged: The Inner City, the Underclass, and Public Policy* (Chicago: The University of Chicago Press, 1987), 6–8.

9. Richard A. Easterlin, *Birth and Fortune: The Impact of Numbers on Personal Welfare*, Second Edition (Chicago: University of Chicago Press, 1987), Chapter 6.

10. Robert Darnton, *The Great Cat Massacre and Other Episodes in French Cultural History* (New York: Basic Books, Inc., Publishers, 1984), Chapter 7.

11. For a statement about the importance of demography and ecology for sociological understanding, see Krishnan Namboodiri, "Ecological Demography: Its Place in Sociology," *American Sociological Review* 53 (August 1988), 619–33.

12. Marvin Harris, *Cultural Materialism: The Struggle for the Science of Culture* (New York, Vintage, 1979), 55–56.

13. I use *cause* simply as an expository shortcut for the longer phrases.

14. Excepting the null case where group size equals one.

15. See Paul C. Siu, "The Sojourner," *American Journal of Sociology* 58 (July 1952), 34–44.

16. For example, see Petersen, pp. 528–546.

17. Calvin Goldscheider and Peter Uhlenberg, "Minority Group Status and Fertility," *American Journal of Sociology* 74 (January 1968), 361–72.

18. See Jiobu, Chapter 3.

19. Jiobu, 77–82.

20. I previously called this the "job squeeze ratio." See Jiobu, Chapter 3.

21. See Hubert M., Blalock, Jr., *Toward a Theory of Minority-Group Relations* (New York: John Wiley & Sons, Inc., 1967); Jiobu, Chapter 5.

22. Barbara Tomaskovic-Dewey, and Donald Tomaskovic-Dewey, "The Social Structural Determinants of Ethnic Group Behavior: Single Ancestry Rates among Four White American Ethnic Groups," *American Sociological Review* 53 (August, 1988), 650–59.

23. Jiobu, Chapter 5.

24. Parker W. Frisbie and Lisa Neidert, "Inequality and the Relative Size of Minority Populations: A Comparative Analysis," *American Journal of Sociology* 82 (March 1977), 1007–1030.

25. To empirically resolve this problem would require (1), separate measures of group political power and majority discrimination; and (2) a method of scaling the measures in order to compare their strengths. Such data are not available in the 1980 Census. Theoretically resolving the problem would require a theory that distinguishes among the three hypotheses. That theory is not available.

26. Jiobu, 1988, Chapter 3.

27. This problem often goes under the heading of "multicollinearity."

28. Not shown are the so-called regression diagnostics: statistics to evaluate the goodness of the equation. These statistics occasionally indicated that Mexicans, Asians, Native Americans, and Swedes have strong influences on some equations, suggesting that they should be eliminated from the analysis. However, because seven different dependent variables are being analyzed, eliminating these groups would produce equations based on different samples, and comparisons would be ambiguous. See David A. Belsley, Edwin Kuh, and Roy E. Welsch, *Regression Diagnostics: Identifying Influential Data and Sources of Collinearity* (New York: John Wiley & Sons, 1980).

29. John Neter, William Wasserman, and Michael H. Kutner, *Applied Linear Regression Models* (Homewood, Illinois: Richard D. Irwin, 1983), 400–411.

30. Some studies drop leverage points from the analysis to improve the fit between equation and data.

31. The same caveat applies to Asian groups. Unfortunately, due to the present sampling frame, they could not be separated for analysis.

32. Karen Johnson Freeze, "Czechs," in *Harvard Encyclopedia of American Ethnic Groups,* ed. Stephan Thernstrom (Cambridge, Massachusetts: The Belknap Press of Harvard University Press, 1980), 261–72.

33. Recall Chapter 2.

34. Oscar Lewis, "The Culture of Poverty," in *On Understanding Poverty: Perspectives from the Social Sciences,* ed. Daniel Patrick Moynihan (New York: Basic Books, 1968), 187.

35. For example, see Neter, Wasserman, and Kutner, Chapter 8.

36. Because this is a principal components analysis, the term "factor analysis" does not apply, strictly speaking.

Chapter 5

1. Herbert J. Gans, *The Urban Villagers: Group and Class in the Life of Italian-Americans,* Updated and Expanded Edition (New York: The Free Press, 1982); originally published in 1962 by the Free Press of Glencoe.

2. Oscar Lewis, "The Culture of Poverty," in *On Understanding Poverty: Perspectives from the Social Sciences,* ed. Daniel Patrick Moynihan (New York: Basic Books, 1968), 187.

3. Lewis, 188.

4. Lewis, 191, 197.

5. William Julius Wilson, *The Truly Disadvantaged: The Inner City, the Underclass, and Public Policy* (Chicago: The University of Chicago Press, 1987).

6. Wilson, 3.

7. Wilson, 22.

8. Lewis, 199.

9. Lewis, 199.

10. For example, see Robert M. Jiobu, "Ethnic Hegemony and the Japanese of California," *American Sociological Review* 53 (June 1988), 353–67.

11. This may not be a problem when applied to other ethnic groups in other societies, but in the United States, the socioeconomic levels of the major ethnic groups are common knowledge among social scientists.

12. I follow the presentation and notation of Marshall. See Ray Marshall, "The Economics of Racial Discrimination: A Survey," *Journal of Economic Literature* 12 (September 1974), 849–71.

13. Lester C. Thurow, *Poverty and Discrimination* (Washington, D.C.: The Brookings Institution, 1969).

14. Gary S. Becker, *Human Capital* (New York: Columbia University Press, 1964); Duncan MacRae, Jr., "Review Essay: The Sociological Economics of Gary S. Becker," *American Journal of Sociology* 83 (March 1978), 1244–58.

15. Michael Banton, *Racial and Ethnic Competition* (Cambridge, Great Britain: Cambridge University Press, 1983), 103.

16. Genocide might be an extreme case in which absolutely nothing is allocated to the losing group.

17. I would not want to argue that "greed is good," only that it is involved in the allocation of resources and rewards.

18. Quoted in Amos H. Hawley, *Human Ecology: A Theory of Community Structure* (New York: The Ronald Press, 1950), 201–202.

19. Robert E. Park and Ernest W. Burgess, *Introduction to the Science of Sociology*, Third Edition, revised (Chicago: University of Chicago Press, 1969), 506, italics added; originally published 1921.

20. Hawley, 202.

21. Hawley, 203.

22. See Banton, Chapter 6.

23. Robert E. Park, "The City: Suggestions for the Investigation of Human Behavior in the Urban Environment," in *The City*, Robert E. Park and Ernest W. Burgess, eds. (Chicago: University of Chicago Press, 1967), 1–47; originally published by the University of Chicago Press, 1925.

24. Robert M. Jiobu, *Ethnicity and Assimilation* (Albany, New York: State University of New York Press, 1988), 114; Robert M. Jiobu and Linda Nishigaya, "Residential Segregation Among Asians in Honolulu," presented at the Annual Meeting of the North Central Sociological Association, 1985.

25. Wilson.

26. Robert M. Jiobu, "Ethnic Hegemony and the Japanese of California," *American Sociological Review* 53 (June 1988), 353–67.

27. See Jiobu, *Ethnicity and Assimilation*.

28. As anecdotal evidence, I have often noted that people are surprised to find that the Chinese American population is so small and that the Filipino American population is as large as it is.

29. Recall the discussion in Chapter 3.

30. Edna Bonacich, "Advanced Capitalism and Black/White Relations in the South: A Split Labor Market Interpretation," *American Sociological Review* 41 (February 1972), 34–51.

31. See Alejandro Portes and Robert L. Bach, *Latin Journey: Cuban and Mexican Immigrants in the United States* (Berkeley, California: University of California Press, 1985); Alejandro Portes, and Leif Jensen, "What's an Ethnic Enclave? The Case for Conceptual Clarity" (Comment on Sanders and Nee) *American Sociological Review* 52 (December 1987), 768–71.

32. Portes and Bach, 203.

33. Herbert Mitgang, review of *The New Chinatown* by Peter Kwong (New York: Hill & Wang/Farrar, Strauss & Giroux, 1988), *New York Times*, June 11, 1988: Y 13.

34. Jiobu, "Ethnic Hegemony and the Japanese of California."

35. George Eaton Simpson and Milton J. Yinger, *Racial and Cultural Minorities: An Analysis of Prejudice and Discrimination*, Fifth Edition (New York: Plenum Press, 1985), 44; italics in original.

36. James A. Geschwender, *Racial Stratification in America* (Dubuque, Iowa: Wm. C. Brown Company Publishers, 1978), 252–53.

37. Banton, 136.

38. For a discussion of this theory, see T. S. Chivers, "Introduction: Rationalizing Racial and Ethnic Competition," *Ethnic and Racial Studies*, Special Issue: Rational Choice Revisited: A Critique of Michael Banton's *Racial and Ethnic Competition* 8 (October, 1985), 465–70.

39. Banton, p. 136.

40. Stanley Lieberson, *A Piece of Pie: Blacks and White Immigrants Since 1880* (Berkeley, California: University of California Press, 1980), 6; Hubert M. Blalock, Jr., *Toward a Theory of Minority-Group Relations* (New York: John Wiley & Sons, Inc., 1967).

41. Banton, p. 126.

42. Gunnar Myrdal, *An American Dilemma*, Volume I (New York: Harper and Row, 1944), 60–67.

43. Hawley, p. 189, note 14.

44. John Dollard, *Caste and Class in a Southern Town*, Third Edition (Garden City, New York: Doubleday Anchor Books, 1957); originally published in 1937 by Harper & Brothers.

45. St. Clair Drake, and Horace R. Cayton, *Black Metropolis: A Study of Negro Life in a Northern City*, Volume II (New York: Harper & Row, Publishers, 1962); originally published in 1945 by Harcourt, Brace & Company.

46. Gunnar Myrdal, *An American Dilemma*, Volume II (New York: Pantheon Books, 1972), Chapter 32; originally published by Harper and Row, 1944.

47. See Chapter 1.

48. Myrdal, 68–73.

49. James A. Geschwender, "Race, Ethnicity, and Class," in *Recapturing Marxism: An Appraisal of Recent Trends in Sociological Theory*, ed. Rhonda F. Levine and Jerry Lembcke (New York: Praeger, 1987), 136–60.

50. Geschwender, 1978, p. 264.

51. Geschwender, 1987, p. 152.

52. Ivan Light, "Immigrant Entrepreneurs in America: Koreans in Los Angeles," in *Clamor at the Gates: The New American Immigration*, ed. Nathan Glazer (San Francisco: Institute for Contemporary Studies Press, 1985), 161–78.

53. A caveat is necessary here, for competition is a value. Not everyone would agree that it is the best mechanism for allocating resources, nor would they agree that even if it is the *de facto* method, that it is ethically correct. Alternatives to competition, however, have not been widely accepted in the United States.

54. This point is suggestive. It helps explains why the tiny number of Asians were so feared on the West Coast and why Jews, another tiny group, suffer from such intense anti-Semitism.

55. This argument is based on many precedents. Possibly the most current one is the theory of cultural materialism. This theory reduces the importance of "ideas" and increases the importance of structure. It asserts that superstructure (the category that includes ethnic consciousness) develops as a result of infrastructure (the category that includes economic competition).

56. Compare with Susan Olzak, "Labor Unrest, Immigration, and Ethnic Conflict in Urban America, 1880–1914," *American Journal of Sociology* 94 (May 1988), 1303–33.

Index

Activity,
 church centered, 32
 shady, 32
Age grading, 125, 127
Age potential, 137–138
 defined, 138
Age squeeze, 128–131, 130
Age structure, 125–128
Amalgamation, 6
Americanization, 10
Ancestral diffusion, 18–21
Ancestry, 65
 defined, 12
Anglo American, 14
Anglo Conformity, 10
Annale school, 2, 117, 152
Arrow, Kenneth, 162
Assimilation, 6, 9–11
 ancestral diffusion, 19
 cultural, 37
 defined, 9, 11–12
 rank order, 24
 structural, 37

Banton, Michael, 163, 174, 175
Beck, E. M., 98
Becker, Gary S., 161
Blalock, Hubert, 136, 175
Blau, Peter, 40
Bonacich, Edna, 169, 170
Bonus jobs, 99
Boundary, hard and soft, 175
Burgess, Ernest, 164, 165, 166

Caste, 30, 33
Cayton, Horace, 32, 177

Central city, effect on underclass,
 84–85
Class
 ethnic resources, 179–180
 Weberian, 29
Class consciousness, 184
Competition
 concentric zones, 165–167
 enclave theory, 170–171
 ethnic boundaries, 173–176
 ethnic hegemony, 171–173
 group size, 167–169
 nature of, 163
 rational choice, 174
 sociological theory, 164–165
 split labor markets, 169–170
Competitive framework of ethnic
 relations, 180–183
Cooley, Charles, 164
Core sector, 100
Cottingham, Clement, 42
Cultural materialism, 117, 152
Cultural pluralism, 10
Culture, 158
Culture of poverty, 158–160
Culture of success, 160
Cutright, Phillips, 99

Davis, James, 40
Demographic analysis, 115
 potential, 115–119
  and socioeconomic attainment,
   133
  assumptions of, 118
Dependency ratio, 128
DFBETA, 154
DFFITS, 155

Differential analysis, 116
Dollard, John, 31, 32, 33, 94, 95, 96, 177
Drake, St. Clair, 32, 33, 177
Dual economy, 100–101
Dual labor market, 101
Dummont-Banks model, 34
Duncan, Otis Dudley, 40, 115, 116

Easterlin, George, 117, 252
Economic segment, 101
Education, 91
Educational attainment, 49–52
Edwards, Alba, 41, 42, 118
Ethclass, 37, 39
Ethnic composition of occupational categories, 57
Ethnic
  consciousness, 183
  diversity, 106–108
  heterogeneity, 100
  occupational composition, 57–59
  world systems theory, 178–179
Ethnic-gen class, 38
Ethnicity, 80
  defined, 6–7, 12
  effect on underclass, 80, 86–87
  race, 14–17
  resources, 179
  socioeconomic status, 31
Etic, 118
Expected number, 61

Farley, Reynolds, 93
Feminization of poverty, 79
Fertility ratio, 123–125
Frazier, E. Franklin, 33, 177

Gans, Herbert, 35, 36, 158
Gender, 79
  effect on underclass, 85–86
Genetic determinism, 3

Geschwender, James, 173, 178, 179, 185
Ghetto, 77, 278
Gilbert, Dennis, 41
Glenn, Norval, 99, 113
Gordon, 37, 38, 39, 184
Gould, Stephen, 6
Group size, 135–137

Harris, Marvin, 117
Hauser, Philip, 115, 116
Hawley, Amos, 164, 165, 176

Income attainment, 52–56
Index of diversity, 103
Infrastructural determinism, 2, 118
Inner city, 77–79
Intermarriage, 90
Internal colonialism, 10

Kahl, Joseph, 40, 41
Kallen, Horace, 10
Kitano, Harry H. L., 38
Kwong, Peter, 171

Leverage point, 141, 154
Lewis, Oscar, 158, 159
Lieberson, Stanley, 98, 99, 175
Life chances, 29
  of blacks, 38
Light, Ivan, 179

Majority and minority, 7, 8
Majority gains, 94–98
Marketplace, 164
Marshall, Ray, 162
Marx, 28, 145, 164
Marxian approach, 28–29, 97, 100, 102, 112, 177
Material resources, 179
Melting pot, 9

Miller, Delbert, 42
Minoritization, 11
Minority percentage, 107–108
Moore, Joan, 96
Multicollinearity, 154
Multiple ancestry, 13, 90
Myrdal, Gunnar, 32, 33, 96, 175,
    177, 183

National Opinion Research Center,
    41
Nature versus nurture, 3
Neoclassical model of discrimina-
    tion, 161–163
Nonmaterial resources, 179

Only, criterion of, 57

Pachon, Harry, 96
Parity, socioeconomic, 61–64, 93
Park, Robert, 9, 164, 165, 166,
    171
Partialing error, 154
Pearce, Diana, 79
Periphery sector, 101
Petersen, William, 7
Place of birth, 90
    and ancestral diffusion,
    21–24
Political power
    minority status, 7–9
    proportionate share, 9
Population studies, 115
Portes, Alejandro, 170
Power, 29
Prestige, 40
Primary labor market, 101

Queuing theory, 98–100

Race, 3–6
Rational choice theory, 174

Reich, Michael, 97
Reserve labor army, 95
Ross, Edward, 9

Sahlins, Marshal, 6
Saxton, Alexander, 80, 99
Secondary labor market, 101
Segment, 101
Sex composition, 120–123, 135
Sex ratio, 121
Shryock, Henry, 115
Siegel, Jacob, 115
Silent trade, 165
Single ancestry, 18
    and ancestral diffusion, 22
Single parenthood, 79–80
    effect on underclass, 86
Social demography, 116
Socioeconomic differentiation,
    110
Socioeconomic status
    correlates of, 64–65, 89–91
    defined, 31
    education, 73–74
    ethnicity, 48–49, 56–57, 59–61,
        89, 176–178
    gender, 69–73
    intermarriage, 65–69
    majority socioeconomic status,
        108
    nature of, 88–89
    of the ethnic group, 56, 59
    place of birth, 69
    structure of, 45–48
Sojourning, 120
Spencer, Herbert, 164
Srole, Leo, 34, 35
Status, 29, 31, 40
Status groups, 29, 34
Steiner, Frederich, 9
St. John De Crevecoeur, 9
Stratification, categories of,
    40–42
Subsociety, 38
Successive replacement, 35

Sumner, William Graham, 164
Syzamanski, Albert, 97, 98

Taeuber, Alma, 166
Taeuber, Karl, 166
Thomas, W. I., 183

Underclass, 38–39, 116
  and ethnicity, 91–92
  model of, 76
  operational definition, 42–45
United States born, 131–133

Veblen, Thorstein, 34

Warner, Lloyd, 34, 35
Weber, Max, 9, 30, 34, 39, 145
Weberian approach, 29–31
Wilson, Edward O., 3, 4
Wilson, William Julius, 38, 39, 42,
  116, 117, 166, 152, 159, 167
Wright, Erick Oflin, 28, 30

Zangwill, Israel, 9